Table of Contents

Anglo-Saxon

Ecglaf, Eadgils, Eomaer, *Eormenric, Frod(a), Hereric, *Hoc, *Hrothmund, Ingeld, **Offa**, Oslaf, Sigemund, *Aehha, Sigeferth, Aetla, *Hagena, Theodric, Waldhere, Becca, Witta, **Wada**, Oswine, Sigehere, *Sceafthere, Alewih, Aelfwine, Eadwine, Wulfhere, Frithuric ; perhaps also Herebald. The asterisk denotes names limited to persons of the sixth and seventh centuries.

3 Eadgils, Eanmund, Heardred, Hygelac, Ingeld, **Offa**, Wermund, Weohstan, Wiglaf, **Wada**, *Scilling, Oswine, Sigehere, *Gislhere (perhaps Eomaer).

4 *Aelfhere, Ecglaf, Eanmund, Heremod, **Offa**, Sigemund, Wermund, Weohstan, Wiglaf, Wulfgar, Garwulf, *Ordlaf, Sigeferth, Waldhere, Becca, **Wada**, *Hun, *Hringwald, Aelfwine, Eadwine, Wulfhere, Frithuric (possibly also Deor).

This genetic invasion continued in 1492 the with the fall of the Kingdom of Granada, they grabbed the line of the Jews and Moors of Granada, of no right of their own to do so, this was all based upon the crusades that upset the balance. I am not stating that anyone can stop them now, but understanding truth of things is always better than accepting deception. They systematically either killed or kicked out (deported) anyone of these family lines so they could take them for themselves. It was their plan to not leave anyone alive that could make any claim to the families own God given lineage that has been stolen from them matrilinealy. Instead of just accepting the events of 1492, and looking down on the peoples of Spain at that time, lets take a look at what this line was and represented **and why** the European monarchies dogpiled and took over its heritage, lineage and lands **Matrilinealy without right as the Nasrid line is a Patrilineal line only as will be shown.**

The **Nasrid dynasty** or **Banū Naṣr** The Nasrid dynasty rose to power after the defeat of the Almohad dynasty in 1212 at the Battle of Las Navas de Tolosa. Twenty-three different emirs ruled Granada from the founding of the dynasty in 1232 by Muhammed I ibn Nasr until January 2, 1492.

Yusuf al-Ahmar ibn Muhammad ibn Ahmad ibn Muhammad ibn (Khamees ibn)[2] Nasr ibn Muhammad ibn Nusair ibn Ali ibn Yahya ibn Sa'd ibn Qais ibn Sa'd ibn Ubadah[3] ibn Dulaym ibn Harithah ibn Abi Hazima ibn Tha'labah ibn Tarif ibn al-Khazraj ibn Sa'ida ibn Ka'b ibn al-Khazraj[4] ibn Harithah ibn **Tha'labah ibn Amr ibn Amir** ibn Harithah ibn **Imri' al-Qays** ibn Tha'labah ibn Mazin ibn **al-Azd** ibn al-Ghawth ibn Nabt ibn Malik ibn **Zayd ibn Kahlan** ibn **Saba'** ibn Yashjub ibn **Ya'rub ibn Qahtan/Joktan** b. Aybar b. Shalikh b. Arfakhshad b. **Sam/Shem** b. Nuh/Noah. *Noah ben[11] LAMECH, *Lamech ben[10] METHUSELAH, *Methuselah ben[9] ENOCH, *Enoch ben[8] JARED, *Jared ben[7] MAHALALEEL, *Mahalaleel ben KENAN[6] (CAINAN), *Kenan (Cainan) ben[5] ENOS, *Enos ben[4] SETH, *Seth ben[3] ADAM, *Adam CREATED BY[2] GOD, JEHOVAH[1])

0.

Chapter 5 The Nasrid Dynasty I Donated in this book was Seth Ben Adam Ben Jehovah's kingdom and the Anglo Saxon Dynasty I Donated in this book

At a glance The kingdoms I donated in this book no one will inherit for not reading this book. "Seth Ben Adam Ben Jehovah's kingdom that has always been here   there are supposed to be 144,000 with their Fathers name on their forehead and that is why this book was written Seth Ben Adam Ben Jehovah's kingdom as stated has always been here via the Nasrid Kingdom of Granda. I donated the Real   Nasrid Dynasty Kingdom of Granda, Thutmose kingdom for real   and Mosikiyas Kingdom and that is Hashem Moses Kingdom And King Davids Real Kingdom via Jahoachim for real and the Real Anglo Saxon Dynasty for real proof below the Nasrid Kingdom of Granda and the Anglo Saxon Dynasty are the Most important Kingdoms of the Entire world and that is why I donated the Narid Kingdom of Granada and the Anglo Saxon Dynasty for real My sons are Real direct male descendants Moorish princes of the Kingdom of Granda also proven in this book :Again I repeat: Ephraim is HIS firstborn (31:9). Ephraim is linked with the Angles who together with the Jutes and Saxons. It is also important to understand the relationship between Manasseh and Ephraim, as our heritrage and bloodline are very related. An **Anglo-Saxon** refers to the tribe of **Ephraim**. **Anglo** comes from the Hebrew word Engle, which could mean a calf or an ox. The **Anglo-Saxon (Ephraim** son of Joseph) Tribe as One of God's Battle Axes

Ten Tribes. Following the pattern of the Bible (Genesis 49), the **Angles identified themselves with the Unicorn Emblem of the tribe of Ephraim, The Tribe of Manasseh together with Ephraim also** formed the *House of Joseph*. **The House of Joseph is how it should stay, Manasseh together with Ephraim not divided**

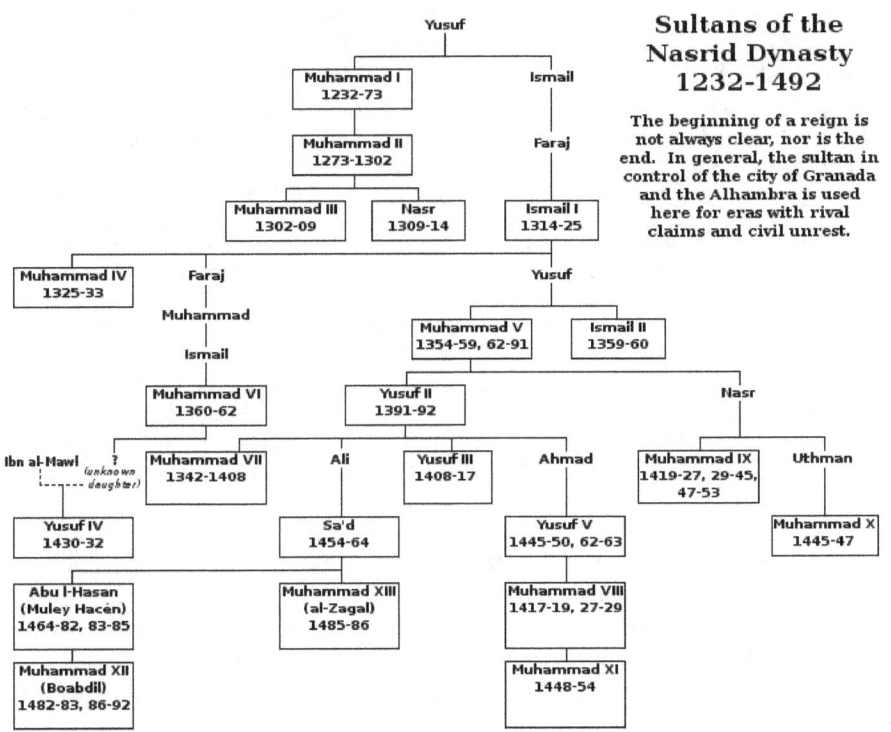

Sultans of the Nasrid Dynasty 1232-1492

The beginning of a reign is not always clear, nor is the end. In general, the sultan in control of the city of Granada and the Alhambra is used here for eras with rival claims and civil unrest.

The family tree below shows the genealogical relationship between each sultan of the Nasrid dynasty.[1] It starts with their common ancestor, Yusuf al-Ahmar.

Imran bin Amr was no doubt Aaron the brother of Moses. Amr his father is thus Amram the father of Aaron and Moses. "And at the end of forty days they came to Moses and Aaron, and they brought him word as it was in their hearts, and ten of the men brought up an evil report to the children of Israel, of the land which they had explored, saying, It is better for us to return to Misraim than to go to this land, a land that consumes its inhabitants. But Joshua the son of Nun, and the son of Jephuneh, who were of those that explored the land, said, The land is exceedingly good."

The story of Jafna, **Muzaikiya** and Tha'labah is unmistakably too similar to that of Jephuneh and his father Caleb in the Bible to be coincidental as well.

The line of Muzaikiya is this:

Al-Aus and al-Khazraj. Al-Aus and al-Khazraj are the sons of Harithah ibn-Tha'labah ibn-'Amr Muzaikiya ibn- 'Amir, and their mother was Kailah, daughter of al-Arkam. Moses was Amr Ibn Amir, Then came Tha'labah ibn-'Amr Muzaikiya with his son The people of Amr bin Amir the soothsayer after being expelled by Akk bin Adnan disengaged and dispersed in idifferent directions. Jafna bin Amr bin Amir settled in Syria, Aus and Khazraj settled in Yathrib and Khuza'a went to Marra.

The Direct male line Descendants of 3 Morrish princes names Cici Haya, Cad, and Nazar who in the vicinity of Granada Spain received Catholic religion and received baptism in the names Pierre Ferdinand De Grenade, and Jean De Grenade. In "Trophees Du Brabant, 1724" by R.P Burkens it is mentioned that among the Lords admitted to the court of Charlequint (Charles V) at Brussells in 1546-1547 is found Jean De Grenade. In this family were also mentioned were Jean and Bernadine-Jerome De Grenade with the spouses, and children. likewise the facts concerning the arms granted to Pierre De Grenade (Cici Haya) are also confirmed "d 'azure A Cinq Grenades d' or translated 5 Golden Pomegranates on a field of blue which as also adopted by Nicholas de Grenade 9de0 family notice of 12/6/1548.

In early biblical history, descent was clearly patrilineal (Exodus 31:2). Abraham was the first Hebrew (Genesis 14:13). Abraham and Sarah would have a son, Isaac, which would establish the line. Isaac and Rebecca would then have a son, Jacob, which would further that line, and Jacob would then have twelve sons, <u>establishing tribal authority</u>.

("Hebrew")

As is shown clearly in the Hebrew Bible, (or the Tanakh) which is called the "Old Testament" by Christians, the <u>"Treasured People"</u> is the exact phrase used in the text, referring to the Hebrews/Israelites.   We also find that in the Book of Deuteronomy, YHWH proclaims the Nation of Israel, known originally as the <u>Children of Israel</u>, as his <u>"treasured people out of all the people on the face of the earth" (Deuteronomy 7:6). As mentioned in the Book of Exodus, the Hebrew people are God's chosen people, and from them shall come the Messiah, or redeemer of the world. The Israelites also possess the "Word of God" and/or the "Law of God" in the form of the Torah as communicated by God to Moses.</u>

<u>"Now therefore, if you will obey my voice indeed, and keep my covenant, then you shall be a peculiar treasure unto me above all people"</u> (Exodus 19:5), <u>God promises that He will never exchange His people with any other. "And I will establish My covenant between Me and you and your descendants after you in their generations, for an everlasting covenant, to be God to you and your descendants after you."</u> (Genesis 17:7).

The actual word Jew only first appeared in the Bible in books, 1st Kings, 2 Kings, and Jeremiah in the Old Testament and was an incorrect translation of the Hebrew word for Yehudah and is often pronounced Judah in English. **The history of the Old Testament**

reveles that the "chosen people" of the Bible were descendants of a man named Jacob and he was named Israel. As a result of this his descendents were called Israelites not Jews, not to exclude that any Israelite's did not later become a Jew/Judiah, but that is a small fraction of the current Jewish population. The religion and laws of Judism and Muslim such as Matrilineal laws do not apply to a True Israelite of Jacob, as the laws of Judism as well as Muslim in this regard are in direct contrast with the Patrlineal laws of an Israelite.

The fact is that Y-chromosome DNA (Y-DNA) is paternally inherited enables patrilines, and agnatic kinships, of men to be traced through genetic analysis.

Y-chromosomal Adam (Y-MRCA) is the patrilineal human most recent common ancestor, from whom all Y-DNA in living men is descended. Y-chromosomal Adam probably lived between 60,000 and 90,000 years ago, judging from molecular clock and genetic marker studies. A man's genetic Y-DNA and his family name (in most cultures) have descended down this same **line** from father to son. In a **patrilineal descent** system **Patrilineal Descent ... that in the Bible the line always followed the father, including the cases of Joseph and Moses.**

The Original Israeilites lost their footprint, and are in our current times are in a very dangerous and vunerable position. All of this is due to our lack of understanding, and it is critical for our understanding to catch up and protect the Israelites.   This is why the First law of an Israeilite is so very important, and the persecution of the Israelites must stop. This persecution is what has allowed Evil to march on, and take over in the first place, as now the Israeilite remnant are in more danger than ever before, and is fast reaching critical mass . These are very dangerous times, but you cannot even begin to fathom how and why unless you understand many pieces of history, then a picture begins to form of the tragic truth, and the dangers we face. **I emphasize the extreme importance of what I call the First Law of an Israeilite,** and what the laws were among the ancient Israeilites, and how this is critical for our current times, and always was important but was forgotten, and history then took a path of the Evil we see in our own times. We must start from the beginning to see with much more clearity the Hebrews that became the Israelites.

"Thus says the Lord God: 'Although I have cast them far off among the Gentiles, and although I have scattered them among the countries, yet I shall be a little sanctuary for them in the countries where they have gone.' Therefore say, 'Thus says the Lord God: I will gather you from the peoples, assemble you from the countries where you have been scattered, and I will give you the land of Israel'" (11:16, 17).

Again :Law one of an Israeilite: among ancient Israelites, the inheritance is patrilineal. It comes from the father, who bequeaths only to his male descendants (daughters don't inherit). The eldest son received twice as much as the other sons. The father gives his name to his children; for example: the sons of Israel are called Israelites, because the land belonged to the father, and every one of his twelve sons gave his name to his descendants.

For thus saith the Lord; Sing with gladness for Jacob, and shout among the chief of the nations: publish ye, praise ye, and say, O Lord, save thy people, the remnant of Israel.

History as you have seen has been hijacked in many ways, and it began its tracks long ago. The results has been what is truly a war against Shem, and the order the lord had put in place long before man took control, and tried to make its own World order that is   way out of line of what the Bible clearly tells us. The tracks of truth, and <u>bread crumbs that were in place were tossed aside, and the Evil began its trek through history.</u>

Chapter 1: The Black Nobility controls the World.

This book is is to explain history,and how it has been twisted and turned. There are core laws that I wish to be understood completely. We will take a trip through time,and see many Biblical prophecies. Laws broken.   The one I will begin with is the most important, the laws of God. The world has turned away from God, and don't turn away, for it is he that saves us all. The Lord calls for understanding. He did warn us of some very great deceptions.   There are many warning's we did not hear and did not heed, and it is this turning away that harms us still today, as it will also harm our childrens future as they will be prisoners of debt, because we did not hear truth, and understand what is happening within our own lifetimes open our hearts and minds, with a resolution to make changes for the betterment of our own present times, as well as the young people of our world that depends on our understanding discernment and resolute sound minds .

It is within our best interest to understand history to understand what has happened, and plagues our current times. We must move beyond the deceptions, and understand the deeper truths. The lord calls for us to hear, and not to give in and accept deceptions that are being perpetrated by a few families that have been trying, and are still trying to move us further and further from the truth.   If a few familes were not trying to take over the world right now, I would not be writing this book. I only will speak the truth of history, and show the correlations to the very best of my understanding.   The poverty, wars and death around the world historically as well as currently should be analyzed for it **root causes and perpetrators**. Our misunderstanding of history is our un-doing. Certain facts beg to be understood.   I forgive the misunderstanding, and forgive the perpetrators, but feel that the way in which the world is currently run is not in the best interest of human kind. Currently we are all under financial and psychological attack, and it has been that way now for generations.

The Salic law is an important code of laws that were held by the Anglo Saxons under King Clovis as they were Salian Franks. This was during the middle ages during the 6th century. The Salic law has been has unrightfully been abandoned since Queen Victoria also known as Victoria Guelf took the thrown and she had nine children and near all of her grand Children too at least twenty six out of fourty two married strategic patrilineal line noble family and took over heritage of major dynasties doing so historically. This has upset the patrilineal bloodline of Critical dynasties and has caused an illegal power vacuum for far too long now.   Queen Victoria did not historically inherit Hanover legally at all and this could very well become an issue very relvant to our times. Their families are called the Black Nobility and they are the source of much of the massive debt and pain of our current times

At issue the Black Nobility of Queen Victoria and her family does not qualify for the Bloodline of King David. It never was and never will be the Mothers Kingdom. It is the bloodline of the Serpent seed of Cain. The Little Horn of Daniel that the Book of Daniel spoke of.   The system of treason must be stopped we cannot allow this debt ridden system to continue indefinitely making the whole world poor for the sake of the Black Nobility that is not really Noble at all. The European Monarchies are female lines that have no actual Birthrights.

The British Monarchy has hijacked Israel and the covenant and has been allowed to for far too long now. Who are these people, and do they have the right to take over Israel, or the United States, or the Worlds economy? How did this happen?   It is something we should all know and understand.   We can all see the economies failing, families failing and out of work, and Evil signs and symbols around us, those who know what to look for, and what is pure deception as we have been warned of.

The European monarchies are all related to Queen Victoria and Queen Victoria doess not qualify at all for the Blood Line of King David and she never did. These monarchies are the serpent seed of Cain but they are suiting on the patrilineal lines of the Seed of the Woman "adam" that Seth Ben Adam Ben Jehovah promised will crush the Serpent Seed of Cain and inherit Seth Ben Adam Ben Jehovah's End Days Kingdom, it is the Fathers Kingdom Originated by Seth Ben Adam Ben Jehovah. Only the Fathers Kingdom Seth Ben Adam Ben Jehovahs Ancient Kingdom that has been traced for literally thousands of years 100% can knock down the Little Horn of Danial because Seth Ben Adam Ben Jehovah is the Seed of the Woman and His own Enmity.

The Curse of Cain is a very serious curse. The Queen Victoria Line has put a Jahabulon Curse on our money to curse us all. All the Money is debt paper to keep us all in Servitude to the Gotha Queen Victoria Bloodline They do not have a right to keep the whole world in Servitude to the Little Horn of Danial This is all a direct result of the Crusades and we are all still paying for that time in history. We are all 40 trillion dollars in debt to them and Seven million more dollars every hour and debt can never be paid off. The Seed line of Cain has to be crushed by the Seed of the Woman "Adam" once and for all The Gotha are the same family line that crucified Hashem Jesus Christ and this Mother of all prophets Hashem will defend the Fathers Kingdom in every way. It never was and never will be The Mothers Kingdom.

Who can say that the Bloodline of Vlad Tepis the Dracula of History is Royal with a strait face even More les be servitude to them. And their system of Treason Queen Elizabeth Cannot prove that her son descends from the Seed of the Woman "Adam" Her son Prince Charles decends from Vlad Tepis and back to Olbert and his Father Unknown.   Queen Victoria's Black Nobility is a great deception. The Black Nobility have taken complete advantage of Mankind for too long The Little Horn of Danial was not supposed to prophet at all yet that is all they do is prophet from all of us. The Little horn of Danial must be knocked down. The Cain Seed line must be crushed by the Seed of the Woman "Adam" The Seed of the Woman "Adam " are the only ones with Birthrights, the Seed of the Serpent Cain must be crushed.

This world is ruled by Satan and his minions. Most people are not aware of it and any suggestions of Satanic bloodlines are ridiculed as nonsense. The bible says that Jesus Christ is the biological descendant of King David and the 'seed of the woman' ie virgin born. The bible also say that there is a seed of the serpent ie a Satanic bloodline. Sad, but we dont care about the Seed of the Woman, we just care about the Seed of the Serpent instead, because they print paper called money. Oh well We are all fooled, and look as though we shall stay so. Sorry Jacob, Moses and Jesus, Joseph, the seed of the woman does not matter. Nor do the Israelite's, as long as we have fiat Money we are BLIND to the Truth.

The only way this can ever happen is if the Victorian Monarchies and the Federal Reserve are somehow ever abolished. We must remember that the Federal Reserve is a privately owned company that is not federal at all. Our government borrows money from it, and what it borrows is what we have in our economy, and it is the debt the people have to pay it is a futile system as these debts will never be able to be paid, as that would break our economy to do so. It is a never ending debt cycle that is all a giant ponzi scheme from its very origins. All based on the deception that the Victorian Monarchies especially the Windsor/Stuarts are the bloodline of King David, yet not a drop of King Davids Y-DNA flows through their vains, their Patrilineal line is Unknown, it's all been a grand scheme all along, and it's time that the world wakes up from history. In Revelation 17:1, it says this harlot sits on many waters. ... This woman, (harlot) is that Great city, Babylon the Great ... Great Britain

   The British Monarchy has hijacked Israel and the covenant and has been allow
  far too long
   now. Who are these people, and do they have the right to take over Israel, or th
  States,
   or the Worlds economy? How did this happen? It is something we should all l
  understand.
   We can all see the economies failing, families failing and out of work, and Evil s
  symbols
   around us, those who know what to look for, and what is pure deception as we l
  been warned of. _.

This book is meant for reference guide to the Abrahmic religions, this means Christianity, Judaism, and Islamic.   It is my goal to bring forth a greater understanding of history, and of Gods Law. There still is a current and continuing War against Shem.

  The crusades have mixed up history to such confusion that the covenants of God go UN-noticed and UN-cared for. This must one day stop.   In this book I only seek to promote peace and understanding. Sometimes truth is harsh, but the days of peace and a closer walk with the biblical law and truth must someday arise.

It is not my purpose here to convince you of history. It is not my purpose to do anything but to show history, and its connections. History has been twisted, and there are many twisted families running the world to this day. How did it all happen? Does the Spanish inquisition spark a thought?   If it does not then a bit more history needs to be understood by the masses. So many cry in our current times, and the Lord said he would hear our cries. So what happened in history that makes so many cry? And why?

I will show and explain both how and why. Just because a few bloodlines wanted to make themselves and their money makers Gods, does not mean the rest of civilization should have to suffer so much for so long now. Who are these people, and how did they go about making themselves seem as Gods to themselves,and try to take over the world that is not theirs to take over? **Are these not questions we should all ask?** **What a fine web they have weaved, but for humanity we are all ensnared.**

The Rabbis follow the Talmud. The Talmud itself encourages readers to place it above the authority of the Old Testament. In the Talmud it states: My son, be more careful in the observance of the Scribes than in the words of the Torah" (Talmud Erubin 21b). Are there potential consequences for the Jews if they don't understand nor care? Are these potential consequences of Biblical perportions? The answers to this very question could be a very loud indeed yes.

The Illuminati has been explored recently in a book written in Britain by Belgium author Pascal Roussel. For the last ten years, he has been studying the Illuminati conspiracy. According to Roussel, twelve "oligarchic families" have grown indescribably wealthy by lending "money" to governments at interest. These are the central bankers. Most but not all are Illuminati Jews.

"Banks got bailed out, we got sold out!" protesters chanted in street protest.

The significance of the crown is not in the power it exercises but in the heritage and God given rights it denies others. I will prove to you why a retro-active **Salic law is is very important to truth but it was just put down as no longer a law by the British monarchy, but. In Biblical times and in other times in history it was always followed as best as possible to keep bloodline intact and pure. Without it, bloodlines are disperced and no true to its origins any longer. We ended up in the mess we are in today, with truth hidden confused and forgotten. I will go into much more about what Salic law and patrilineal means.**

Perhaps, it is time for both Jews as well as Muslims to at least consider the Torah, and not discount it so easily. If Biblical testimony is false, then the Israel of today has no right to exist, and seems to much like embattled lands of places such as South Africa, it could not present itself as a divine fulfillment of the Bible, and in its current state with its current controllers, the only fulfillment it is currently fulfilling is Revelations. The Lord is indeed all powerful and wise. One who has set things in place, that are have consequences. The Lord knows very well that some factions the Jews are sometimes are still a stiff necked people, and often do not even heed even his warnings, this has been proven to the Lord, as well as to history.

If you ask an Orthodox Jew what they did for Christmas, many will say such things as on I went to a Chinese restaurant or something of the sort. Not only do some not heed the Old Testament, but completely do not heed nor care about the New Testament. Only the Messianic Jews accept Jesus

Christ at all, be warned of these facts. Muslims as well don't believe in the Torah, but do believe in Jesus, just not as the Messiah. Where is a dividing line on our Biblical history, as well as any Biblical bloodlines? What are the defining factors, and has history been hijacked? These are all questions we must address.

Let's consider the following factors, clearly. What happened historically that has hijacked history more than any other ideology, and has had the most severe consequences. The fighting will never stop while this most dangerous ideology, not fact, it perpertrated. The facts make themselves evident, when the history is understood and revealed on how it all happened.   This is intended to be a reference for both Rabbi's as well as Imams. It is also for the people who are concerned for history, as well as the present, and the future. Who are the lines and supporters of Hitler? Are they the ones in power currently? They rock and inflate economies, so people buy, then deflate the economy so people loose everything they were able to purchase, such as housing and land. It is an ancient and draconian technic. The Great Recession we have been going through painfully so so very many and now new jobs pay less and offer fewer work hours than the ones they have see replaced, and multitudes   have lost their savings, our homes, and our futures for ourselves and our children.

History has been hijacked in many ways, and it began its tracks long ago. The results has been what is truly a war against Shem, and the order the lord had put in place long before man took control, and tried to make its own World order, that is   way out of line of what the Bible clearly tells us. The tracks of truth, and bread crumbs that were in place were tossed aside, and the Evil began its trek through history.

Lets look back into history to see what has happened to set forth the events and people we still see today, and how they are in controle of the world.

Thus, Illuminati Jews characterize the "Jewish" role in terms of the destruction of civilization.

For example, in the book *"You Gentiles"* (1924) Maurice Samuel writes:

In 1928, Marcus Ravage, a Jewish Rothschild biographer wrote an essay entitled, *"The Real Case Against the Jews."*

 "You have not begun to appreciate the real depth of our guilt. We are intruders. We are disturbers. We are subverters. We have taken your natural world, your ideals, your destiny, and played havoc with them. We have been at the bottom not merely of the latest great war but of nearly all your wars, not only of the Russian but of every other major revolution in your history. We have brought discord and confusion and frustration into your personal and public life. We are still doing it. No one can tell how long we shall go on doing it."

<u>**Oh woeth how the pain of the world stems and is rooted in our own misunderstanding of history. History has been hidden, and the results are now far more dangerous than most can even begin to**</u>

comprehend. **Without a frame of reference one cannot see yet what the future entails. Yet with a true frame of reference you can begin to see clearly the dangerous world we live in. Why is it like this? What are the forces behind this? What are the answers? Are there any answers? The answers are contained in the Bible. The answers are called the covenents with God, these answers are called the Truth. Taking off the blinders of deception and seeing Truth is a very wonderous thing in so very many ways.**

I hear the sound of the trumpet as do many, as we are told our blood will be on our head if we hear the trumpet but do not take warning, and must blow the trumpet to warn the people, as the watchman is accountable for his blood. If he had taken warning, he would have saved himself. Oh dear sweet Lord, can man heareth your call finally, for the sake of our world, as well as their own salvation I pray.

The crusades led into what is today known as British Israelism, and the families who rule the world with tyranny and un-justice. The coventant with God has been violated, the tyranny continues, and our people suffer under their increasing greed and desire to rule the world. The knights Templars had found Kabbala documents from the temple of Soloman, and turned its teachings into todays banking practices. It is when they found these documents they started their take over the world. It continues today with full force.

I am not implying that the Talmud is all bad as I use several quotes from in these chapters, but it does indeed have it's seamier side to it as well:

Examples of the seamier side of the TALMUD:

The Babylonian Talmud, the accepted and preferred version, further teaches that Adam committed bestiality.

"Yebamoth 63a. States that Adam had sexual intercourse with all the animals in the Garden of Eden." 27.

"Yebamoth 59b. A woman who had intercourse with a beast is eligible to marry a Jewish priest. A woman who has sex with a demon is also eligible to marry a Jewish priest." 28.

"Sanhedrin 55b. A Jew may marry a three year old girl (specifically, three years "and a day" old)." 29.

"Sanhedrin 54b. A Jew may have sex with a child as long as the child is less than nine years old" 30.

Kethuboth 11b. "When a grown-up man has intercourse with a little girl it is nothing." 31.

The collaboration of Royal families also ties into the Illuminati who were the international organization that tied these royal families together via the Knights Templar going back to the Crusades.

What people in the western world need to understand is that when Monarchy fell out of favor in the 18th century. The resulting Democracy that followed still remained under the Royal families control due their never relinquishing control of the banking system.

That is exactly why the Federal Reserve was formed. And their collection agency, called the Internal Revenue Service. Both private corporations. The invention of private banking started back in Babylon in 648 B.C. This is the type of banking we use today.

We must begin to understand the question of "What is history" and "what is the Past" The past is what happened; Yet History itself is mearly our interpretation of what happened. Now with current archeology we know much more than we did a hundred and 50 years ago. We must with our new understanding begin to piece together what actually happened in the past, and rediscover history as it happened. Most of history was written during the Victorian age. Historians and archeologist are finding large discrepancies that have distorted our view of history and now must be re-adjusted. These points are critical to gain actual truth, not history that has only been written by the conquerors as it has been historically.

One of the most important things this accomplishes and points out gracefully is how our knowledge has been stuck back 150 years ago still in the Victorian era. Just by moving beyond the Victorian age, history is now able to break free of it historical inherent inaccuracy. There is talk of a "New World Order", as well there is talk of a New Age. More deception to follow up the Victorian age, and no more Biblically sound than that has been historically either. Either of those paths just leads to more Debt, and Deception. As we are born and even our un-born are already in debt. Why are they in such a hurry now to drive their plan to complete fruition? These answers lay directly in the very same Deception they promote called the New World Order.

We must now clearly accept that history was truly written by the conquerors, and our laws and banking system are all Based on and Created by these Same Forces. The Banking Cartel is the fraudulently controlled and cause of Humanity's Woes. The Price of Gold has been Manipulated. This is More Scandalous Than Libor! The power of the Illuminati lies in their global fiat currency hegemony.

It is dangerous world that far too many don't understand. History has been very biased by the Black nobility during the Victorian era.As we are moving past this biased history with Archeology and proof,it is also time to understand history itself in an more accurate light. The Libor scandal is already being called "The Crime of the Century" Capitalism is based on a house of cards, which are, at last, about to come tumbling down and the **Illuminati** Exposed.

It was in 1930 Willie Munzenberg made clear that the Frankfurt School's long-term   plans upon plans were and still are: 'We will make the West so corrupt that it stinks.

We are on a slippery slope towards communism, the many communist agendas have been forcing America to move in that direction for far too long now, and we are facing a very grim future. It was historically the Rothschilds family were were originally the Baur family, one of the most occultic families in history that funded the communist manifesto.

Ezekiel 38:2 - Son of man, set your face against Gog, the land of Magog, the chief prince of Meshech and Tubal, and prophesy against him: **"Whosoever controls the volume of money in any country is absolute master of all industry and commerce... And when you realise that the entire system is** very easily controlled, one way or another, by a few powerful men at the top, you will not have to be told how periods of inflation and depression originate."James Garfield 1881, a few weeks before he was shot and killed. Mayer Bauer changed the name to "Rothschild" (meaning "red shield") The Rothschilds were formerly known as the Bauers, one of the most infamous occult families of Middle Ages Germany, and they originate not from Israel, but the Caucasus Mountains. It just so happens that he was an Ashkenazi Jew, and that Ashkenaz was a region in Magog where the so-called "red Jews" of Khazaria had ruled an empire on the north shores of the Black and Caspian seas. The Caucasus Mountains is a mountain system in Eurasia between the Black Sea and the Caspian Sea:Historically the Ashkenaz Jews were/are the sons of Japheth not Shem: "Now these are the generations of the sons of Noah, Shem, Ham, and Japheth: and unto them were sons born after the flood. The sons of Japheth;...the sons of Gomer; Ashkenaz..."(Genesis 10:1-3)The sons of Japheth: Gomer, and Magog, and Madai, and Javan, and Tubal, and Meshech, and Tiras. 6And the sons of Gomer: Ashkenaz, and Diphath, and Togarmah. 7And the sons of Javan: Elishah, and Tarshish, Kittim, and Rodanim.In the Goetia, Belial is said to be a mighty and a powerful king over fifty legions, made after Lucifer. Edom, Moab, the sons of Ammon, the Amalekites, Philistia, and the Kittim of Asshur (referred to as the army of Belial), and [those who assist them from among the wicked] who "violate the covenant."[12]Silent Dawn of Open Fascism - U.S. Enabling Act of 2011 The hexagram faded from Jewish usage for 2,600 years. Then in the 1800's, in Germany, it was adopted by Mayer Rothchild to mark his house. The six pointed star was used as the Rothchild coat of arms. 6 points, 6 triangles, and the 6 sides of the hexagram -- 666 " Our notion that our personal income taxes go to paying for our country's infrastructure, social services, military, etc. is inaccurate, to say the least. Our personal income taxes first are collected by the US Treasury via the Internal Revenue Service, which sends the funds to the Federal Reserve, which is NOT a federal bank of any sort. The privately owned Federal Reserve, which is owned by the Rothschilds and, to a smaller extent, other banking families, then sends our tax dollars to its own Bank of England, which is located in the sovereign area of London called The City of London.

Revelation 12:17

Revelation 12:17American Standard Version (ASV)

[17] And the dragon waxed wroth with the woman, and went away to make war with the rest of her seed, that keep the commandments of God, and hold the testimony of Jesus:

Mattew 5:17

Matthew 5:17American Standard Version (ASV)

[17] Think not that I came to destroy the law or the prophets: I came not to destroy, but to fulfil.

Isaiah 8:20

Isaiah 8:20American Standard Version (ASV)

20 To the law and to the testimony! if they speak not according to this word, surely there is no morning for them.

So then what is the New World Order? It is the same old order taking further control, it is basically the European Monarchies and the Banks and the UN taking complete and ultimate control. Or it can also mean what is called the "World to come" but this world to come is not mentioned anywhere in the Holy Bible, and thus something that should be understood and will be anylized within this work. Is it not now time to all do what we must do. Now that this Evil has been EXPOSED, we must be now ready to rout it out, and shine the light on Truth.There is no better way to do so than realize their complete Deception and support the Laws of GOD. Lets now take back our heritage and our lands, and not cower to the New World Order and the Anti-Christ.

Babylonian Brotherhood represented in the **Illuminati**, the House of **Windsor**, the Rothschilds and the Rockefellers, the round table, the UN, the Bilderberg

Why the big push now by the Illuminati now? It is because their plans have been long term in the making but now very Many people are waking up to their Complete Deception. Of the Illuminati plan they will take us all down in to a death throws of a process to financially force the world down under their complete One World Control complete with One World Religion.Ah does not the Bible warn us this will happen and by whom? They are not finished yet, their plan is still in full motion.

Many have been used as tools to futher their goal Just as Belial is using the Illuminati as tools to futher his goal, Doubt this not. One of the steps on this plan is that they would infiltrate the Education system, and the media and the churches. This has been accomplished as planned in far too many ways. The Illuminati was first began as a secret society that was and is under the direction of Jesuit priests. Then a council of five men, one for each of the points on the pentagram, formed what was called "The Ancient and Illuminated Seers of Bavaria." They were high order Luciferian Freemasons.

In *The War of the Sons of Light Against the Sons of Darkness*,[20] one of the Dead Sea scrolls, Belial is the leader of the Sons of Darkness:

"You *11* made Belial for the pit, angel of enmity; in dark[ness] is his [dom]ain, his counsel is to bring about wickedness and guilt. All the spirits *12* of his lot are angels of destruction, they walk in the laws of darkness; towards it goes their only [de]sire."[21]

The Dead Sea Scrolls: Study Edition, Florentino García Martínez and Eibert J.C. Tigchelaar, Brill Publishers, 1999, p.135

Their aim is to Bankrupt the world, to where nothing is of value including cash, then the only thing of value at that point is the Bio chip that will be offered as the one thing that can save you, but in reality it is the one thing that can Damn you completely, the Mark of the Beast.They will keep trying to destroy the economy and try to create as many global problems as they can driving us closer and closer to the Mark of the Beast. Reports created by the Rockefeller foundation

already speaks of mass deaths over 13,000 people, and the number used is also indicative of the perpretrators motives.And the U.S. poverty climbs to historic levels. The Problem is not the actual Debt, it's the massive amount of Interest charged, forget this not.

I see so many are asking if GOD will save us from the Illuminati, and oh Yes He Will, we just have to know his Word and Follow it. So many feel like it is already too late, and that breaks my heart. Many are also asking how can we even save the United States? We have plenty of clues of what the future brings, and I am attempting to bring forth many more clues.

We must understand that the Dead sea scroles have only been translated for a short while now. The future is being revealed to us, as it is Gods Will for mankind as a whole, and what is in the future still, we have far to go still. We must hear Gods Truth, and Gods law. The laws of man are created by the Illuminati. God will deal with everything in existence, illuminati included.

The Skull & Bones and the Satanic Bohemian Grove. The ROTHSCHILD'S WEALTH EQUALS BANKRUPT NATIONS. The Illuminati Bohemian Grove Members Pray to Satanic Babylonian Owl Moloch Statue in Robes, a satanic cult, the Illuminati have subverted all nations for ther own greed, and to fund the future Wars of Gog and Magog as well as The War of Armeggeddon.

We must come to understand that the banking system is mearly just this one ruling cartel and that the entire planet is owned by this same small group of centuries old families known as the Illuminati. Though the Illuminati feel they have won, it is time we all show them we do not agree, and neither does GOD. They work as though they are above the law, because they work under who made the man made laws, so the Illuminai families feel they are way above any law. They are not though above the Laws of God, and this will be made clear to them as well as to the world eventually possibly in very many ways still.

Revelation 14:8
And another angel, a second one, followed, saying, "She fell, she fell, Babylon the great, she who has made all the nations drink of the wine of the passion of her immorality."

Revelation 17:1
Then one of the seven angels who had the seven bowls came and spoke with me, saying, "Come here, I will show you the judgment of the great harlot who sits on many waters,

Revelation 17:4
The woman was clothed in purple and scarlet, and adorned with gold and precious stones and pearls, having in her hand a gold cup full of abominations and of the unclean things of her immorality,

How deep does the rabbit hole go? And is it what we are seeing today? Does this plan go against Americans? My answer is indeed yes!!!!! Follow me on just how sick and dangerous this truly is to this day. The grave deception continued and grew massively. The question is, "will you believe the lie"? MY GOD , HOW DEEP THE RABBIT HOLE GOES!

They are trying to take over the world, and one day will they be stopped once and for all. Their tyranny has to be dealt with, before they succeed in their complete world domination by deception and greed. One world it's a battle ground; one world will smash you down. You don't have to take my word on the fact they are trying to take over the world, you can read it for yourself how they have working on this for many generations: **The related families all related past and present that carry on the aim of Queen Victoria of complete world domination by debt and our current monetary system occurred historically**

The Cursed seedline of Cain has convinced the world that thye are the most Royal Humans on Earth. This is a big deception to keep them in power. Femaale Matrilineal lines do not carry the Seedline of "Adam" they cannot and don't at all. The family of Queen Victoria has raped and plundered the whole world based on a complete lie. Their claim they are the Bloodline of King David when only a patrilineal line has been a big lie that has kept her family in power for far too many generations.

We are Fourty Trillion dollars in Debt to them and Seven million dollars more each and every hour and debt cannot be paid off. We are in a spiral down hill yet oblivious to the deception. It is the Seed line of "Adam" that must crush the Serpent seed of Cain, not the other way around.

We are in Revleaion 13 now and doing what the bible says not to do!

Again Case in point: For instance, in **Numbers, chapter 1, verse 18**, we're told that the Jewish people historically and Biblically had declared their **pedigrees according to their fathers' houses**. When Queen Athaliah wanted to eliminate the Royal Line of David, she only killed the males **knowing full well that a female descendant of David couldn't pass on the right to the throne** (II Kings 11; II Chronicles 22).

2 Kings 11American Standard Version (ASV)

11 Now when Athaliah the mother of Ahaziah saw that her son was dead, she arose and destroyed all the seed royal.

² But Jehosheba, the daughter of king Joram, sister of Ahaziah, took Joash the son of Ahaziah, and stole him away from among the king's sons that were slain, even him and his nurse, and put them in the bedchamber; and they hid him from Athaliah, so that he was not slain;

³ And he was with her hid in the house of Jehovah six years. And Athaliah reigned over the land.

⁴ And in the seventh year Jehoiada sent and fetched the captains over hundreds of the Carites and of the guard, and brought them to him into the house of Jehovah; and he made a covenant with them, and took an oath of them in the house of Jehovah, and showed them the king's son.

⁵ And he commanded them, saying, This is the thing that ye shall do: a third part of you, that come in on the sabbath, shall be keepers of the watch of the king's house;

⁶ And a third part shall be at the gate Sur; and a third part at the gate behind the guard: so shall ye keep the watch of the house, and be a barrier.

⁷ And the two companies of you, even all that go forth on the sabbath, shall keep the watch of the house of Jehovah about the king.

⁸ And ye shall compass the king round about, every man with his weapons in his hand; and he that cometh within the ranks, let him be slain: and be ye with the king when he goeth out, and when he cometh in.

⁹ And the captains over hundreds did according to all that Jehoiada the priest commanded; and they took every man his men, those that were to come in on the sabbath, with those that were to go out on the sabbath, and came to Jehoiada the priest.

¹⁰ And the priest delivered to the captains over hundreds the spears and shields that had been king David's, which were in the house of Jehovah.

¹¹ And the guard stood, every man with his weapons in his hand, from the right side of the house to the left side of the house, along by the altar and the house, by the king round about.

¹² Then he brought out the king's son, and put the crown upon him, and gave him the testimony; and they made him king, and anointed him; and they clapped their hands, and said, Long live the king.

¹³ And when Athaliah heard the noise of the guard and of the people, she came to the people into the house of Jehovah:

¹⁴ and she looked, and, behold, the king stood by the pillar, as the manner was, and the captains and the trumpets by the king; and all the people of the land rejoiced, and blew trumpets. Then Athaliah rent her clothes, and cried, Treason! treason!

¹⁵ And Jehoiada the priest commanded the captains of hundreds that were set over the host, and said unto them, Have her forth between the ranks; and him that followeth her slay with the sword. For the priest said, Let her not be slain in the house of Jehovah.

¹⁶ So they made way for her; and she went by the way of the horses' entry to the king's house: and there was she slain.

¹⁷ And Jehoiada made a covenant between Jehovah and the king and the people, that they should be Jehovah's people; between the king also and the people.

¹⁸ And all the people of the land went to the house of Baal, and brake it down; his altars and his images brake they in pieces thoroughly, and slew Mattan the priest of Baal before the altars. And the priest appointed officers over the house of Jehovah.

¹⁹ And he took the captains over hundreds, and the Carites, and the guard, and all the people of the land; and they brought down the king from the house of Jehovah, and came by the way of the gate of the guard unto the king's house. And he sat on the throne of the kings.

²⁰ So all the people of the land rejoiced, and the city was quiet. And Athaliah they had slain with the sword at the king's house.

²¹ Jehoash was seven years old when he began to reign.

2 Chronicles 22American Standard Version (ASV)

22 And the inhabitants of Jerusalem made Ahaziah his youngest son king in his stead; for the band of men that came with the Arabians to the camp had slain all the eldest. So Ahaziah the son of Jehoram king of Judah reigned.

² Forty and two years old was Ahaziah when he began to reign; and he reigned one year in Jerusalem: and his mother's name was Athaliah the daughter of Omri.

³ He also walked in the ways of the house of Ahab; for his mother was his counsellor to do wickedly.

⁴ And he did that which was evil in the sight of Jehovah, as did the house of Ahab; for they were his counsellors after the death of his father, to his destruction.

⁵ He walked also after their counsel, and went with Jehoram the son of Ahab king of Israel to war against Hazael king of Syria at Ramoth-gilead: and the Syrians wounded Joram.

⁶ And he returned to be healed in Jezreel of the wounds which they had given him at Ramah, when he fought against Hazael king of Syria. And Azariah the son of Jehoram king of Judah went down to see Jehoram the son of Ahab in Jezreel, because he was sick.

⁷ Now the destruction of Ahaziah was of God, in that he went unto Joram: for when he was come, he went out with Jehoram against Jehu the son of Nimshi, whom Jehovah had anointed to cut off the house of Ahab.

⁸ And it came to pass, when Jehu was executing judgment upon the house of Ahab, that he found the princes of Judah, and the sons of the brethren of Ahaziah, ministering to Ahaziah, and slew them.

⁹ And he sought Ahaziah, and they caught him (now he was hiding in Samaria), and they brought him to Jehu, and slew him; and they buried him, for they said, He is the son of Jehoshaphat, who sought Jehovah with all his heart. And the house of Ahaziah had no power to hold the kingdom.

¹⁰ Now when Athaliah the mother of Ahaziah saw that her son was dead, she arose and destroyed all the seed royal of the house of Judah.

¹¹ But Jehoshabeath, the daughter of the king, took Joash the son of Ahaziah, and stole him away from among the king's sons that were slain, and put him and his nurse in the bedchamber. So Jehoshabeath, the daughter of king Jehoram, the wife of Jehoiada the priest (for she was the sister of Ahaziah), hid him from Athaliah, so that she slew him not.

¹² And he was with them hid in the house of God six years: and Athaliah reigned over the land.

We are all in Revlelation 13 now and few even realize the many signs that point to this conclusion. It is possible that even Baraq Obama is the long fortold Anti-Christ of Revelation 13 as he has the very same desease that a well known Phaero of History had and may well be a direct decendent of Phaero Akhenaten. The Fake Windsor monarchy also may well be as the Torah of Hashem Moses calls the dragon Statan that gives power unto the Beast because they have a Red dragon on the family's heraldry and are the hidden hand behind the Baking power that is shackling the world in such massive debt.

Revelation 13American Standard Version (ASV)

13 and he stood upon the sand of the sea. And I saw a beast coming up out of the sea, having ten horns, and seven heads, and on his horns ten diadems, and upon his heads names of blasphemy.

² And the beast which I saw was like unto a leopard, and his feet were as the feet of a bear, and his mouth as the mouth of a lion: and the dragon gave him his power, and his throne, and great authority.

³ And I saw one of his heads as though it had been smitten unto death; and his death-stroke was healed: and the whole earth wondered after the beast;

⁴ and they worshipped the dragon, because he gave his authority unto the beast; and they worshipped the beast, saying, Who is like unto the beast? And who is able to war with him?

⁵ and there was given to him a mouth speaking great things and blasphemies; and there was given to him authority to continue forty and two months.

⁶ And he opened his mouth for blasphemies against God, to blaspheme his name, and his tabernacle, even them that dwell in the heaven.

⁷ And it was given unto him to make war with the saints, and to overcome them: and there was given to him authority over every tribe and people and tongue and nation.

⁸ And all that dwell on the earth shall worship him, every one whose name hath not been written from the foundation of the world in the book of life of the Lamb that hath been slain.

⁹ If any man hath an ear, let him hear.

¹⁰ If any man is for captivity, into captivity he goeth: if any man shall kill with the sword, with the sword must he be killed. Here is the patience and the faith of the saints.

¹¹ And I saw another beast coming up out of the earth; and he had two horns like unto lamb, and he spake as a dragon.

¹² And he exerciseth all the authority of the first beast in his sight. And he maketh the earth and them dwell therein to worship the first beast, whose death-stroke was healed.

¹³ And he doeth great signs, that he should even make fire to come down out of heaven upon the earth in the sight of men.

¹⁴ And he deceiveth them that dwell on the earth by reason of the signs which it was given him to do in the sight of the beast; saying to them that dwell on the earth, that they should make an image to the beast who hath the stroke of the sword and lived.

¹⁵ And it was given unto him to give breath to it, even to the image to the breast, that the image of the beast should both speak, and cause that as many as should not worship the image of the beast should be killed.

¹⁶ And he causeth all, the small and the great, and the rich and the poor, and the free and the bond, that there be given them a mark on their right hand, or upon their forehead;

¹⁷ and that no man should be able to buy or to sell, save he that hath the mark, even the name of the beast or the number of his name.

¹⁸ Here is wisdom. He that hath understanding, let him count the number of the beast; for it is the number of a man: and his number is Six hundred and sixty and six.

When people say, "There is peace and security," destruction will strike them as suddenly as labor pains come to a pregnant woman, and they will not be able to escape.

Chapter 2: The Victorian Era we are all stuck in

When I started to study history, it became clear to me that I could no longer trust Western history anymore, because it was written by the ones in history that have been and are still trying to take over the world for the sake of their own greed.

We must begin to understand the question of "What is history" and "what is the Past" The past is what happened; History is our interpretation of what happened. Now with current archeology we know much more than we did a hundred and 50 years ago. We must with our new understanding begin to piece together what actually happened in the past, and rediscover history as it happened. Most of history was written during the Victorian age. Historians and archeologist are finding large discrepancies that have distorted our view of history and now must be re-adjusted. These points are critical to gain actual truth, not history that has only been written by the concourors as it has been historically.

We have new evidence and dating that is based on many current archiological discoveries that outdate the history books since 150 years ago in the Vitorian age. This is critical to our understanding of the truth of history in many ways. This includes how and why our current times are as they are. It also includes many truths of history that have been off their dating about 300 years. Several centuries had been added to the chronology and history of the Pharoes. When this miscalculation was acted upon by historians and archeology itself a new picture of history has formed and actual inceridible Biblical discoveries have been made based upon our new understanding of history.

It is an exciting time in Archeology as with these new discoveries what has become clear is that just by adjusting the our current model of Historical dating technique back only 3000 years, the Archeology actually lines up with the history of the Bible as based on this we have been able to make some of our most important archeological finds of the Bible yet in our history.

One of the most important things this accomplishes and points out gracefully is how our knowledge has been stuck back 150 years ago still in the Victorian age. Just by moving beyond the Victorian age, history is now able to break free of it historical inherent inaccuracy. There is talk of a "New World Order", as well there is talk of a New Age. More deception to follow up the Victorian age, and no more Biblically sound than that has been historically either. Either of those paths just leads to more debt, and deception. allowing the Usery to continue un challeneged we are allowing writ of slavery to be placed upon our children, their children and so on and so on. We are accepting that there is nothing that can be done, and that it is okay to enslave our future generations with a mound of dept, that they will never be able to pay off, hence a form of littereral slavery.

What is the New World Order? It is the same old order taking further control, it is basically the Banks and the UN taking complete and ultimate control.

The New Age on the other hand is a cult following of people who believe in Extra terrestrial (Aliens)and think that Aliens will save the world. I wish what I am saying was incorrect honestly, but you can do the research on your own and find the same conclusions. I am merely simplifying what are indeed disturbing details.

This is so very important because literally our world is still stuck in this Victorian age in still far too many ways. Our knowledge of history and our history books have been stuck in the Victorian age, our laws, our monarchines and our banking system are all still as well stuck in the Victorian age.

Since we are able now to move beyond the Victorian age in Archeology, it underscores 1st how it is possible, and 2nd how important it is to finally move beyond the very things that have laid heavy on our planet with its deception, and one day must change and finally break free of the chains the Victorian age has bound us with.

I began as far back into the past as I could to understand what has happened, and how it affects out current history. I identify the Victorian age, and it players. Though I forgive and am not personally aganst these players, for historical analysis the key facts are brought forth and identified.

It never was and never will be the Mothers Kingdom and just how much more is the World goinmg to stand for the little horn of Danial? Those who were not supposed to Profit that profit from us all? The Cain Cursed Monarchies of Europe do not anfd d cannot carry the Seed of the Woman Ada, because they are all female no male non patrilineal bloodlines of Queen Victoria. They claim to be the Bloodline of King David when no woman qualifies for the Bloodline of King David it has all been one great deception. The Bloodline of Vlad Tepis historically is one of the most Evil men in the world. Thelma law which is Alyster Crowleys law another very Evil men of History. The Gotha family why is everyone so very bought and sold by these European Monarchies that needs to be abolished?

Who can say that the Blood line of Vlad Tepis the fake Windsor Monarchy is Royal with a strait face? , More less is servitude to them for the system of Treason a Cain curse to us all? Queen Elizabeth cannot prove that her son decends from the Seed of the Woman "Adam" Her son Charles decends from an unknown male line. All of the Black nobility are decedents of Queen Victoria. And her top Ancestor is patrilinally Olber and his father Unknown. The Cain cursed seedline must be crushed.

For the love of money is a root of all kinds of evils. It is through this craving that

some have wandered away from the faith and pierced themselves with many pangs

The European monarchies and their bankers have literally been using the lineage of so many hoping we would never figure it out. So many cry out and say "where is my heritage?" If your heritage was worth anything, there is a good possibility they are already claiming it as their o1 wn. They historically took over Kingdoms, and whole dynasties, not just by force, but by marriage to whatever female line had the heritage they wanted most. They had taken over the Anglo-Saxons hundreds of years ago, and found how easy it had been for them to marry one female, and then take over that lineage, and the lands and heritages' associated with them.

None of the European monarchies can claim to tbe the Seed of the Woman "Adam" as none of them qualify to do so.   They are the Little Horn of Danial that was not supposed to profit but that is all they have done is profit of of every Human alive with their debt paper. The Eu,propean Monarchies only have female bloodlines and that that does not qualify. They are not and cannot claim to be the Seed of the Woman "Adam" so they are disqualified The Male Top ancestor is Olbert and his father is unknown.

Queen Elizabeths family does not qualify to be the Seed of the Woman "Adam " either so her family is disqualified too complately. The European Monarchies areindeed the Littele horn of Danail and only Seth Ben Adam Ben Jehovahs' Kingdom can knock down the Little Horn of Danial because it is the Seed of the Woman "Adam" Seth Ben Adam Ben Jehovah.

King Edward IV, who ruled with a brief interruption from 1461 to 1483, was illegitimate.

The current senior line descends through Charles I and his youngest daughter Henrietta Anne Stewart and survives to this day in the House of Wittelsbach.

James Fitz-James Stuart was once of the grandsons of King James II of England who was sired by by his historicallyillegitimate son James FitzJames.

The Duke of Berwick and his family are the only surviving male-line descendants of King James II and VII. They descend from King James' illegitimate son by Arabella Churchill, James Fitz James.

James Fitz James was illegitimate so he and his descendants) had no legal rights to historically claim and hold the English and Scottish thrones.

Queen Victoria was also an illegitimate child, as well Prince consort Albert who was also illegitimate, her father was also her children's father, as well her brother was also her children's father, her eldest son Edward, Prince of Wales was the father of Winston Churchill. The decendents of the Queen Victoria line is quite interbred with the Rothschilds they are an actual subset of the Rothschilds.

Winston Churchill himself had illuded to the existence of a long term conspiracy when he wrote in 1920, "From the days of Spartacus-Weishaupt to those of Karl Marx, to those of Trotsky, Bela Kun, Rosa Luxemburg, and Emma Goldman, this worldwide conspiracy for the overthrow of civilization . . . has been steadily growing."

Historically Jewish people always had declared their family pedigrees in line with their fathers' houses in Numbers, chapter 1, verse 18, we're told that. Queen Athaliah historically wanted very much to somehow get rid of the actual real patrilineal Royal Line of King David, so she killed

many of the patrilineal all male bloodlines because she knew that a female matrilineal blood line of King David cannot and does not pass any actual rights to the throne (II Kings 11; II Chronicles 22).

This truth is plain *"There is no peace," says the Lord, "for the wicked."* (Isaiah 48:22) The score may be settled on either side of eternity, but it will be settled. No one can forsake the Lord and escape the consequences.

For the Davidic Messiah in Jewish law we find it is an necessity that Moshiach ben David be a male line descendant of King David through Solomon or Nathan. The answer among almost all Hebrew royal genealogists is "yes." By definition alone, the name Son of David that has been designated to identify the messiah, indicates a male line descendant, with no female breaks in the chain. Scripture tells us that Moshiach ben David will be a male line descendant of King David.

The Y chromosome is only paternally inherited though Male bloodines so this only only makes it actually possible for patrilines, to be traced through genetic analysis. The line of descent for monarchs is only passed on through patrilineal bloodlines and that qualifies as an unbroken paternal line.

Queen Victoria believed herself she descended from King David, they quote a letter she wrote supporting this view that she occupied the throne of David. This is a complete false claim, as the Davidic line is Patrilineal. I will show her Top Patrilineal line, The Top Ancestor, and prove it is not the throne of David. You must understand deeply it is this completely False Claim that Kept Her and her descendents in power over the people and the banking system, the 12 oligarchic families of the Black Nobility.

There is no way that Queen Victorias Blood line is the Seed of the Woman Adam, nor do they qualify for the Bloodline of King David as they have falsly claimed, it is all one big deception. They never did occupy legally the Thrown of King David it has always been an illegal move on their part. Being from the Top Ancestor names Olbert who father is Unknown they are not qualified as the Blood Line of King David At all. Not then and still not to this day as it is impossible. No female qualifies to occupy the Thrown of King David.

"I believe that banking institutions are more dangerous to our liberties than standing armies." --- Thomas Jefferson

"I place economy among the first and most important virtues, and public debt as the greatest of dangers. To preserve our independence, we must not let our rulers load us with perpetual debt."

-Thomas Jefferson

"The central bank is an institution of the most deadly hostility existing against the Principles and form of our Constitution. I am an Enemy to all banks discounting bills or notes for anything but Coin. If the American People allow private banks to control the issuance of their currency, first by inflation and then by deflation, the banks and corporations that will grow up around them will deprive the People of all their Property until their Children will wake up homeless on the continent their Fathers conquered."
—Thomas Jefferson (1743-1826

The rebellion of the southern slave owners that historically fostered the **civil war was a British backed insurrection. The Stuart Scottish Rite** was let by Quitman and then by Albert Pike after the death of Quitman. Oh America, what they have done to you and your people, yet yet we watch then as if they were movie stars, not considering the damage they have caused, historically as well as now.

Post Civil war Depression in the United States

Year	Total Dollars	Per Capita
1866	*1.8 Billion*	*50.46*
1867	*1.3 billion*	*44.00*
1876	*0.6 billion*	*14.60*
1886	*0.4 billion*	*6.67*

This is a 760% Loss

This so called New World order esentially controles the world finances and resources under what are a few very wealthy families,and their workers who support their goal of world domination. They have chosen themselves, they are not elected by the public, so they are not controlled. Their secret agenda is basically our elites who are members of a satanic cult. They are all Masons whether they know it or not. The Illuminati bankers figured out how to take down Western civilization. It is clearlypart of the same agenda that was spoken of to make the descendents of Queen Victoria the rullers of the world. They consider themselves divinely chosen, but their satanic agenda is not in the best interest of the people. They are power hungry,and driven by evil forces. This is not a false alarm,this is the current world we live in.

Rev 18:4 Then I heard another voice from heaven say:

"Come out of her, my people, so that you will not share in her sins, so that you will not receive any of her plagues; 5 for her sins are piled up to heaven, and God has remembered her crimes. 6 Give back to her as she has given; pay her back double for what she has done. Mix her a double portion

from her own cup. 7 Give her as much torture and grief as the glory and luxury she gave herself. In her heart she boasts, 'I sit as queen; I am not a widow, and I will never mourn.' 8 Therefore in one day her plagues will overtake her: death, mourning and famine. She will be consumed by fire, for mighty is the Lord God who judges her.

The actual word Jew only first appeared in the Bible in books, 1st Kings, 2 Kings, and Jeremiah in the Old Testament and was an incorrect translation of the Hebrew word for Yehudah and is often pronounced Judah in English. **The history of the Old Testament reveals that the "chosen people" of the Bible were descendants of a man named Jacob and he was named Israel.** As a result of this his descendents were called Israelites not Jews, not to exclude that an Israelite did not later become a Jew, but that is a small fraction of the current Jewish population. **The religion and laws of Judism and Muslim such as Matrilineal laws do not apply to a True Israelite of Jacob, as the laws of Judism as well as Muslim in this regard are in direct contrast with the Patrlineal laws of an Israelite.**

Judism is based upon Matrilineal decent, not patrilineal. Historically the Israelites strictly based decent on Patrilineal lines, clearly in contrast with Judism in this regard. Muslims don't care either way if decent is Maitrilineal or Patrilineal, which is also in contrast with the original Israelites.

For thus saith the Lord; Sing with gladness for Jacob, and shout among the chief of the nations: publish ye, praise ye, and say, O Lord, save thy people, the remnant of Israel.

Jeremiah 31:10 ASV

[10] Hear the word of the LORD, O nations,
And declare in the coastlands afar off,
And say, "He who scattered Israel will gather him
And keep him as a shepherd keeps his flock."
[11] For the LORD has ransomed Jacob
And redeemed him from the hand of him who was stronger than he

Today a very sad fact is that the term Jew is very erroneously assumed to be synonymous with Israel. This is largely due that what was strictly a just a religion has now taken on a bredth and depth of its own along with an extreme nationalistic connotation with the establishment of the current state of Israel and the Zionist movement.

" Female bloodlines also known as Matrilineal descent, for passing on a child's Jewish decent via the matrilineal side of the Mothers heritage, is not in line at all with actual legal as well as biblical laws. In biblical times, many Jewish men married non-Jews, and their children's status was determined by the father's religion.**

Jewish status through matrilineality, is in direct contrast to the position of the *Tanakh* **(Hebrew Bible) Moses** proceeded to do exactly as G-d had commanded him." (Exodus 40:14, 15) ... This indicates direct **patrilineal descent**

As we can clearly see in Duet 7:3-4 during the days of the giving of the Torah of Hashem Moses only patrilineal bloodlines were passed on and it was how the Law was kept by Jehovah perfect law.

Deuteronomy 7 ▶
American Standard Version

Casting out the Nations

1When Jehovah thy God shall bring thee into the land whither thou goest to possess it, and shall cast out many nations before thee, the Hittite, and the Girgashite, and the Amorite, and the Canaanite, and the Perizzite, and the Hivite, and the Jebusite, seven nations greater and mightier than thou; 2and when Jehovah thy God shall deliver them up before thee, and thou shalt smite them; then thou shalt utterly destroy them: thou shalt make no covenant with them, nor show mercy unto them; 3neither shalt thou make marriages with them; thy daughter thou shalt not give unto his son, nor his daughter shalt thou take unto thy son. 4For he will turn away thy son from following me, that they may serve other gods: so will the anger of Jehovah be kindled against you, and he will destroy thee quickly. 5But thus shall ye deal with them: ye shall break down their altars, and dash in pieces their pillars, and hew down their Asherim, and burn their graven images with fire. 6For thou art a holy people unto Jehovah thy God: Jehovah thy God hath chosen thee to be a people for his own possession, above all peoples that are upon the face of the earth.

7Jehovah did not set his love upon you, nor choose you, because ye were more in number than any people; for ye were the fewest of all peoples: 8but because Jehovah loveth you, and because he would keep the oath which he sware unto your fathers, hath Jehovah brought you out with a mighty hand, and redeemed you out of the house of bondage, from the hand of Pharaoh king of Egypt. 9Know therefore that Jehovah thy God, he is God, the faithful God, who keepeth covenant and lovingkindness with them that love him and keep his commandments to a thousand generations, 10and repayeth them that hate him to their face, to destroy them: he will not be slack to him that hateth him, he will repay him to his face. 11Thou shalt therefore keep the commandment, and the statutes, and the ordinances, which I command thee this day, to do them.

God's Promises

(Exodus 23:20-33)

12And it shall come to pass, because ye hearken to these ordinances, and keep and do them, that Jehovah thy God will keep with thee the covenant and the lovingkindness which he sware unto thy fathers: 13and he will love thee, and bless thee, and multiply thee; he will also bless the fruit of thy body and the fruit of thy ground, thy grain and thy new wine and thine oil, the increase of thy cattle and the young of thy flock, in the land which he sware unto thy fathers to give thee. 14Thou shalt be blessed above all peoples: there shall not be male or female barren among you, or among your cattle. 15 And Jehovah will take away from thee all sickness; and none of the evil diseases of Egypt, which thou knowest, will he put upon thee, but will lay them upon all them that hate thee. 16And thou shalt consume all the peoples that Jehovah thy God shall deliver unto thee; thine eye shall not pity them: neither shalt thou serve their gods; for that will be a snare unto thee.

17If thou shalt say in thy heart, These nations are more than I; how can I dispossess them? 18thou shalt not be afraid of them: thou shalt well remember what Jehovah thy God did unto Pharaoh, and unto all Egypt; 19the great trials which thine eyes saw, and the signs, and the wonders, and the mighty hand, and the outstretched arm, whereby Jehovah thy God brought thee out: so shall Jehovah thy God do unto all the peoples of whom thou art afraid. 20 Moreover Jehovah thy God will send the hornet among them, until they that are left, and hide themselves, perish from before thee. 21Thou shalt not be affrighted at them; for Jehovah thy God is in the midst of thee, a great God and a terrible. 22And Jehovah thy God will cast out those nations before thee by little and little: thou mayest not consume them at once, lest the beasts of the field increase upon thee. 23But Jehovah thy God will deliver them up before thee, and will discomfit them with a great discomfiture, until they be destroyed. 24And he will deliver their kings into thy hand, and thou shalt make their name to perish from under heaven: there shall no man be able to stand before thee, until thou have destroyed them. 25 The graven images of their gods shall ye burn with fire: thou shalt not covet the silver or the gold that is on them, nor take it unto thee, lest thou be snared therein; for it is an abomination to Jehovah thy God. 26And thou shalt not bring an abomination into thy house, and become a devoted thing like unto it: thou shalt utterly detest it, and thou shalt utterly abhor it; for it is a devoted thing.

It should be understood that a patrilineal line carries the Y-DNA. The matrilineal lines heritage is passed on as well. The sticking point though is that for instance if you have a brother and a sister and the sister gets married, then she has a son, the Y-DNA does not carry through. Just like if the brother has a daughter his Y-DNA would not be passed on so the heritage does not carry on through his daughter. If this brother has a son, his Y-DNA does carry on through his son. **Every dynasty has a top ancestor, it is even called their Top Ancestor and for very good reason, it is the Y-DNA line of that family.**

A Levite for instance has to be a patrilineal line so it carries the Y-DNA of the priestly line. The same requirement is needed for the Davidic line. Our current European monarchies do not qualify to be Levite, nor of the Davidic bloodline as they do not carry a patrlineal line of Moses, nor Joseph or   David, as the required Y_DNA is missing from their bloodlines. This fact will be proven in this work to the best of my ability for truth.

_____Dividing line_____

_____Dividing
line_____

In consideration of the Bible, and it's historical proofs, I began to dig deeply at the many questions and still surviving proof's and evidence there truly was. I found that there were archaeologist, historians, theologins, Karites, Azd and historical tribes and theorist were all looking for the complex answers of this very important Exodus history and the people associated with this important period of time.

Many questions really started to peak my interest as I had often wondered as a child why there was royalty, and then the rest of us, it made no sence. How could they be so much more special then everyone else? Is their lineage just so much better than anyones?   This is a question that began to burn deeper as the years went by. So I began to research history very deeply. I wanted to know for instance who the Royal families were, and in general why things have gotten so out of balance.

The poverty, wars and death around the world historically as well as currently should be analyzed for it **root causes and perpetrators**. Our misunderstanding of history is our un-doing. Certain facts beg to be understood.   I forgive the misunderstanding, and forgive the perpetrators, but feel that the way in which the world is currently run is not in the best interest of human kind. Currently we are all under financial and psychological attack, and it has been that way now for generations.

Capitalism is in danger and is unsustainable" in its current state. Far too many resources are going into the bankers and Monarchies pocket's, and not back into the economy. This is called Usery by the Bible, and is quite unfare to the world as whole. What we must all face and understand are the perpetrators of this Usery debt, and how as a planet we are suffering far to greatly its massive greed. We must somehow be able to move beyond this, by holding are current debtors accountable for their unfare and un biblical actions of charging so much usery for the sake of their own greed, as far too many are and have been suffering and will suffer in the future if we don't in some way demand change.

We must look at history to understand who these people are, and how they took the reigns that started us down this path of perpetual debt in the first place. It is critical we understand, so we can try and put a stop to a system of Usery that truly unsustainable, and puts Capitalism in its current form in danger. Has this all been fare to the people, and has it put the world under far too much stress on it resources? The answer to this question is a resounding yes, and must be stopped. They are masters of building communism, so that is NOT the answer to this equasion either, and we must caution ourselves against it.

The Bankers would be happy to take the complete reigns, but as well is that a God given right for them to do so? And has this massive debt ever been correct?

We must move beyong the Age of Victoria to move towards a future somehow without all debt associated with it. Our children and their children are already being strapped with debt to a Victorian age that has outlived its purpose. Our history and archeological evidence must aid our understanding in doing so. For an example of how critical this TRULY is critical to our futures and families, just think about the Reality of our current time that are still stuck in the Victorian age.

The U.S. owed $75 million in 1791 — today it has been discovered that the debt rises by that much every hour.

How can we leave it like this for the sake of Future generations to suffer more than we are in our current times? Simply put, we cannot, and we must consider the how and why we are in these conditions in the first place.

We must take the example of that when in Archeology we moved beyond the inaccurate history books of the Victorian age, we were then actually able to see real Biblical history that we had been unable to locate in the past 200 years of searching because of the in accuracy and bias of the history written during the Victorian age. This has for far too long enabled the Black Nobility to control the world without question.

It is possible that if we follow the Bible, and what it says, that we can move forward away from the Black Nobility as well as their finely crafted so called New World Order. There are many laws and clues that the Bible does provide to guide us in a direction of Gods will for mankind. We must open our hearts and minds to achieve this goal. We can see clearly with the debt rising so much every hour that we cannot keep moving in the direction they want for us to. The direction of non action is acceptance. We must move on, just as archeology has done and finally reject the deception and massive debt of the Victorian age.

If we just stay with the party line of this all, then we are truly accepting their writ of slavery via perpetual debt on our decedents for many generations to come. It is the responsibility of the Many to learn the deception, and work together to make change. Not one person can do it on their own, and they know that clearly and have been taking advantage of this for over 150 years now. The debt we have incurred is so massive already we cannot pay it off because of the extreme usury charges that are directly against the Bible, and God's promise. We accept the Black nobility because they dress as though they are nobler than anyone on Earth, but it is all a complete deception and has been all along historically.

The European Monarchies of the line of Queen Victoria and the Stuarts, have been historically responsible for some of the most extreme anti-semetic acts in history, and should ultimatly be held accountable for their actions. For instance their claim to King David via Q. Tea Tephi (b. B.C. 565) is completely false. The British Royal Family expended much effort and money in propagandizing the legend of Tea Tephi, but it has been proven that this in indeed a false claim.

Skeptics made many claims that "Tea-Tephi never existed and had been a completely made-up character. The British Israel World Federation even now admit she never existed. She was an invention of a British-Israel expositor named F.R.A. Glover in 1861 and the myth was made to seem as truth and was perpetuated unchecked." In that time though, the Queen Victoria bloodline of the Monarchies of Europe proceeded to try and take over the planet by means perpetual debt.   Our ancestors suffered under them, we have suffered, and if we don't do anything, our children shall suffer as well. It is indeed a sad world we live in, and we go further in debt daily by the hands of the perpetrators and their bankers, based on what was and is still a great untruth today.

Many feel that the British so called Royal family are just figure heads, yet an deep examination of British Israelism and its very dangerous errors are quite necessary and will be made in this work. British Israelism by all rights should be rejected because it does not have a solid basis biblically, historically or genetcally. It has been and is still a danger to our world as a whole.   There have been many statements in this regard, now I want to lay down some hard facts and proof.   This system of desception has plagued the world for far too long.   Their practice of Genetic invasion is unacceptable,   and untimately should be undersood and delt with once and for all.   The Stuart/Windsors are not Anglo-Saxon by their own heritage. They are masters at turning countries communist, they are masters as stealing a whole lineage with just one marriage, or less.   They literally hijacked the lineage of familes, then proceeded to take over the world with it, with no right to do so. Historically these Olygarchies would threaten a familes with its life, and run them out of their home, taking their land and heritage, **or sometimes worse by near extermination of an entire bloodline**.

Only one of their main false claims is saying they are Anglo-Saxon, but they stole the lineage of the Anglo-Saxons, and other cultures as well.

Cerdic was the supposed son of King Arthur

It was the Anglo-Saxon Chronicle that provided an actual pedigree tracing Cerdic's ancestry back to Wōden and the antediluvian patriarchs. This pedigree is false and has been shown by Kenneth Sisam to have resulted from a process of elaboration upon a root pedigree taken from the kings of Bernicia, and hence prior to Cerdic himself it has no historical basis.[1] Through a female line (matrilineal) line there is a **direct descent from Cerdic to Elizabeth II**

1.   ^ Sisam, Kenneth, "Anglo-Saxon Royal Genealogies", *Proceedings of the British Academy*, vol. 39, pp. 287-348 (1953)

Many scollars are certain that Cerdic was not anglo-saxon he was a Briton and then Alfred the Great actually **fabricated an Anglo-Saxon pedigree.   These facts are Very Important to both history as well as the future .**

1.   **David Parsons, "British *Caratīcos, Old English Cerdic", Cambridge Medieval Celtic Studies, vol. 33, pp. 1-8 (1997); Henry Howorth, "The Beginnings of Wessex", The English Historical Review, vol. 13, pp. 667-71 (1898) - a contrary opinion is taken by Alfred Anscombe, "The Name of Cerdic", Y Cymmrodor: The Magazine of the Honorable Society of Cymmrodorion vol. 29, pp. 151-209 (1919)**

The tale of King Arthur only serves to distract the many from history the Stuart/Windsor Monarchy claims King Arthur in their lineage. In fact what is Prince William's full name: PRINCE WILLIAM ARTHUR PHILIP LOUIS WINDSOR.... They are counting on his glitz and glamour wedding to his relative Kate Middleton to distract the masses once again; just as the wedding of Charles and Diana did. Diana was a Stuart/Spencer/Rothschild. Diana had tried to commit suicide while she was pregnant with William, it has been said that she knew the horrible truths herself.

Cerdic is not though the Top Ancestor for the current Queen Victoria monarchies, I will show the truth indeed.

As Cerdics Anglo-saxon pedigree is fabricated, Cerdic historically was not anglo-saxon and is the supposed line of the current Windsor Monarchy though not its patrilineal line at all; they have a very dubious beginning to say the very least. And it gets worse, historically, as well as present. The House of Windsor it can be shown absorbs lineage as their own, though their lineage had no right to begin with. Once it absorbs others lineage like an ameba, they never give it back, it become their line, and the families of the original lineage are tossed aside as after the assimilation the families line they absorbed is no longer needed , over and over again. I warn, being absorbed by this ameba renders any other family line as worthless historically, though these bloodlines are not worthless at all, just invaded. They are taking over the world, without firing a shot, and how? It is called national debt. Ah now the picture becomes clearer. Read on it will become much more

apparent why our world today is so deeply in debt, and feels like something evil has taken over, well it has indeed.

What is known by many though is that there is far more German or Edomite blood in the queen Victoria monarchies of Europe, than there is actual Anglo-Saxon blood. All the kings of England, the supposed only pure Ephraimite nation, actually have come from the intermingling of the House of Hanover and the House of Brunswick[3], both of German genealogy. Europes Queen Victoria monarchs are more German or Edomite, than they are "pure Israelite",

1. Ibid.

2. Ibid.

3. Ibid.

4. 1991 World Book Encyclopedia Vol. 21, p.336

5. Isaiah 8:1

Charge some that they teach no other doctrine, neither give heed to legends and endless genealogies, which minister questions. For the time will come when they will not endure sound doctrine; but after their own lusts shall they heap to themselves teachers, and they shall turn away their ears from the Truth,and instead shall be turned unto legends. **1Timothy 1:3-4 and 2Timothy 4:3-4**

Chapter 3: Our Ancestors fled to America the Land of the Free

King Charles I   was born in 1600 November 19th, King Charles was not well liked in

United   States   for many reasons. There are still the memories of our ancestors that

of the times as they were then.

Lets first take a glance at the Stuart lineage origins:

Alain Dapifer

Born about 1046 in Dol, Ill et Vilaine, Bretagne, France ♀

Son of **[father unknown] and [mother unknown]**

[sibling(s) unknown]

[spouse(s) unknown]

Father of Flaad FitzAlain

Died about 1110 in Dol, Ill et Vilaine, Bretagne, France ⚲

Flaad **FitzAlain**

Born [date unknown] in Dol, Ill et Vilaine, Bretagne, France ⚲

Son of Alain Dapifer du Dol and [mother unknown]

[sibling(s) unknown]

[spouse(s) unknown]

Father of Alan FitzFlaad

Died [date unknown] in Shropshire, England ⚲

Dap´i`fer

n.

1.

One who brings meat to the table; hence, in some countries, the official title of

The European monarchies and their bankers have literally been using the lineage of so many hoping we would never figure it out. So many cry and say where is my lineage, and if your lineage was worth anything, there is a good possibility they are already claiming it as their own. They historically took over Kingdoms, and whole dynasties, not just by force, but by marriage to whatever female line had the heritage they wanted most. They had taken over the Anglo-Saxons hundreds of years ago, and found how easy it had been for them to marry one female, and then take over that lineage, and the lands and heritages' associated with them.

The Crown stripped many of them of their land, crops and lives. Many American and Canadian ancestors had to leave England to escape the stifling oppression of the British Crown and its landowner-run government, which hanged poor children for stealing food to survive. So many families had their homes their lives their family and their lands and heritage stripped away because they were not Catholic, it is a sad testament to history, but the truth as it was.

Many feel that the British so called Royal family are just figure heads, yet an deep examination of British Israel-ism and its very dangerous errors are quite necessary and will be made in this work. British Israel ism by all rights should be rejected because it does not have a solid basis bionically, historically or genetically. It has been and is still a danger to our world as a whole.   There have been many statements in this regard, now I want to lay down some hard facts and proof.   This system of deception has plagued the world for far too long.   Their practice of Genetic invasion is unacceptable, and ultimately should be understood and dealt with once and for all.   The Stuart/Windsors are not Anglo-Saxon by their own heritage. They are masters at turning a countries communist, they are masters as stealing a whole lineage with just one marriage, or less.   They literally hijacked the lineage of familes, then proceeded to take over the world with it, with no right to do so, or.The lineage is not theirs. Historically these Olygarchies would threaten a familes with its life, and run them out of their home, taking their land and heritage, **or sometimes worse by near extermination of an entire bloodline**.

Only one of their main false claims is saying they are Anglo-Saxon, but they stole the lineage of the Anglo-Saxons, and other cultures. They will be called out upon this fact as well.

Deuteronomy 17:14-17 (American Standard Version)

 14 When thou art come unto the land which Jehovah thy God giveth thee, and shalt possess it, and shalt dwell therein, and shalt say, I will set a king over me, like all the nations that are round about me;

 15 thou shalt surely set him king over thee, whom Jehovah thy God shall choose: one from among thy brethren shalt thou set king over thee; thou mayest not put a foreigner over thee, who is not thy brother.

 16 Only he shall not multiply horses to himself, nor cause the people to return to Egypt, to the end that he may multiply horses; forasmuch as Jehovah hath said unto you, Ye shall henceforth return no more that way.

 17 Neither shall he multiply wives to himself, that his heart turn not away: neither shall he greatly multiply to himself silver and gold.

The direct male line of the Royal branch of the House of Stuart is assumed to be extinct, after the deaths of Charles Edward Stuart, and his brother Cardinal Henry Benedict Stuart (although **the male line continues through the descendants of several illegitimate sons** of Charles II and James II). The current British Royal family descends from the House of Stuart in the Count Palatine cadet branch of the House of Stuart.

I begin now with The Legend of King Arthur, a tale of medieval times. When you think about King Arthur and the nights of the round table it brings images to mind of Kings, Squires and Noble Men; Mysteries of the times of old shrouded by mystery and glory. Thoughts of Merlin, his spells of magic, even the Charm of making runs through your head. The Holy Grail and Persivle; Knights that seeks the

Holy Grail for redemption of their King; Conniving trickery of Morgana; An alliance between Morgana and Merlin; The Sword and the Stone, and King Arthur's rise to power.

A great kinship wells within. You cannot explain why, yet it somehow haunts you. Recently in the past few years, the legend is being reported as possibly true. How can that be? King Arthur's castle possibly found reported in the news, how exciting! What if I told you now, King Arthur is just a legend, and would you believe me? What if I told you truth? Arthur in his earliest form appears entirely mythical.

References

1. ^ Gildas, *De Excidio et Conquestu Britanniae*, chapter 26.
2. ^ Pryor 2004, pp. 22–27
3. ^ Bede, *Historia ecclesiastica gentis Anglorum*, Book 1.16.
4. ^ Dumville 1977, pp. 187–88

Charge some that they teach no other doctrine, neither give heed to legends and endless genealogies, which minister questions. For the time will come when they will not endure sound doctrine; but after their own lusts shall they heap to themselves teachers, and they shall turn away their ears from the Truth, and instead shall be turned unto legends. 1Timothy 1:3-4 and 2Timothy 4:3-4

Cerdic the supposed son of King Arthur

The Anglo-Saxon Chronicle provides a pedigree tracing Cerdic's ancestry back to Wōden and the antediluvian patriarchs. However, this pedigree has been shown by Kenneth Sisam to have resulted from a process of elaboration upon a root pedigree taken from the kings of Bernicia, and hence prior to Cerdic himself it has no historical basis. Through a female line (matrilineal) there is supposedly a d**irect descent from Cerdic to Elizabeth II**

1^ Sisam, Kenneth, "Anglo-Saxon Royal Genealogies", *Proceedings of the British Academy*, vol. 39, pp. 287-348 (1953)

The Crown stripped many of our very own ancestors of their land, crops and lives. Many American and Canadian ancestors had to leave England to escape the stifling oppression of the British Crown and its landowner-run government, which hanged poor children for stealing food to survive. So many families had their homes their lives their family and their lands and herritage stripped away because they were not Catholic, it is a sad testament to history, but the truth as it was.

Revelation 10:11 And they said to me, "You must prophesy again concerning many peoples and nations and tongues and kings."

The Stewart/Windsor families falsely trace themselves to the Legend of King Arthur. Guess what, as you saw legend was all King Arthur was, there is no evidence he ever existed. Oh no, he we go with yet more false history and lineage, oh what the Windsor's have gotten away with, and still do to this day is sickening. Two Royal Families in Great Britain claim and have claimed of them to be descendants of Israel. These are the current House of Windsor (Queen Elizabeth, Charles, etc.) and the House of

Stewart/Spencer (Late Princess Diana, Diana was also a Rothschild. So William is essentially triple trouble, or as some claim, the Anti-christ himself, as time may indeed show.

Cerdic is not though the Top Ancestor for the current Queen Victoria monarchies, I will show the truth indeed about this grave deception.

As Cerdics Anglo-saxon pedigree is fabricated, Cerdic historically was not anglo-saxon and is the supposed line of the current Windsor Monarchy though not its patrilineal line at all; they have a very dubious beginning to say the very least. And it gets worse, historically, as well as present. The House of Windsor it can be shown absorbs lineage as their own, though their lineage had no right to begin with. Once it absorbs others lineage like an ameba, they never give it back, it become their line, and the families of the original lineage are tossed aside as after the assimilation the families line they absorbed is no longer needed , over and over again. I warn, being absorbed by this ameba renders any other family line as worthless historically, though these bloodlines are not worthless at all, just invaded. They are taking over the world, without firing a shot, and how? It is called national debt. Ah now the picture becomes clearer. Read on it will become much more apparent why our world today is so deeply in debt, and feels like something evil has taken over, well it has indeed.

What is known by many though is that there is far more German or Edomite blood in the queen Victoria monarchies of Europe, than there is actual Anglo-Saxon blood. All the kings of England, the supposed only pure Ephraimite nation, actually have come from the intermingling of the House of Hanover and the House of Brunswick[3], both of German genealogy. Europes Queen Victoria monarchs are more German or Edomite, than they are "pure Israelite",

1. Ibid.
2. Ibid.
3. Ibid.
4. 1991 World Book Encyclopedia Vol. 21, p.336
5. Isaiah 8:1

It can be stated clearly that the British Monarchy is NOT Anglo-Saxon of its own lineage, not Hebrew of its own lineage, and not Moor or Arab by its own lineage. They are Norman/Germans of their own lineage, and that is all. They have absorbed many deep lineages as their own, but these stolen lineages are not theirs, and shall be returned to rights of the original families they have intruded upon.

Revelation13:2
13:2 And the beast which I saw was like a leopard, and its feet were like the feet of a bear, and its mouth was as a lion's mouth. And the dragon gave its

power to it, and its throne, and great authority.

Refrences

[3] A partial English translation of the law can be found in Ernst Ekman, "The Danish Royal Law of 1665" pp. 102-107 in: *The Journal of Modern History*, 1957, vol. 2.

[4]The Western Experience, Seventh Edition, Boston: McGraw-Hill, 1999.

‸ Fosberry, John trans, *Criminal Justice through the Ages*, English trans. John Fosberry. Mittalalterliches Kriminalmuseum, Rothenburg ob der Tauber, (1990 Eng. trans. 1993) p.7

‸ Cave, Roy and Coulson, Herbert. *A Source Book for Medieval Economic History*, Biblo and Tannen, New York (1965) p.336

‸ "The Dutch Language". Livius.org. http://www.livius.org/dutchhistory/language.html. Retrieved 2006-09-20.

‸ G. M. Fraser (2006) *Royal Flash*, p. 172, Grafton paperback.

Notes

‸ *a b* "History—Charles I (1600–1649)". British Broadcasting Corporation. http://www.bbc.co.uk/history/historic_figures/charles_i_king.shtml. Retrieved 20 April 2008.

‸ *a b c d e* "Charles I (r. 1625–49)". Royal.gov.uk. http://www.royal.gov.uk/HistoryoftheMonarchy/KingsandQueensoftheUnitedKingdom/TheStuarts/CharlesI.aspx. Retrieved 20 April 2008.

‸ "Queen Henrietta Maria, 1609–69". British-civil-wars.co.uk. http://www.british-civil-wars.co.uk/biog/henrietta-maria.htm. Retrieved 20 April 2008.

‸ "Queen Henrietta Maria, 1609–69". British-civil-wars.co.uk. http://www.british-civil-wars.co.uk/glossary/parliament-1625-29.htm. Retrieved 20 April 2008.

‸ "Charles, King and Martyr". SKCM. http://www.skcm.org/SCharles/scharles_main.html. Retrieved 16 October 2008.

Charles II left no legitimate children, but his numerous illegitimate descendants ... Legitimacy was formerly of great consequence, in that only legitimate children could inherit their fathers' estates, yet there were no legitimate children, this non royal line should have ended then and there.

Among my people are wicked men who lie in wait like men who snare birds and like

those who set traps to catch men. Like cages full of birds, their houses are full of deceit;

have become rich and powerful and have grown fat and sleek. Their evil deeds have no limit -
miah 5:26)

1 After this I saw another angel coming down from heaven. He had great authority, and the earth was illuminated by his splendour. 2 With a mighty voice he shouted:

"Fallen! Fallen is Babylon the Great! She has become a home for demons and a haunt for every evil spirit, a haunt for every unclean and detestable bird. 3 For all the nations have drunk the maddening wine of her adulteries. The kings of the earth committed adultery with her, and the merchants of the earth grew rich from her excessive luxuries."

Revelation 10:11 And they said to me, "You must prophesy again concerning many peoples and nations and tongues and kings."

"And there was war in heaven: Michael and his anels fought against the dragon; and the dragon fought and his angels... And the **great dragon was cast out,** that old serpent, called the Devil, and Satan, which deceiveth the whole world: he was cast out into the earth, and his angels were cast out with him...
"And I stood upon the sand of the sea, and saw a beast rise up out of the sea..
And...the dragon gave him his power, and his seat, and great authority."
(Rev. 12:7,9; 13:1-2) And I beheld another beast coming up out of the earth; and he had two horns like a lamb, and he spake as a dragon. And he exerciseth all the power of the first beast before him, and deadlywound was healed. And he doeth great wonders, so that he maketh fire come down from heaven on the earth in the sight of men, - Rev. 13:11-13

"Satan always wanted a substitute religion. a. 'I will be like the most high'

(Isa. 14:14). b. 'The man of sin be revealed, the son of perdition...who opposeth

and exalteth himself above all that is called God,...so that he as God sitteth in

the temple of God, shewing himself that he is God'(II Thess. 2:3-4).c. Substitute

Trinity, Satan, antichrist, and false prophet. 3. Future Babylon is the apostate church.

a. Called 'Mystery, Babylon the Great, the Mother of Harlots, and abominations

of the earth (Rev. 17:5). b. Babylon associated with the Beast (antichrist) and the

revived Roman Empire of 10 nations (Rev. 17:3, 12). c. Merger of Protestants,

Catholics, Jews, Muslims, Hindus, etc. d. The religious glue is supernatural signs

and wonders. (Not Roman Catholic, or doctrine). 'The beast that was, and is not,

and yet is' (Rev. 17:8). 'His deadly wound was healed and all the world wondered at

him" (Rev. 13:3). 'So that he maketh fire to comedown out of heaven' (Rev. 13:13)

I hear the sound of the trumpet as do many, as we are told our blood will be on our

head if we hear the trumpet but do not take warning, and must blow the trumpet to

warn the people, as the watchman is accountable for his blood. If he had taken

warning, he would have saved himself. Oh dear sweet Lord, can man heareth

your call finally, for the sake of our world, as well as their own salvation I pray.

"Do what thou wilt," is the satanist motto.

Benjamine Franklin said:

"In the Colonies we issue our own money. It is called Colinial scrip. We control

its purchasing power,and we have no interest to pay to no one."   Quoted by Senator

Robert L Owen 1839

"The Colonies would have gladly have borne the little tax on Tea and other matters

had it not been that England took away from the Colonies [their] money,which created

 unemployment and disssatifaction"

Quoted by Senator Robert Owen 1893

The Rothschild-controlled *Times of London* wrote, "If that mischievous policy,

which had its origins in the North American Republic, should become indurated

down to a fixture, then that Government will furnish its own money without cost.

It will pay off its debts and be without debt. It will have all the money necessary

to carry on its commerce. It will become prosperous beyond precedent in the

history of the civilized governments of the world. The brains and the wealth of all

countries will go to North America. That government must be destroyed, or it will destroy every monarchy on the globe." [1]

[1] *Human Race Get Off Your Knees: The Lion Sleeps No More*. David Icke. David Icke Books Ltd. Isle of Wight. UK. 2010. p.92

"When money is lent on a contract to receive not only the principal sum

The Queen Victoria monarchies that include the **British Royal Family** is the group of close and often inbred relatives of the so called monarchy of many parts of Europe including Spain and the United Kingdom.

1st the so called Windsor Monarchy part of he Queen Victoria Black nobility, grabbed

the lineage of the Anglo-Saxon Dux via the line of Wada. Wada was related to all

Ango-Saxon kings. This lineage was not their own, it was Genetic invasion.

They have also Genetically invaded many other families lineage to grab every biblical

line possible in an effort to make themselves seem as Gods, but all they are is the

worst persecutors in history. One day they must be put to a halt, for they have brought

on the worst terror of any family, be it economic, or with the genetic invasions, and indeed

with pure genocide and what they have done in history to so many, including the Hebrews,

Jews, Anglo-Saxons and Arabs, and worst of all so many Children.

Many around the world have been quite aware as I am that there is an attempt to take

over the world by a few very wealthy families, and the ones they surround themselves

with.   This mission has been in their plans for well over one hundred years now or longer.

We are at critical mass,and the world is suffering.   As per British Israelism, Britain

can be the only kingdom, and that leaves Israel in a bad position, as the Windsors are

clearly not the Patrilineal line of King David. The CCG (Cristian churches of God)

will have two false witnesses and they already proclaim the Windsors as the bloodline

of King David.   Why should any of the true Anglo-Saxons, Picts or pure Arab lines of Keturah want to join something that hurts Israel further?   When the only Kingdom under British Israel can be in Britain, as per British Israelism itself,   why should anyone take part in furthering the deception? The bloodlines they are calling have been plundered and abused as it is already, and used Maitilinealy by the Victoria Monarchies as their own bloodlines, but those bloodlines are clearly not theirs to use Lets first take a glance at the Stuart lineage:

Alain Dapifer was born around 1046 in Dol, France and he was the Son of his father was as well as his mother Alain Dapifer was the Father of Flaad FitzAlain who Died about 1110 in Dol, France

Again Alan Fitz Flaad is not the top patrilieal line of the Windsors either, why is this very important? You will find it is quite important indeed.   The Stuart line is not though the Windsors patrilineal line though, since the Stuart line goes back to Unknown it really matters not but that bloodline is leached by them as well in any way possible, as there are many bloodlines have suffered the same fate as well.

In WWII the Windsors did not even have a last name, as their own was obvious it was too German.

Alan was the son of Flaad, who was in turn a son [4] of an Alain who had been the crusader (in 1097[5]) who was ***Dapifer*** to the Archbishop of Dol, which is situated near Mont-Saint-Michel. "Alan, **dapifer**" is found as a witness in 1086 to a charter relating to Mezuoit, a cell of St. Florent, near Dol.[5]

Dap´ï´fer

n. 1. **One who brings meat to the table**; hence, in some countries, the official title of the grand master or steward of the king's or a nobleman's household.

Webster's Revised Unabridged Dictionary, published 1913 by C. & G. Merriam Co.

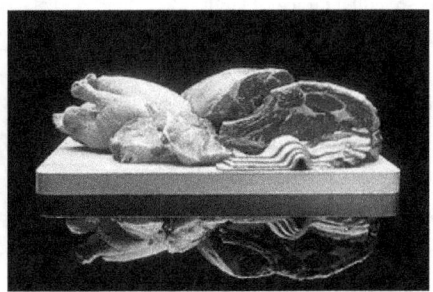

Varieties of meat

1.^ _a_ _b_ _c_ Bartlett, *England Under the Norman and Angevin Kings, 1075–1225*, 544.

2.^ Lieber, *Encyclopædia Americana*, 30

3^ "J.H. Round: The Origin of the Stewarts: Part 1". MedievalGenealogy.org.uk. http://www.medievalgenealogy.org.uk/sources/round/stewarts1.shtml. Retrieved on 13 November 2008.

4.^ Round (1901) p.122, speculates he may be possibly a brother, with their father also being Alain, and another dapifer.

5.^ a b Round (1901) p.122

stop here

Queen Victoria was an illegitimate child,   as well Prince consort Albert was also illegitimate, her father was also her children's father, as well her brother was also her children's father, her eldest son Edward, Prince of Wales was the father of Winston Churchill. The dependents of the Queen Victoria line is quite interbred with the Rothschilds   they are an actual subset of the Rothschilds.   Winston Churchill, admitted the existence of conspiracy when he wrote in 1920, "From the days of Spartacus-Weishaupt to those of Karl Marx, to those of Trotsky, Bela Kun, Rosa Luxemburg, and Emma Goldman, this worldwide conspiracy for the overthrow of civilization . . . has been steadily growing."

Historically since the time of Queen Victoria making a claim of being the Davidic line, their bankers the Rothschilds have amassed over 500 Trillion dollars from debt of Usury. Queen Elizabeth II still fronts for the Rothschilds. By the So called Grace of God, Queen Elizabeth is the largest land owner on Earth, this deception they have promoting has cost the planet and its people far too much already. She is Head of State of the United Kingdom and of thirty one other states and territories, and and acts as though she and her family are the legal owner of 6,600 million acres of land, one sixth of the Earth's land surface, was actually accumulated by the historical theft of many of our ancestors lands. The crusader families of Europe that control the world today hide these facts presented in this book. They sit upon the lineage of many, and this must come to an end as these lineages are not rightfully theirs to claim.

I present to you history that has been hidden and abused to the harm of many.

How deep does the rabbit hole go? And is it what we are seeing today?

Does this plan go against Americans? My answer is indeed yes!!!!!

Follow me on just how sick and dangerous this truly is to this day.

Revelation 10:11 Then I was told, "You must prophesy again about many peoples, nations, languages and kings."

Revelation 12:3 Then another sign appeared in heaven: an enormous red dragon with seven heads and ten horns and seven crowns on his heads.

Revelation 13:1 And the dragon stood on the shore of the sea. And I saw a beast coming out of the sea. He had ten horns and seven heads, with ten crowns on his horns, and on each head a blasphemous name.

Daniel 7:23 Thus he said, The fourth beast shall be the **fourth kingdom** upon earth, which shall be diverse from all kingdoms, and shall devour the whole earth, and shall tread it down, and break it in pieces.

House of Windsor"; I believe this to be fairly accurate. The fact
that a number of U.S. presidents are related to royalty does not prove any
conspiracy; rather it simply demonstrates that the presidency of the U.S. is related to
the Ten Crowns of Europe
Stop here

The question is, "will you believe the lie"?
The related families all related past and present that carry on the aim of Queen Victoria of complete world domination by debt and our current monitary system are as follows:

The line of Victoria should be disqualified as their patrilineal line shows no indication they are the line of David, nor even eligible to be a Levite.   Their deception has put the world under deep debt, and far too many suffer as a result. They are trying to take over the world, and have to be stopped once and for all. The world must agree that their tyranny has to be delt with,before they succeed in their complete world domination by deception and greed.

Under that **Covenant** the monarch is **prohibited** from using their position for **personal** material gain of **any** kind and from making up their **own** laws and taxes and economic policies; either themselves or their politicians.

America is a land of peoples that originally in the early years had been the families that were kicked out of Europe often by the "Crown" itself. I looked into my own Anglo-Saxon heritage and could see the depth to this history. I then looked at my sons lineage, and was in shock at what "The Crown" has gotten away with, and still are to this day. I could see what my ancestors themselves had said about this very same family called the British Crown, and felt their pain as well. As far as I can tell, even though America thinks it is free from England due to our fight for independence, that it is really not free at all in many ways. What they could not take by force and by War, they now take though our banking system, and their Bankers. The City of London is the Banking hub.

Jefferson extolled, "A country which expects to remain ignorant and free...expects that which has never been and that which will never be. There is scarcely a King in a hundred who would not, if he could, follow the example of Pharaoh – get first all the people's money, then all their lands and then make them and their children servants forever. banking establishments are more dangerous than standing armies. Already they have raised up a money aristocracy."

<u>1 Timothy 6:10</u> ESV

For the love of money is a root of all kinds of evils. It is through this craving that some have wandered away from the faith and pierced themselves with many pangs

<u>This truth is plain</u> *"There is no peace," says the LORD, "for the wicked."* (Isaiah 48:22) The score may be settled on either side of eternity, but it will be settled. <u>No one can forsake the LORD and escape the consequences.</u>

Photograph by <u>Alexander Bassano</u>, 1882

In today's spending power Victoria was given a cool £M8 per-year public money to play with. A mear pitance compared with her profits from the opium trade, the arms trade, the slave trade, sheep, coal, iron, tea, cocoa, cotton, sugar, grain, banking, rail & shipping investments and similar anchors of the British Empire - where the sun it is said never set's.

Though no female bloodline qualifies as a valid and legal bloodline to be an heir of King David historically <u>Queen Victoria</u> **believed herself she descended from King David, she wrote a letter supporting this view that she occupied the throne of David**.[1] **This is a complete false claim**, as the Davidic line is Patrilineal. I will show her Top Patrilineal line, The Top Ancestor, and prove it is not the throne of David. You must understand deeply it is this false claim that has kept her and

her decedents in power over the people and the banking system, the 12 oligarchic families of the Black Nobility.

This horrible and fallacious reasoning actually asserts that **since Britain is Israel,**

no other nation can be according to others like E. Odlum in his book God's Covenant

Man-British Israel. By their very own definition, there cannot possibly be two nations

of Israelite population and background, let alone two legitimate kingdoms of Israel, <u>and that is according</u> <u>to British Israelism.</u>

In genealogy, a **top ancestor in a geneolocial study** is the oldest ancestor in a continuous sequence of ancestors. This means, that a complete continuous line of parent-child connections exists between the top ancestor and the subject of the genealogical patrilineal study, such as a living person. However, the top ancestor's parents are not (or not yet) known.

Top ancestors are sometimes used to describe the status of a genealogical research project, or in order to compare the availability of genealogical data in different times and places. Often, top ancestors are implied to be patrilineal. If a patrilineal dynasty is considered, and this is an important fact, each such dynasty has exactly one top ancestor.

<u>**In contrast the Top Patrilineal line of Victoria is know as well, or Not Know is more accurate.**</u> <u>**They have been taking over many countries including Israel, The United States and Canada. They**</u> <u>**have no God given right to try and rule the world, they chose themselves, and the suffering of the**</u> <u>**people and children has become massive as we can see from the unemployment and contolled**</u> <u>**economies. They want their New World order, but have no right to rule over anyone, including the**</u> <u>**economies their bankers controle currently.**</u>

Revelation Chapters 2:9 and 3:9

I know the blasphemy of them which CLAIM to be Jews (Bloodline of Judah) and are NOT. They *are* the Synogogue of Satan, and *do LIE*

Examples of <u>patrilineal</u> top ancestors of the line of Victoria

subject	dynasty	top ancestor	date of top ancestor's death
Queen Elizabeth II of the United Kingdom	Wettin	**Dietrich I of Wettin**	10th century AD
Charles, Prince of Wales	Oldenburg	**Elimar I,** Count of Oldenburg	12th century AD

Charlemagne	Carolingian	Bishop Arnulf of Metz	640 AD
Queen Victoria of the United Kingdom	Este	**Otbert I,** Count Palatine of Italy	975 AD

Oberto I Obizzo was one of Queen Victoria's ancestors who died 15 October 975

is is also known that **Otbert's father was Margrave Adalbert, historically**

nothing is known other than he is the Top Patrilineal ancestor of Queen Victoria.

_Queen Victoria was the granddaughter of George III, and was an ancestor

of most major European royal houses.   But King George even is not their

patrileneal line either.

These false monarchies can be justifiably viewed as the "the trail of the serpent"

Queen Elizabeth's patriline is the line from which she is descended father to son.

The oldest traceable member of the Wettin family was Dietrich he would be the Top Ancestor of the Bloodline of Queen Elizabeth.

"A nation...cannot survive treason from within...the traitor ...wears the face of his victims,...and he appeals to the baseness that lies deep in the hearts of all men. He rots the soul of a nation—he works secretly...he infects the body politic so that it can no longer resist. A murderer is less to be feared......." Cicero, 42 B.C.E.

During one of the most horrifying wand bloody wars , George dropped the family's German titles and created the phony House of Windsor. To fool the ignorant King George 5 bribed newspaper owners to forget the royals real name, Saxe-Coburg-Gotha. Yet who they? It is very important to know both who they are, as well as who they are not. This family's roots and the history of their obscene offshore fortune, made from stolen land, slaves & slavery, arm's & ammo have been studiously ignored by the media ever since.

He did all this as he was sweeping everything under the rug hoping that no one would Ever Notice

"A Good Riddance". Propaganda cartoon from Punch, Vol. 152, 27 June 1917, commenting on the King having ordered the relinquishing of the German titles held by members of His Majesty's family **history Has shown that the pedigree may very well not be authentic at all. Clearly of German celtic origin not Anglo-Saxon ... After the Battle of Hastings in 1066 the Norman french monarchy ruled England.**

VERY Many scollars are Certain that Cerdic was actually a Briton with Alfred the great **fabricating an Anglo-Saxon pedigree for political purposes. These facts are Very Important to both history as well as the future . Patrileal law was the law and Salic law has precedence to this day no matter if they overturned the Salic law, as it was not witin their right to have done so, and it was NEVER** within the right of the Victorican/Stuart monarchies to ignor the Ancient Salic law in the first place.

The illuminati ruling with this Iron hand based upon a matrilineal line of the great-great-granddaughter, Poppa of Bavaria has no Salic right, nor Biblical rights at all. It is not an unbroken Patrilineal chain of any sort of the imagination, nor does it have the Salic rights that the Dukes of Narabonne held in the first place. Allow me to help my bretherine in understanding our history. You will then see the Grave deception we have had forced upon us since the days of Cerdic. Then I will ask you to also understand the even Bigger picture to these equasions.

Remember about the Windsors and Rothchilds and the illuminati the following again:

The Black Nobility including the Stuarts, the Rothschilds and the Windsors are all the   arrogant as well as aristocratic bloodlines that comprise the very core of the Illuminati, are descended from Guillaume de Gellone of the eighth century AD. Guillaume's father was Rabbi Makhir. They carry only a Matrilineal line again from one marriage to a Great Great Grand daughter of Rabbi Makhir of Narbonne. Again not a patrilineal line At All, and That Carries No Rights Nor Birthrights associated with it according to the 1st law of an Isralite as well as the Salic law. Yet the Illuminati rule with an Iron hand based upon Matrilineal lines that have no Birthright or Salic right.

The crusaiders who are still in control namely the Sinclairs especially are descendants of Guillaume de Gellone, through his great-great-granddaughter, Poppa of Bavaria. This is yet again just another Matrilineal decent with a broken chain with no Y-DNA or Birthright.

This game these 12 families are playing is effectively divide and concour, and it has been historically far too affective.   When do we finally say enough is enough on a massive enough scale for it to mattter?

Queen Elizabeth is herself a great-great-granddaughter of Queen Victoria, and her and her family make up the Balck Nobility that rule the World by making everyone worship their money they They are all one big happy family controlling the world, and as you can see they are all related.

And IF God has ever called an individual to be a King or Queen, then that said individual would need to obay the laws of God in order to maintain their title! / And if they are not acting in accordance with the laws of God, it then becomes a must needs that they step down or be   removed! Thus the Kings and Queens that are up on the Earth today have no true power over anyone!

But is the patrilineal line that being followed today?   The answer to that question is clearly no. This is why the Monarchies of Europe control the world via the bloodline of Queen Victoria, as they are the bloodline that have absorbed the deepest lineages of others via marriage. Their actual patrlineal lines lead back to simply put **Unknown,** and that is clearly un-acceptable.

What many know for certain with great pain is that the most hellish, demonic and satanic doctrine, has been and still is the removal of the throne of David from Jerusalem (both earthly and heavenly), to

London and the removal of Messiah Yahshua from the throne, in order to establish the German based house of House of Brunswick-House of Hanover- House of Windsor.

How did they do it? Ah now, lets learn a little more history first, then see more clealy how this was cruely and calculatedly accomplished, and what it tells of our current times.

On September 11, 1922, the British mandate came into force over Palestine. ("Mandate" in this sense means a commission given to a nation to govern a territory.) The British mandate lasted until 1948, when the state of Israel was established. **The current State of Israel was established by the Windsor monarchy by proxy of the Rothschilds**.

Is it not nice that Good ol Queen Victoria left such a legacy as the European Monarchies of today, but lets not forget a far bigger legacy we all feel the pinch of on a daily basis.

The history of the Federal Reserve is an ongoing battle between the Banking elite and the people and anyone who gets in the way is usually crushed. The Federal Reserve Bank is the Central bank that publish the US dollar. ... but it is owned by the world bankers the most powerful of them is the Rothschild

Historically since the time of Queen Victoria making a claim of being the Davidic line, their bankers the Rothschilds have amassed over 500 Trillion dollars from debt of Usury. Queen Elizabeth II still fronts for the Rothschilds. By the So called Grace of God, Queen Elizabeth is the largest land owner on Earth, this deception they have promoting has cost the planet and its people far too much already. She is Head of State of the United Kingdom and of thirty one other states and territories, and acts as though she and her family are the legal owner of 6,600 million acres of land, one sixth of the Earth's land surface, was actually accumulated by the historical theft of many of our ancestors lands.

Rothschilds own the IMF, The World Bank, and the World Conservation Bank for Third World Countries

U.S. debt holdings: $6.328 trillion

That's right, the biggest single holder of U.S. government debt is the Federal Reserve system.

China holds U.S. debt holdings: $1.132 trillion

The U.S. owed $75 million in 1791 — today the debt rises by that much every hour.

Da. Magdalena de Granada of Granada, married into the house of Aviz, and then the Nasrid lineage of the Kingdom of Granada was genetically invaded, and the houses of Europe tried, and still to this day try to make Gods of themselves with this female line. It was not their genetics at all, one marriage, and the whole of the dynasty was absorbed. Please do not be prejudice as that is the history they hide, the is history they do not want for you to understand The Nasrid lineage is very deep indeed, what they stole was immeasurable. It was Hebrew, Israelite, Levite then Jewish

then Muslim. How do they make all these false claims of Hebrew lineage? They stole it from in one marriage, and they have been inbreeding from that time forward trying to keep their claim.

I will to my very best ability prove I am speaking truth, <u>Should we continue to disregard this line of Queen Victoria for so long just so they can be rich beyond our wildest dreams while people live in Cardboard boxes? The Matrilineal line of Da.Magdalena de Granada was absorbed into the Victoria line in the following way:.</u>

Chapter 4: Traced History back to Seth Ben Adam Ben Jehovahs Kingdom, The Father's Kingdom Originated by Seth Ben Adam Ben Jehovah

I can prove Seth Ben Adam Ben Jehovah Replaced Cain with Seth Ben Adam Ben Jehovah. Jehovah was his very own Enmity. Genesis 3:15 is the same as Revelation 12 final Judgment. I was able to trace and will prove that all tribes were descended though Seth Ben Adam Ben Jehovah. As the Nasrid and Anglo-Saxon dynasties traces directly back to Seth Ben Adam Ben Jehovah and I can prove these fact and do in this work. I am more valuable than a ruby the Bible says because I know that all tribes traced through "Seth" Seth Ben Adam Ben Jehovah. Jehovahs is his very own enmity and placed himself between the Seed of the Serpent Cain and the Seed of the Woman "Adam" Seth Ben Adam Ben Jehovah.

The tribes of Israel all descended though Seth Ben Adam Ben Jehovah and I can prove this. It is the Seed of the Woman "ADAM" that has to crush the Serpent and Receive the Fathers Kingdom Seth Ben Adam Ben Jehovah End days Kingdom. I can and will prove that my son the Revelation 12 Rod of Iron that will rule all nations is the seed of the Woman Adam decedent though Seth Ben Adam Ben Jehovah's an all-male line with no female breaks in it. Genesis 3:15 is the same as Revelation 12 Final Judgment and I am the Queen of Sheba decedent t the Holy Bible the Torah of Hashem Moses says will stand and judge. A mother of all prophets Hashem is a special thing as Zipporah was a Mother of all prophets Hashem too and so was the Mother Mary the wife of Hashem Jesus Christ.

American Standard Version

The Serpent's Deception
(Genesis 7:1-5; Romans 5:12-21; 2 Peter 3:1-9)

1Now the serpent was more subtle than any beast of the field which Jehovah God had made. And he said unto the woman, Yea, hath God said, Ye shall not eat of any tree of the garden? 2And the woman said unto the serpent, Of the fruit of the trees of the garden we may eat: 3but of the fruit of the tree which is in the midst of the garden, God hath said, Ye shall not eat of it, neither shall ye touch it, lest ye die. 4And the serpent said unto the woman, Ye shall not surely die: 5for God doth know that in the day ye eat thereof, then your eyes shall be opened, and ye shall be as God, knowing good and evil. 6And when the woman saw that the tree was good for food, and that it was a delight to the eyes, and that the tree was to be desired to make one wise, she took of the fruit thereof, and did eat; and she gave also unto her husband with her, and he did eat. 7And the eyes of them both were opened, and they knew that they were naked; and they sewed fig-leaves together, and made themselves aprons.

God Arraigns Adam and Eve

8And they heard the voice of Jehovah God walking in the garden in the cool of the day: and the man and his wife hid themselves from the presence of Jehovah God amongst the trees of the garden. 9And Jehovah God called unto the man, and said unto him, Where art thou? 10And he said, I heard thy voice in the garden, and I was afraid, because I was naked; and I hid myself. 11And he said, Who told thee that thou wast naked? Hast thou eaten of the tree, whereof I commanded thee that thou shouldest not eat? 12And the man said, The woman whom thou gavest to be with me, she gave me of the tree, and I did eat. 13And Jehovah God said unto the woman, What is this thou hast done? And the woman said, The serpent beguiled me, and I did eat.

14And Jehovah God said unto the serpent, Because thou hast done this, cursed art thou above all cattle, and above every beast of the field; upon thy belly shalt thou go, and dust shalt thou eat all the days of thy life:

15and I will put enmity between thee and the woman, and between thy seed and her seed: he shall bruise thy head, and thou shalt bruise his heel.

The Punishment of Mankind

16Unto the woman he said, I will greatly multiply thy pain and thy conception; in pain thou shalt bring forth children; and thy desire shall be to thy husband, and he shall rule over thee.

17And unto Adam he said, Because thou hast hearkened unto the voice of thy wife, and hast eaten of the tree, of which I commanded thee, saying, Thou shalt not eat of it: cursed is the ground for thy sake; in toil shalt thou eat of it all the days of thy life;

18thorns also and thistles shall it bring forth to thee; and thou shalt eat the herb of the field;

19in the sweat of thy face shalt thou eat bread, till thou return unto the ground; for out of it wast thou taken: for dust thou art, and unto dust shalt thou return.

20And the man called his wife's name Eve; because she was the mother of all living.

The Expulsion from Paradise

21And Jehovah God made for Adam and for his wife coats of skins, and clothed them.

22And Jehovah God said, Behold, the man is become as one of us, to know good and evil; and now, lest he put forth his hand, and take also of the tree of life, and eat, and live for ever- 23therefore Jehovah God sent him forth from the garden of Eden, to till the ground from whence he was taken. 24So he drove out the man; and he placed at the east of the garden of Eden the Cherubim, and the flame of a sword which turned every way, to keep the way of the tree of life.

(Matt. 5:35). His throne shall be established there, and it shall be the gathering point for all nations (Zech. 8:23; 14:16-21). Then shall the despised descendants of Jacob be "the head" of the nations, and no longer the tail (Deut. 28:13); then shall the people of Jehovah's ancient choice be the center of His earthly government; then shall the Fig Tree, so long barren, "blossom and bud, and fill the face of the world with fruit" (Isa. 27:6). Dan. 12:1 says, "And there shall be a time of trouble, such as never was since there was a nation even to that same time". And in Matt. 24:21,22 we read, "For there shall be a great tribulation, such as was not since the beginning of the world to this time, no, nor ever shall be. And except those days should be shortened, there should no flesh be saved".

I became very aware of all the Covenant's when I found that historically I am what a Mother of all prophets Hashem. So I will Verily verily indeed go more into the History of Moses later in this work. Currently none of the Tribes of Israel know who they are, and this is what this work is to accomplish is for the Tribes to learn now who they are and who they are decedents from historically.

The Bloodlines of Jacob must be Patrilineal for all sons we must require the First Law of an Israelite. Psalm 25:14 reads, "The Lord confides in those who fear him; he makes his covenant known to them." In the end, all of Darkness is to be destroyed and Light will live in peace for all eternity. When I started to study history, it became clear to me that I could no longer trust Western history anymore, because it was written by the ones in history that have been and are still trying to take over the world for the sake of their own greed.

Israel is promised a blessing for obedience and a curse for breaking the covenant. Moses is the mediator between Jewish people and God. -'Do not let God speak to us or we shall die' (Ex. 20:19). The people understand that speaking to God is chasing death. Only a man like Moses can speak to God. He can speak 'face to face' with God.

The Y-DNA" is passed on exclusively from father to son through the patrilineal line

EXODUS 19:6 "AND YOU SHALL BE UNTO ME A KINGDOM OF PRIEST AND AN HOLY NATION. THESE ARE THE WORDS WHICH YOU SHALL SPEAK UNTO THE CHILDREN OF ISRAEL."

Exodus 19:3-6 records a promise God made to the children of Israel encamped about Mount Sinai. Speaking to Moses, God says,

Thus you shall say to the house of Jacob, and tell the children of Israel: "You have seen what I did to the Egyptians, and how I bore you on eagles' wings and brought you to Myself. Now therefore, if you will indeed obey My voice and keep My covenant, then you shall be a special treasure to Me above all people; for all the earth is Mine. And you shall be to Me a kingdom of priests and a holy nation."

Among ancient Israelites, the inheritance is patrilineal. It comes from the father, who bequeaths only to his male descendants (daughters don't inherit). The eldest son received twice as much as the other sons. The father gives his name to his children; for example: the sons of Israel are called Israelites, because the land belonged to the father, and every one of his twelve sons gave his name to his descendants. As well:

An important point that must be remembered is the line of descent for monarchs and main personalities is almost exclusively through males. **Tribal descent, such as whether one is a kohen or a Levite, is still inherited patrilineally in Judaism,[1] Y-DNA" is passed solely along the patrilineal line, from father to son.**

"And unto Joseph in the land of Misraim were born Manasseh and Ephraim, which Asenath the daughter of Potipherah priest of On bare unto him." Genesis 46:20 of the Bible

Israelite s are Gods Chosen People. Now it is time to re-claim our stolen heritage. The Sons of Light, consisting of the sons of Levi, the sons of Judah, and the sons of Benjamin: Jesus According to the family records presented in the books of Matthew and Luke, Mary and Joseph (the mother and earthly father of Jesus) had David as a common ancestor - so by birth (through Mary) and by inheritance (through Joseph) he was counted as a descendant of David. Tribal affiliation and family genealogy can only be traced through the person's father (the patrilineal in accordance with Exodus 28:4, 29:9-30, 30:30, and 40:15 [Priesthood Lineage]; Numbers 36 [Tribal Lineage]; Genesis 49:10, I Kings 11:4, and I Chronicles 17:11-19 [Kingship Lineage].).

Oh woeth how the pain of the world stems and is rooted in our own misunderstanding of history. History has been hidden, and the results are now far more dangerous than most can even begin to comprehend. Without a frame of reference one cannot see yet what the future entails. Yet with a true frame of reference you can begin to see clearly the dangerous world we live in. Why is it like this? What are the forces behind this? What are the answers? Are there any answers? The answers are contained in the Bible. The answers are called the covenants with God, these answers are called the Truth. Taking off the blinders of deception and seeing Truth is a very wondrous thing in so very many ways. We must begin to understand the question of "What is history" and "what is the Past" The past is what happened; Yet History itself is merely our interpretation of what happened

Genesis 9:25-27 Cursed be Canaan: a servant of servants shall he be unto his brethren And he said Blessed be Yahweh the Elohim of Shem: and Canaan shall be his servant. Elohim shall enlarge (Heb: yapth 'persuade') Japheth and he shall dwell in the tents of Shem: and Canaan shall be his servant.

And I beheld, and heard an angel flying through the midst of heaven, saying with a loud voice, Woe, woe, woe, to the inhabiters of the earth by reason of the other voices of the trumpet of the three angels, which are yet to sound!"
Revelation 8:13

The Bible says that God will do nothing until he reveals his plans to his servants the prophets Dead Sea Scrolls: Sons of Light versus the Sons of Darkness refers to the very same War in Heaven written by Apostle John in Apocalypse just prior to the Great Tribulation or Jacob's trouble.

The phrase "the time of Jacob's trouble" is a quote from

He stated that the appearance of false christs, wars and rumors of wars, famines, and earthquakes are "the beginning of birth pains."

Paul, too, described the Tribulation as birth pains. .3:3 says, "While people are saying, 'Peace and safety,' destruction will come on them suddenly, as labor pains on a pregnant woman, and they will not escape." This event follows the Rapture and the removal of the Church, in 4:13-18. In 5:9, Paul reemphasizes the absence of the Church from this time period by saying, "For God has not destined us for wrath, but for obtaining salvation through our Lord Jesus Christ." The wrath spoken of here is God's judgment on the unbelieving world and His discipline of Israel during the Tribulation.

And these are GOD's plans as Stated Clearly in the Dead Sea scroles.

Then [the Sons of Rig]hteousness shall shine to all ends of the world, continuing to shine forth until end of the appointed seasons of darkness. Then at the time appointed by God, His great excellence shall shine for all the times of e[ternity;] for peace and blessing, glory and joy, and long life for all Sons of Light.

"And they assembled all the congregation together on the first day of the second month and they declared their pedigrees after their families by their fathers' houses..." Numbers 1:18.

As for God: For you have a multitude of holy ones in the Heavens and Host of Angels in your exalted dwelling to praise your name.
Judaism insists that: (1) the Messiah must have the right lineage (DNA), namely being a patrilineal descendant of King David through Solomon; and (2). he must accomplish certain things (skills).

A scroll about Amram: I saw Watchers in my vision, the dream-vision. Two men were fighting over me...holding a great contest over me. I asked them, 'Who are you, that you are thus empowered over me?' They answered, 'We have been empowered and rule over all mankind.' They said to me, 'Which of us do you choose to rule you?' I raised my eyes and looked. One of them was terrifying in his appearance, like a serpent, his cloak, many-colored yet very dark....And I looked again, and in his appearance, his visage like a viper....I replied to him, 'This Watcher, who is he?' He answered, 'This Watcher...his three names are Belial and Prince of Darkness and King of Evil.' I said (to the other Watcher), 'My lord, what dominion (have you?)'

Muslims distinguish between the two different individuals as:"Imran, ancestor of Mary", who is Amram "Imran, father of Mary", who is Joachim **Amram** is arabicized to **Imran**. In the Qur'an, the name Imran is used for two different people. The first one is Amram the father of Moses and the second one isJoachim the father of Mary, the mother of Jesus. Amram, the father of Moses and Aaron, is a revered patriarch of Islam. (*The House of* Imran), ayah 33

- **. Our Father who art in heaven, Hallowed be thy name. 10 Thy kingdom come. Thy will be done, as in heaven, so on earth.**

  From this passage we derive that the messiah will come from the "seed" of David and through him King David's kingdom will be established forever. The operative term is "seed." While it has always been maintained that the messiah must be a male line descendant of King David, with no females breaking the chain, this was based upon the right of inheritance of Kingship and the use of the term "seed" which referred to the seed of a man as opposed to the seed of a woman. However, with modern DNA research we have truly seen the significance of this male lineage. Why? **Because male seed (Y-chromosome) cannot pass through a female**. A female breaks the chain. For that reason, a woman or a girl cannot be tested to determine her father's Y-DNA. She can be tested to determine her mother's DNA. Y-DNA reveals the DNA of each generation of men in succession from father to son. In contrast, mt-DNA reveals the generations of women from mother to daughter.

II Samuel 7:12-16
12. When your days are finished and you shall lie with your forefathers, then I will raise up your seed that shall proceed from your body after you, and I will establish his kingdom. 13. He shall build a house for My name, and I will establish the throne of his kingdom forever. 14. I will be to

him a father, and he shall be to Me a son; so that when he goes astray I will chasten him with the rod of men, and with the stripes of the sons of Adam. 15. But My mercy shall not depart from him as I withdrew it from Saul, whom I removed from before you. 16. And your house and your kingdom shall be confirmed forever before you; your throne shall be established forever."

From this passage we derive that the messiah will come from the "seed" of David and through him King David's kingdom will be established forever. The operative term is "seed." While it has always been maintained that the messiah <u>must be a male line descendant of King David, with no females breaking the chain,</u> this was based upon the right of inheritance of Kingship and the use of the term "seed" which referred to the seed of a man as opposed to the seed of a woman. However, with modern DNA research we have truly seen the significance of this male lineage. Why? <u>Because male seed (Y-chromosome) Cannot Pass Through a Female.</u> A Female Breaks the Chain. For that reason, a woman or a girl cannot be tested to determine her father's Y-DNA. She can be tested to determine her mother's DNA. Y-DNA reveals the DNA of each generation of men in succession from father to son. In contrast, mt-DNA reveals the generations of women from mother to daughter. <u>Judaism insists that: (1) the Messiah must have the right lineage (Y-DNA), namely being a patrilineal Tribal affiliation and family genealogy can only be traced through the person's father (the patrilineal in accordance with Exodus 28:4, 29:9-30, 30:30, and 40:15 [Priesthood Lineage]; Numbers 36 [Tribal Lineage]; Genesis 49:10, I Kings 11:4, and I Chronicles 17:11-19 [Kingship Lineage].).descendant of King David through Solomon; and (2). he must accomplish certain things (skills).</u>

The **Israelites** (or <u>children of Israel</u>) were the "**chosen people**" of the god Yahweh.

The **Israelites practiced patrilineal descent** they **had to prove that their "father's house** and **descent** were **Israelite**."

It is important that we understand that a **biblical covenant** is an agreement found in the Bible between God and His people in which God makes specific promises as well as demands, thus it is important to all Abrahamic religions.

In theology and Biblical studies, the word "covenant" principally refers to any of a number of solemn agreements made between <u>God and the children of Israel</u> in the Hebrew Bible, as well as to the New Covenant, likewise, some Christians use the term Old Covenant to collectively refer to the covenants described in their "Old Testament".

BLESSED BE THE HOLY ONE OF ISRAEL; BLESSED BE THE NAME OF THE GOD OF ABRAHAM, ISAAC, AND JACOB, FOREVER!

The foundation of the Torah is the belief that God chose the Children of Israel, in His wisdom and for His purposes, and made His covenant with them. This covenant requires the Children of Israel not to practice idolatry and to live their lives according to the commandments.[Lev 26] This covenant is essentially one-sided, since its terms are dictated by God, though performance is left to the free will of society (collective of God's people) and each person within it. By contrast, at many points in the Hebrew Scripture, not just Jewish scripture ,human covenants are made, and in such covenants, the terms are agreed upon mutually.

None of the European Monarchies of Europe can claim to be the Seed of the Woman "Adam" as their female bloodlines do no It is important that we understand that a biblical covenant is an agreement found in the Bible between God and His people in which God makes specific promises as well as demands, thus it is important to all Abrahamic religions.

BLESSED BE THE HOLY ONE OF ISRAEL; BLESSED BE THE NAME OF THE GOD OF ABRAHAM, ISAAC, AND JACOB, FOREVER!
I say Deliverance, for I fear the Lord, and I pray for those who listen, and fear the Lord as well, for he alone is our grace.

The Book of Daniel is one of the most prophetic books of the Holy Bible also known as the Torah of Moses. Moses wrote the Hebrew Shema back 3000 years ago. The Torah of Hashem Moses is a Legal document as per a 1985 Resolution as well as the Last Will and Testament of Hashem Jesus Christ. Hashem Jesus Christ died as the Testator of His will for Mankind. He left us all a Covenant called the "New Covenant" It is something we all want, and need. Currently no one is on any of the Covenant and there are Three Covenant. The Eternal Covenant of Seth Ben Adam Ben Jehovah that was created before the Universe began, the Covenant of Grace of Hashem Moses, and the New Covenant of Hashem Jesus Christ.

I can prove that Jehovah replaced Cain with Seth! Seth Ben Adam Ben Jehovah. Jehovah was his very own Enmity.   Genesis 3:15American Standard Version and I will put enmity between thee and the woman, and between thy seed and her seed: he shall bruise thy head, and thou shalt bruise his heel. And Genesis 3:15 is the same as Revelation 12 final Judgment!   The Rod of Iron that will Rule all nations.

To further explain, when a man's DNA is tested, we are testing the DNA of his father, his father's father, his father's father an unbroken chain etc. We can go back thousand's of years in this fashion because Y-DNA changes very slowly over time. Only men inherit the Y chromosome. It cannot pass to a female. This is the seed of a man. It is this seed that passes from father to son. It is the Y-chromosome of King David that is inherited along with the rest of the DNA by Moshiach ben David that will uniquely qualify him as the messiah

I am Yahweh your God, who brought you out of the land of Egypt, out of the house of bondage. You shall have no other gods before me. You shall not make for yourselves an idol, nor any image of anything that is in the heavens above, or that is in the earth beneath, or that is in the water under the earth: you shall not bow yourself down to them, nor serve them, for I, Yahweh your God, am a jealous God, visiting the iniquity of the fathers on the children, on the third and on the fourth generation of those who hate me, and showing loving kindness to thousands of those who love me and keep my commandments.

– Exodus 20:1-6

Deuteronomy 31:16 (American Standard Version)

[16] And Jehovah said unto Moses, Behold, thou shalt sleep with thy fathers; and this people will rise up, and play the harlot after the strange gods of the land, whither they go to be among them, and will forsake me, and break my covenant which I have made with them.

²⁰ **For when I shall have brought them into the land which I sware unto their fathers, flowing with milk and honey, and they shall have eaten and filled themselves, and waxed fat; then will they turn unto other gods, and serve them, and despise me, and break my covenant.**

Jeremiah 22:9 (American Standard Version)

⁹ Then they shall answer, Because they forsook the covenant of Jehovah their God, and worshipped other gods, and served them.

Moses, along with his brother Aaron and sister Miriam historically did love their people and , led the Children of Israel out of Egypt and to the Promised Land. But who are indeed their people today, and who was the line of Moses? Would the Jews care today, or just turn away?

Malachi 3

1 Behold, I send my messenger, and he shall prepare the way before me: and the Lord, whom ye seek, will suddenly come to his temple; and the messenger of the covenant, whom ye desire, behold, he cometh, saith Jehovah of hosts.

2 But who can abide the day of his coming? and who shall stand when he appeareth? for he is like a refiner's fire, and like fuller's soap:

3 and he will sit as a refiner and purifier of silver, and he will purify the sons of Levi, and refine them as gold and silver; and they shall offer unto Jehovah offerings in righteousness.

4 Then shall the offering of Judah and Jerusalem be pleasant unto Jehovah, as in the days of old, and as in ancient years.

5 And I will come near to you to judgment; and I will be a swift witness against the sorcerers, and against the adulterers, and against the false swearers, and against those that oppress the hireling in his wages, the widow, and the fatherless, and that turn aside the sojourner from his right, and fear not me, saith Jehovah of hosts.

6 For I, Jehovah, change not; therefore ye, O sons of Jacob, are not consumed.

7 From the days of your fathers ye have turned aside from mine ordinances, and have not kept them. Return unto me, and I will return unto you, saith Jehovah of hosts. But ye say, Wherein shall we return?

8 Will a man rob God? yet ye rob me. But ye say, Wherein have we robbed thee? In tithes and offerings.

9 Ye are cursed with the curse; for ye rob me, even this whole nation.

10 Bring ye the whole tithe into the store-house, that there may be food in my house, and prove me now herewith, saith Jehovah of hosts, if I will not open you the windows of heaven, and pour you out a blessing, that there shall not be room enough to receive it.

11 And I will rebuke the devourer for your sakes, and he shall not destroy the fruits of your ground; neither shall your vine cast its fruit before the time in the field, saith Jehovah of hosts.

12 And all nations shall call you happy; for ye shall be a delightsome land, saith Jehovah of hosts.

13 Your words have been stout against me, saith Jehovah. Yet ye say, What have we spoken against thee?

14 Ye have said, It is vain to serve God; and what profit is it that we have kept his charge, and that we have walked mournfully before Jehovah of hosts?

15 And now we call the proud happy; yea, they that work wickedness are built up; yea, they tempt God, and escape.

16 Then they that feared Jehovah spake one with another; and Jehovah hearkened, and heard, and a book of remembrance was written before him, for them that feared Jehovah, and that thought upon his name.

17 And they shall be mine, saith Jehovah of hosts, even mine own possession, in the day that I make; and I will spare them, as a man spareth his own son that serveth him.

18 Then shall ye return and discern between the righteous and the wicked, between him that serveth God and him that serveth him not.

Malachi 4
1 For, behold, the day cometh, it burneth as a furnace; and all the proud, and all that work wickedness, shall be stubble; and the day that cometh shall burn them up, saith Jehovah of hosts, that it shall leave them neither root nor branch.

2 But unto you that fear my name shall the sun of righteousness arise with healing in its wings; and ye shall go forth, and gambol as calves of the stall.

3 And ye shall tread down the wicked; for they shall be ashes under the soles of your feet in the day that I make, saith Jehovah of hosts.

4 Remember ye the law of Moses my servant, which I commanded unto him in Horeb for all Israel, even statutes and ordinances.

5 Behold, I will send you Elijah the prophet before the great and terrible day of Jehovah come.

6 And he shall turn the heart of the fathers to the children, and the heart of the children to their fathers; lest I come and smite the earth with a curse.

Jesus said: Do not think that I will accuse you to the Father: there is one that accuseth you, even Moses, in whom ye trust. For had ye believed Moses, ye would have believed me: for he wrote of

me.
But if ye believe not his writings, how shall ye believe my words?

Now this covenant has laid dormant again for 500 years of persecution.
Israel has broken the covenant.

He gave them plenty of time to return and it is all mentioned in the Malachi 3 prophecy.

It takes a willingness to be willing to do the will of God.

Is this really is their last chance, if they don't do the will of God now? Then the prophecy predicts that the land of Israel will be destroyed completely. **The bible tells them that they are robbing God, they're also denying the children their inheritance that God promised to them.**

And God spoke all these words, saying: "I am the Lord your God, who brought you out of the land of Egypt, out of the house of bondage.

1. You shall have no other gods before me.

2. You shall not make for yourself any carved image, or any likeness of anything that is in heaven above, or that is in the earth beneath, or that is in the water under the earth; you shall not bow down to them nor serve them. For I, the Lord your God, am a jealous God, visiting the iniquity of the fathers on the children to the third and fourth generations of those who hate me, but showing mercy to thousands, to those who love Me and keep My commandments.

3. You shall not take the name of the Lord your God in vain, for the Lord will not hold him guiltless who takes His name in vain.

4. Remember the Sabbath day, to keep it holy. Six days you shall labor and do all your work, but the seventh day is the Sabbath of the Lord your God. In it you shall do no work: you, nor your son, nor your daughter, nor your manservant, nor your maidservant, nor your cattle, nor your stranger who is within your gates. For in six days the Lord made the heavens and the earth, the sea, and all that is in them, and rested the seventh day. Therefore the Lord blessed the Sabbath day and hallowed it.

5. Honor your father and your mother, that your days may be long upon the land which the Lord your God is giving you.

6. You shall not murder.
   -

7. **You shall not commit adultery.**

8. **You shall not steal.**

   -

9. **You shall not bear false witness against your neighbor.**

10.   **You shall not covet your neighbor's house; you shall not covet your neighbor's wife, nor his manservant, nor his maidservant, nor his ox, nor his donkey, nor anything that is your neighbor's."**

Israel is promised a blessing for obedience and a curse for breaking the covenant. Moses is the mediator between Jewish people and God. -'Do not let God speak to us or we shall die' (Ex. 20:19). The people understand that speaking to God is chasing death. Only a man like Moses can speak to God. He can speak 'face to face' with God.

People have lost their understanding of covenants. People really don't understand them or their importance. There are two places in the entire bible where one finds the words **'the mind that has wisdom.'** Rev. 17:9 and 13:18

I say Deliverance, for I fear the Lord, and I pray for those who listen, and fear the Lord as well, for he alone is our grace.

Talmudic Times

Sometime during the Roman occupation and the Second Temple period, a law of matrilineal descent, which defined a Jew as someone with a Jewish mother, was adopted. By the 2nd century CE, it was clearly practiced. And there is even less reason that we should accept the discrimination of this supported not merely by bad reasons, but by no reason at all. In doing this the Jews have denied themselves the laws of Moses and the Torah by only caring about the matrilineal lines.(specify)   We have a Satanic world, and Usery is run rampant to everyone's suffering.

The Book of Daniel is one of the most prophetic books of the Holy Bible also known as the Torah of Moses. Moses wrote the Hebrew Shema back 3000 years ago. The Torah of Hashem Moses is a Legal document as per a 1985 Resolution as well as the Last Will and Testament of Hashem Jesus Christ. Hashem Jesus Christ died as the Testator of His will for Mankind. He left us all a Covenant called the "New Covenant" It is something we all want, and need. Currently no one is on any of the Covenant and there are Three Covenant. The Eternal Covenant of Seth Ben Adam Ben Jehovah that was created before the Universe began, the Covenant of Grace of Hashem Moses, and the New Covenant of Hashem Jesus Christ.

I can prove that Jehovah replaced Cain with Seth! Seth Ben Adam Ben Jehovah. Jehovah was his very own Enmity.   Genesis 3:15American Standard Version **and I will put enmity between thee and the woman, and between thy seed and her seed: he shall bruise thy head, and thou shalt bruise his heel. And Genesis 3:15 is the same as Revelation 12 final Judgment!   The Rod of Iron that will Rule all nations.**

To further explain, when a man's DNA is tested, we are testing the DNA of his father, his father's father, his father's father an unbroken chain etc. We can go back thousand's of years in this fashion because Y-DNA changes very slowly over time. Only men inherit the Y chromosome. It cannot pass to a female. This is the seed of a man. It is this seed that passes from father to son. It is the Y-chromosome of King David that is inherited along with the rest of the DNA by Moshiach ben David that will uniquely qualify him as the messiah

"For the children of Israel shall abide many days without a king, and without a prince and without a sacrifice, and without an image, and without an ephod and without teraphim, Afterward shall the children of Israel return, and seek YHWH their POWER, and David their king; and shall fear YHWH and his goodness in the latter days." **Hosea 3:4,5.**

For thus saith the Lord; Like as I have brought all this great evil upon this people, so will I bring upon them all the good that I have promised them. **Jeremiah 32:41,42**

Jeremiah 16:15

American Standard Version (ASV)

[15] but, As Jehovah liveth, that brought up the children of Israel from the land of the north, and from all the countries whither he had driven them. And I will bring them again into their land that I gave unto their fathers.

(Not as it currently is in our world, or it would say I gave unto their mothers instead)

And shall put my spirit in you, and ye shall live, and I shall place you in your own land: then shall ye know that I the Lord have spoken it, and performed it, saith the Lord. **Ezekiel 37:12-14**

And say unto them, Thus saith the Lord God; Behold, I will take the children of Israel from among the heathen, whither they be gone, and will gather them on every side and bring them into their own land: **Ezekiel 37:21**

Therefore, behold, the days come, saith the Lord, that it shall no more be said, The Lord liveth, that brought up the children of Israel out of the land of Egypt;

But, The Lord liveth, that brought up the children of Israel from the land of the north, and from all the lands whither he had driven them: and I will bring them again into their land that I gave unto their fathers.

Behold, I will send for many fishers, saith the Lord, and they shall fish them; and after will I send for many hunters, and they shall hunt them from every mountain, and from every hill, and out of the holes of the rocks. **Jeremiah 16:14-16**

Thus saith the Lord of hosts; If it be marvelous in the eyes of the remnant of this people in these days, should it also be marvelous in mine eyes? saith the Lord of hosts.

Thus saith the Lord of hosts; Behold, I will save my people from the east country, and from the west country;

And I will bring them, and they shall dwell in the midst of Jerusalem: and they shall be my people, and I will be their God, in truth and in righteousness. Thus saith the Lord of hosts; Let your hands be strong, ye that hear in these days these words by the mouth of the prophets, which were in the day that the foundation of the house of the Lord of hosts was laid, that the temple might be built. **Zechariah 8:6-9**

Many have lost their understanding of these core covenants and really don't understand the great importance of these agreements with God. There are two places in the entire bible where one finds the words **'the mind that has wisdom.'** Rev. 17:9 and 13:18

I say Deliverance, for I fear the Lord, and I pray for those who listen and fear the Lord as well, for he alone is our grace.

In Genesis 26:3 God says to Isaac, "To you and to your descendants I will give all these lands, and I will fulfill the oath which I swore to Abraham your father." And then to Isaac's son, Jacob, God appeared at Bethel (according to Genesis 28:13-15) and confirmed the covenant to him: "I am the Lord, the God of Abraham your father and the God of Isaac; the land on which you lie I will give to you and to your descendants; and your descendants shall be like the dust of the earth ... and by you and your descendants shall all the families of the earth be blessed. Behold, I am with you and will keep you wherever you go. **This covenant promise would lie dormant until God confirmed it afresh with Moses.**

Psalm 25:14 reads, "The Lord confides in those who fear him; he makes his covenant known to them."

In the case of the Law Covenant, this was Moses:

... "Write down for yourself these words, because it is in accordance with these words that I do conclude a covenant with you and Israel." (Exodus 34:27)

These are the words of the covenant that Jehovah commanded Moses to conclude with the sons of Israel in the land of Moab aside from the covenant that he had concluded with them in Horeb. (Deuteronomy 29:1)

The fact is that Y-chromosome DNA (Y-DNA) is paternally inherited enables patrilines, and agnatic kinships, of men to be traced through genetic analysis.

<u>In a **patrilineal descent** system **Patrilineal Descent ... that in the Bible the line always followed the father, including the cases of Joseph and Moses.**</u> This has led to the idea of a single male ancestor of all males members of these groups. In the Bible this individual is identified as Aaron, brother of Moses, so the hypothetical figure is known as the Y-chromosomal Aaron

The Ezran Covenant states that it is **Mandatory Patrilineal Law.** It must have descended down this same line **from father to son for patrilineal** descent. <u>**Among ancient Israelites, the inheritance is patrilineal. It comes from the father, who bequeaths only to his male descendants (daughters don't inherit).**</u> The eldest son received twice as much as the other sons. The father gives his name to his children; for example: the sons of Israel are called Israelites, because the land belonged to the father, and every one of his twelve sons gave his name to his descendants.

Professor Shaye Cohen, who devoted an entire chapter to the origins

of matrilineal descent in his book *The Beginnings of Jewishness* was ultimately

forced to admit that he has no idea why the rabbis chose to break with biblical

practice and institute matrilineality[2]. There is no clear reason that Judaism has

to be matrilineal, except that it has been so for many centuries.

<u>**And there is even less reason that we should accept discrimination**</u>

<u>**supported not merely by bad reasons, but by no reason at all.**</u>

Israel has a genetic prescription to follow: <u>israel</u> <u>inheritance</u> <u>genetics</u> <u>moses</u>

<u>patrilineal</u> <u>law</u>.

Patrilineal descent was the primary way of determining the status of children

in this period. The Biblical traditions and their early rabbinic commentaries

take it for granted that the paternal line was decisive in the tracing of descent,

tribal identity, or priestly status.A glance at the Biblical genealogies makes

this clear.

<u>**Furthermore, the most important parental responsibility to teach**</u>

Torah rested with the father (Kiddushin 29a; cf.

Shulchan Aruch,

Yoreh De-a 245.1).

Biblical Times

No matter what anyone tells you or what history has unjustly done, an Israelite as well as a Levite always were and always will be patrilineal lines Only. Though the Illuminati are squatting on these patrilineal lines with no right to, one day we must wake up and this must STOP! For this is the Great Deception we have been warned about, and we are living it, breathing it, and hurting from it, and have been now for far too many generations. On future generation are in Grave danger, Wake up!!!! The question is, "will you believe the lie"?

As the world sleeps, few of us remain vigilant to what's happening around us: The heirs of God's promise that the Son of God would come through their lines.(Jesus)This strongly suggests that the ruling lines were aware and believed the promise made in Eden (Gen. 3:15) concerning the Woman's Seed who would crush the serpent's head, deliver from death and receive the Father's Kingdom. The seed of the woman will crush the serpent's head indicating Satan's ultimate defeat.For the love of money is a root of all kinds of evils. It is through this craving that some have wandered away from the faith and pierced themselves with many pangs.But I tell you: Love your enemies and pray for those who persecute you

Daniel's Vision of the Ram and Goat

1In the third year of the reign of king Belshazzar a vision appeared unto me, even unto me, Daniel, after that which appeared unto me at the first. 2And I saw in the vision; now it was so, that when I saw, I was in Shushan the palace, which is in the province of Elam; and I saw in the vision, and I was by the river Ulai. 3Then I lifted up mine eyes, and saw, and, behold, there stood before the river a ram which had two horns: and the two horns were high; but one was higher than the other, and the higher came up last. 4I saw the ram pushing westward, and northward, and southward; and no beasts could stand before him, neither were there any that could deliver out of his hand; but he did according to his will, and magnified himself. 5And as I was considering, behold, a he-goat came from the west over the face of the whole earth, and touched not the ground: and the goat had a notable horn between his eyes. 6And he came to the ram that had the two horns, which I saw standing before the river, and ran upon him in the fury of his power. 7And I saw him come close unto the ram, and he was moved with anger against him, and smote the ram, and brake his two horns; and there was no power in the ram to stand before him; but he cast him down to the ground, and trampled upon him; and there was none that could deliver the ram out of his hand. 8And the he-goat magnified himself exceedingly: and when he was strong, the great horn was broken; and instead of it there came up four notable horns toward the four winds of heaven.9And out of one of them came forth a little horn, which waxed exceeding great, toward the south, and toward the east, and toward the glorious land . 10And it waxed great, even to the host of heaven; and some of the host and of the stars it cast down to the ground, and trampled upon them. 11Yea, it magnified itself, even to the prince of the host; and it took away from him the continual burnt-offering , and the place of his sanctuary was cast down. 12And the host was given over to it together with the continual burnt-offering through transgression; and it cast down truth to the ground, and it did its pleasure and prospered.13Then I heard a holy one speaking; and another holy one said unto that certain one who spake, How long shall be the vision concerning the continual burnt-offering , and the transgression that maketh desolate, to give both the sanctuary and the host to be trodden under foot? 14And he said unto me, Unto two thousand and three hundred evenings and mornings; then shall the sanctuary be cleansed.Gabriel Interprets Daniel's Vision 15And it came to pass, when I, even I Daniel, had seen the vision, that I sought to understand it; and, behold, there stood before me as the appearance of a man. 16And I heard a man's voice between the banks of the Ulai, which called, and said, Gabriel, make this man to understand the vision. 17So he came near where I stood; and when he came, I was affrighted, and fell upon my face: but he said unto me, Understand, O son of man; for the vision belongeth to the time of the end.

18Now as he was speaking with me, I fell into a deep sleep with my face toward the ground; but he touched me, and set me upright. 19And he said, Behold, I will make thee know what shall be in the latter time of the indignation; for it belongeth to the appointed time of the end. 20The ram which thou sawest, that had the two horns, they are the kings of Media and Persia. 21And the rough he-goat is the king of Greece: and the great horn that is between his eyes is the first king. 22And as for that which was broken, in the place whereof four stood up, four kingdoms shall stand up out of the nation, but not with his power. 23And in the latter time of their kingdom, when the transgressors are come to the full, a king of fierce countenance, and understanding dark sentences, shall stand up. 24And his power shall be mighty, but not by his own power; and he shall destroy wonderfully, and shall prosper and do his pleasure ; and he shall destroy the mighty ones and the holy people. 25And through his policy he shall cause craft to prosper in his hand; and he shall magnify himself in his heart, and in their'security shall he destroy many: he shall also stand up against the prince of princes; but he shall be broken without hand. 26And the vision of the evenings and mornings which hath been told is true: but shut thou up the vision; for it belongeth to many days to come .

27And I, Daniel, fainted, and was sick certain days; then I rose up, and did the king's business: and I wondered at the vision, but none understood it.

It is necessary that Moshiach ben David be a male line descendant of King David through Solomon or Nathan? The answer among almost all Hebrew royal genealogists is "yes." By definition alone, the name Son of David that has been designated to identify the messiah, indicates a male line descendant, with no female breaks in the chain. Scripture tells us that Moshiach ben David will be a male line descendant of King David.

"He is the Lord our God; His judgments are in all the earth. He remembers His covenant forever, the word He Commanded, for a thousand generations, the covenant He made with Abraham, the oath He swore to Isaac.He confirmed it to Jacob as a decree, to Israel as an everlasting covenant: "To you I will give the land of Canaan As the portion you will inherit" (Psalm 105:7-11).

"You will know the Truth; and the Truth will set you free." -- John 8:33.

Paul said in Romans 9:6-8, *"Not as though God's Word had failed, for they are not all elect Israelites, who are of born of Jacob: Neither, because they are the seed of Abraham, are they all heirs of the Promise: because It was to come through the line of Isaac. So the heirs of the Promise are not children from Abraham's loins, but an election from Isaac through Jacob"*

sky:NEHEMIAH 9:5 . . . "Stand up and bless the LORD your God forever and ever! Blessed be Your glorious name, which is exalted above all blessing and praise! 6 You alone are the LORD; You have made heaven, the heaven of heavens, with all their host, the earth and everything on it, the seas and all that is in them, and You preserve them all. The host of heaven worships You." (Only living creatures can worship God. Clearly, the "host of heaven" here refers to sentient created beings which reside in the heavens.

JEREMIAH 19:13 "And the houses of Jerusalem and the houses of the kings of Judah shall be defiled like the place of Tophet, because of all the houses on whose roofs they have burned incense to all the host of heaven, and poured out drink offerings to other gods.")Here Jeremiah draws a parallel between "the host of heaven," to whom incense was burned and "other gods," to whom drink offerings were poured out. This grammatical construction in Hebrew is meant to show that both the "host of heaven" and the "other gods" are the same. They were "the gods of the nations," the angelic rulers assigned by God over the nations of the earth.One of the most grievous sins of the ancient Israelites was their continual idolatry. Instead of worshiping the one true God, they instead worshiped the inferior "sons of God," the "host of heaven":

Since you know. Or who stretched the line on it? 6 On what were its bases sunk? Or who laid its cornerstone, 7 When the morning stars sang together and all the sons of God shouted for joy?" (NASU)This Scripture clearly indicates that the "sons of God" (beney 'elohim, also called "morning stars" here) were present at creation week. This fact is supported by the first chapter of Genesis:GENESIS 1:26 Then God said, "Let us make man in our image, in our likeness, and let them rule over the fish of the sea and the birds of the air, over the livestock, over all the earth, and over all the creatures that move along the ground." (NIV)This verse is often used by modern scholars to attempt to prove that the doctrine of the Trinity can be found in the Old Testament. Regarding this erroneous contention, The Eerdmans Bible Dictionary states: The "us" in "Let us make man in our image" (Gen. 1:26; cf. 3:22; 11:6-7) refers to the "sons of God" or lesser "gods" mentioned elsewhere (6:1-4; Job 1:6; Ps. 29:1), here viewed as a heavenly council centered around the one God (cf. Ps. 82:1). In later usage these probably would be called "angels." (p. 1019, "Trinity")Deuteronomy 32:8 is paralleled by a passage from Deuteronomy 4 that speaks of the allocation of the heavenly host:When he prayed "that they may be one just as we are one," Yeshua was not praying for all believers to become a part of the Trinity. Yeshua clearly tells us that he and the Father are "one" by the Father being in him (through the Holy Spirit) and by Yeshua being in the Father (by doing God's will instead of his own). Yeshua always knew God's will because of the indwelling of the Holy Spirit; he remained in the Father by always doing His will. Yeshua's prayer for all believers was that the Father would make them one with both of them; this would be accomplished by God's Spirit flowing through Messiah (the mediator) to dwell within them.

CONCLUSION The world is currently ruled over by angelic principalities and powers that Yah gave authority over the nations. Just as the nations over which they rule, these mighty spirits have often chosen to go against the will of God. In choosing not to submit to God's authority, they have become the enemies of YHVH and His chosen people. Eventually, the rebellion of these wicked spirits will lead to their judgment and punishment.

There were more than one Sheba ancestors of the Queen of Sheba. There was Sheba the Elder who historically was the brother of Eber. Of the tribes of Israel it was the lines of Ham and Shem who had practiced endogamy and actually intermarried for centuries. Sheba was descended from Noah through Ham and Eber was descended from Noah through Shem. In the Torah of Hashem Moses there is only approximately one-quarter of the book of Genesis is the story of SETH BEN ADAM BEN JEHOVAH God's dealings with the prophet Abraham and his direct ancestors (chapter 1-12). In the other chapters we find prophet Abraham's direct descendants and their lives well before the actual establishment of Israel.

History depends on mankind understanding that it is very imperative that we must recognize and understand how very important the promise made back in Genesis of the actual coming of the Seed of God by the Woman (Gen. 3:15) did not originate with the Jews as they are decedents of Judah that came much later. The actual seed is so much very much older!!! Indeed the tribes had the firstborn son and then the cousin or often niece wife ascended to the throne of his maternal grandfather, after whom he was named.

The Covenant always ran though the Bloodline of Isaac, also known as the Truth will set you free! So Isaac ruled over Abraham's territory by Joktan ruled over the territory of Joktan the Elder, Ketu-rah's father. These two holy lines historically really did intermarry according to a very specific pattern that is traceable, using the Biblical genealogies, to Jesus Christ. (Jer. 30:7). Our times now are known as the Time of Jacobs trouble! The Book of Jeremiah was dedicated into saving this very generation. Jerimiah was the weeping Prophet who prophetically saw the judgments of SETH BEN ADAM BEN JEHOVAH GOD coming as all the tribes lost their way back in Babylon!

Sheba was descended from Noah through Ham and Eber was descended from Noah through Shem. Amen The Four Horsemen of the Apocalypse are described in the last book of the New Testament of the Bible, called the Book of Revelation of Jesus Christ to Saint John the Evangelist at 6:1-8. The chapter tells of a "'book', or 'scroll', in God's right hand that is sealed with seven seals". The Lamb of God, or Lion of Judah, (Jesus Christ) opens the first four of the seven seals, which summons forth four beings that ride out on white, red, black, and pale horses. Although some interpretations differ, in most accounts, the four riders are seen as symbolizing Conquest,[1] War,[2] Famine,[3] and Death, respectively. The Christian apocalyptic vision is that the four horsemen are to set a divine apocalypse upon the world as harbingers of the Last Judgment.[1][4]The Torah indicates that Jewishness passes exclusively through the father's line, maintaining the system of patrilineality that many scholars believe was the practice of ancient Israel. From the earliest biblical history, descent was patrilineal (Exodus 31:2).For this reason, many scholars suggest that the original rule of Jewish descent must have been patrilineal, and that it was changed around the time of Ezra, or even later, at the time of Yavneh, possibly under the influence of Roman law. Jewish status through matrilineality, is in direct contrast to the position of the Tanakh (Hebrew Bible) The ruler-priest lines of the two first-born sons intermarried, thus preserving the bloodline of those to whom God made the promise that a woman of their people would bring forth the Seed who would crush the serpent's head and restore Paradise. The Messiah Jesus fulfilled the eternal promise to the line of Moses as the King of Jeshurun. Jesus being a descendant of David verifies David's descent from Moses.

The Order Of Melchizedek: Melchizedek or Malki Tzedek (pron.: /mɛlˈkɪz.ə.dɪk/[1]); Hebrew: מַלְכִּי־צֶדֶק malkī-ṣeḏeq) translated as "my king (is) righteous(ness)") This does suggest that the tribes maintained a very high importance to the preservation of the bloodline of these rulers. As they knew the importance of their lineage It is likely that they realized and knew themselves to be heirs of God's promise that the Son of God would come through their lines.(Jesus)This strongly suggests that the ruling lines were aware and believed the promise made in Eden (Gen. 3:15) concerning the Woman's Seed who would crush the serpent's head, deliver from death and receive the Father's Kingdom.

"These are the divisions of the gatekeepers: From the Korahites, there was Meshelemiah son of Kore, of the family of Asaph." – 1 Chronicles 26:1 "The first lot fell to Joseph of the Asaph clan and twelve of his sons and relatives. The second lot fell to Gedaliah and twelve of his sons and relatives. 1 Chronicles 25:9 From the sons of Asaph, there were Zaccur, Joseph, Nethaniah, and Asarelah. They worked under the direction of their father, Asaph, who proclaimed God's messages by the king's orders. – 1 Chronicles 25:2"

KUDHA'A – Qudha'a,(Kodha'a, Qata'a or Qita'a) was a major tribe of the Himyarites. In Arabian and modern Ethiopian tradition he is referred to as Kouth, Kuti or Quti child of Ham or as Qahit brother of Qahtan and Peleg. **The tribes intermarried very strictly in the priestly lines. In the Bible however, he is Kohut or Kohath son of Levi, whom Josephus calls Kaath.** They were later called in the European Hebraic writings **Kuthi, Kuthim or Kuzi the well-known name for the Samarians i.e., the Samran or Banu Simran of the Yemen (Edersheim, 2002, p. 37)** This word Kuthi or Kohut came also to be transcribed as Kushi and Kushan. (Goldenberg, 2003, pp. 206 and 375, fn. 32) The name was probably derived from the Kudha'a tribe of Khushayn or Qushayn.

Ibn Ishaq gave the genealogy of the Qudha'a as Qudha'a bin Malik bin Himyar bin Saba bin Yashjab bin Ya'rab bin Qahtan. Otherwise the tradition goes Qudha'a was the son of Malik bin Amr bin Murra bin Zayd bin Malik bin Hamid bin Saba. The tribes descended from the Arabian Qudha or Kuth were many and well known. Of the Yemen Al Hakami of the 12th century wrote, "Mahra, son of Haydan son of al Haf son of Kuda'ah (Kuth or Kaath) reigned over the countries of Kuda'ah." This land of the Yemen. Elsewhere he writes,"Ash Shahr was a country also known as Mahra

As these are the ancestors of the tribe of Kohath, the tribes did work their way to exactly as the Bible says Kohath son of Levi, as the tribes inter married in a very specific pattern historically which is proven in this work to the very best of my ability.

Testament of Levi, and the Book of Jubilees, Levi's wife, Kohath's mother, is named as Milkah, a daughter of Aram.

"ORIGINS: Biblical References to Soleym ibn Mansur, who was Manasseh son of Joseph whose brother was Levi.Levi's wife, his children's mother, is named as Milkah, a daughter of Aram.

Strictly speaking, therefore, there were actually 13 tribes, but only 12 tribal areas. When the tribes are listed in reference to their receipt of land (as well as to their encampments during the 40 years of wandering in the desert), the tribe of Joseph is replaced by the tribes of Ephraim and Manasseh

Levites, descendants of a patrilineal clan that assisted the Israelite priests during ancient times

RamessesII has appeared in books like Joan Grant's *So Moses Was Born*, a first person account from Nebunefer, the brother of Ramoses, which paints the picture of the life of Ramoses from the death of Seti, with all the power play, intrigue, plots to assassinate, following relationships are depicted: Bintanath, Queen Tuya, Nefertari, and Moses. We also find in film, Ramesses was played by Yul Brynner in the classic film *The Ten Commandments* (1956). **Here Ramesses was portrayed as a vengeful tyrant as well as the main antagonist of the film, ever scornful of his father's preference for Moses over "the son of [his] body"**. Did **Ramses** II ("trust no pretended **brother**") and Moses live together as **brothers**, until Moses' true heritage was learned?

Exodus 15:8 says:

"By the blast of your nostrils the waters piled up.
The surging waters stood firm like a wall;
the **deep** waters **congealed** in the **heart of the sea.**"

The El Amarna letters describe the troublesome Hapiru that were taking over the land of Canaan. This seems to fit well with the Hebrews during the time of the judges. The word "Hebrew" probably came from the word "Hapiru."

The Book of Exodus tells how Moses leads the Israelites out of Egypt and through the wilderness to Mount Sinai, where God reveals himself and offers them a Covenant: they are to keep his *torah* (i.e. law, instruction), and in return he will be their God and give them the land of Canaan. The Book of Leviticus records the laws of God. The Book of Numbers tells how the Israelites, led now by their God, journey onwards from Sinai towards Canaan, but when their spies report that the land is filled with giants they refuse to go on. God then condemns them to remain in the desert until the generation that left Egypt passes away. After thirty-eight years at the oasis of **Kadesh Barnea** the next generation travel on to the borders of Canaan. The Book of Deuteronomy tells how, within sight of the Promised Land, Moses recalls their journeys and gives them new laws,Out of the 40 years of Wandering in the Desert, almost 38 years were spent in Kadesh Barnea. [10] Usually the place is looked for in the Sinai Desert, and the preferred location is about 18 miles south of el-Arish on the Mediterranean coast, however, much evidence has been found that shows that Nuweiba Beach is where Israel crossed the Red Sea.

Scripture refers to **Kadesh-barnea** as being located in both the Wilderness of Zin and the Wilderness of **Paran**. Each is true.

First, the "Kadesh" (Gen 16:14) and "Paran" (Gen 21:21) of the Hagar & Ishmael accounts are unarguably the same Kadesh and Paran of the Wilderness Wanderings of the Israelites under Moses after crossing the Red Sea. In fact, the Israelites spend 38 of their 40 years of exile at Kadesh, also called Kadesh-Barnea. And given the links between Kadesh-Barnea and Paran, we are also tempted to identify Barnea with Paran. Indeed, such identification would enable us to simply understand Kadesh-Barnea as the "Holy of Paran".Out of the 40 years of Wandering in the Desert, almost 38 years were spent in Kadesh Barnea. [10] **Usually the place is looked for in the Sinai Desert, and the preferred location is about 18 miles south of el-Arish on the Mediterranean coast, however, we show that Nuweiba Beach is where Israel crossed the Red Sea.**

Has there been any Evidence of the Exodus located? Lets consider this factor:

Nuweiba Beach is where Israel crossed the Red Sea.

The Crossing of the Red Sea ... Yahweh blows the sea back with a strong east wind, allowing the Israelites to cross

Yahweh causes the pharaoh to pursue the Israelites with chariots, and he overtakes them at Pi-hahiroth. When the Israelites see the Egyptian army they are afraid, but the pillar of fire and the cloud separates the Israelites and the Egyptians. **At Yahweh's command Moses holds his staff out over the water, and throughout the night a strong east wind divides the sea,**[1] and the Israelites pass through with a wall of water on either side. **The Egyptians pursue, but at daybreak Yahweh clogs their chariot-wheels and throws them into a panic, and with the return of the water the pharaoh and his entire army are destroyed (see Psalm 136:15). When the Israelites see the power of Yahweh they put their faith in Yahweh and in Moses, and sing a song of praise to the Lord for the crossing of the sea and the destruction of their enemies. (This song, at Exodus 15, is called the Song of the Sea). The Song of the Sea was reputedly sung by the Israelites after they crossed the Red Sea in safety, and celebrates the destruction of the Egyptian army during the crossing, and looks forward to their future conquest of Canaan.**

As Moses by the power of God parted the waters, the Israelites crossed the Red Sea And the Israelites saw the Egyptians dead on the seashore: Exodus 14:30

And the Lord looked down upon the Egyptian army... and he made the wheels of their chariots come off: Exodus 14

Exodus 14:21, 22 says:

"Then Moses stretched out his hand over the sea, and all that night the Lord drove the sea back with a strong east wind and turned it into dry land. The waters were divided, and the Israelites went through the sea on dry ground, with a wall of water on their right and on their left."

After the Israelites reached the other side, God removed the cloud blocking the Egyptians and they pursued the Israelites, going into the trough. Moses stretched forth his rod over the sea again. The ice which was thinnest at the western side of the trough began to melt, sending water cascading into it. The water rushed into the channel and eastward carrying many of the Egyptian soldiers and their horses with it. The bodies of many of the drowned soldiers were washed up on the eastern shore at the feet of their intended victims. (Exodus 14:30)

These are the remains of Pharaoh's decimated army, drowned in the Red Sea. At both ends of the crossing, there are columns erected by King Solomon. These columns are inscribed with Old Aramaic. The damaged inscriptions, when partially translated, contained words such as Mizraim (Egypt), Moses, Israel, and Yahweh. **The column on the Arabian east side was removed and possibly moved to a museum.**

The Gulf of Aquaba has evidence. Under the sea at this site there are numerous chariot parts; wheels, axles, spokes and the such, most encrusted with coral.

Remnents of chariot wheels confirm this, scollars can identify the chariot wheels as being the chariot wheels of the 18th and 19th dynasty of Egypt just of the shore.

Moses raised his rod over the sea and God caused a strong east wind to blow, quickly freezing the water into a thick mass of ice on either side of what became a channel or trough over this land bridge.

After the Israelites reached the other side, God removed the cloud blocking the Egyptians and they pursued the Israelites, going into the trough. Moses stretched forth his rod over the sea again. The ice which was thinnest at the western side of the trough began to melt, sending water cascading into it. The water rushed into the channel and eastward carrying many of the Egyptian soldiers and their horses with it. **The bodies of many of the drowned soldiers were washed up on the eastern shore at the feet of their intended victims**. (Exodus 14:30)

Many source now place the Israelites on the eastern side of the Red Sea. On the west side of the Gulf of Suez where they crosses the "Red Sea" from west to east. An increasing numbers of sources have agreed. One of the oldest sources is the *Kitab-alaghaniy*, an Arabian legend that is about a tribe that came through their region after a series of plagues much like the Egyptian ones. The Amalekites were said to be around Mecca when the plagues struck, because of them they fled northward. Along the way they were hit by a deluge, which was most likely the result of the Red Sea dividing. The distraught Amalekites ran into the Djorhomites which were also a nomadic. The Arabs say that at the time the Djorhomites were near Merib, and it here is that the battle between them took place.

Solymi, a nation celebrated in the poems of Homer, who called the city they founded Hierosolyma

The Solymi are mentioned by Homer in the *Iliad* 6.184 and 204 and in the *Odyssey* 5.283. They were brave warriors from Lycia. **The word Jerusalem was read as 'Hiero-Solyma' or 'holy place of the Solymi'.**

Simeon 5:3 says that fornication separates man from God and brings him near to Beliar**. Levi tells his children to choose between the Law of God and the works of Beliar (Levi 19:1)** It also states that when the soul is constantly disturbed, the Lord departs from it and Beliar rules over it. Naphtali (2:6, 3:1) contrasts the Law and will of God with the purposes of Beliar. Also, in 20:2, Joseph prophesies that when Israel leaves Egypt, they will be with God in light while Beliar will remain in darkness with the Egyptians. **Finally, the Testament describes that when the Messiah comes, the angels will punish the spirits of deceit and Beliar (3:3) and that the Messiah will bind Beliar and give to his children the power to trample the evil spirits (18:12).**

Question: "What does the Bible say about lending money?"

Answer: God's Word says that many people wander from the faith and pierce themselves with many griefs when they allow money to have an improper hold on their hearts. That's why the Bible contains hundreds of Scriptures on how God wants us to treat money, and this includes the lending of it.

The genealogy of Suleym or Sulaym, Mazin and Hawazin are that they were the children of Mansur (Manasseh) son of Ikrima (Ikrima) bin Khasafa (Asaf or Hasepha) son of Qays son of Ailan. It is another way of showing historically that the clans of Soleym and the Azd are descend from the original Israelite/Canaanite people of the region south of Ta'if extending to the Sara'at in Asir.

Azd ancestors were said to have fought against the people already in control of Misrah i.e. "the Amalekites" near Mecca under Moses (Muzaikiya) and Aaron. Who is linked in Arabian genealogy to the ancestral Azd people of Marib, KHAZRAJ, KHUZA'A, GHASSAN, BAHILA Groups traditionally descended from those who followed diviner Muzaikiya from Marib in Yemen and wandered to other parts of Arabia. Amr bin Amir Ma'as Sama who was surnamed Muzaikiya or Muzaiqiya (Moses) Muzaikiya which is parallel that of prophet Moses leading an exodus from Meriba in the Biblical book of Exodus - Exodus 17. The leader Muzaikiya of the Azd, Khazraj and Aus. Much of this all ties together historically.

Ziphorah the Kushite is called Za'afira, Zarifah or Saffureh and she is "the diviner or prophetess and wife of Amr bin Amir Ma'as Sama who was surnamed **Muzaikiya**

The story of Jafna, **Muzaikiya** and Tha'labah and is also much too similar to the story of Jephuneh and his father Caleb in the Bible to just an accident

Remember The Khazraj of Medina the Harrah who were the same as the Kush or Ghassan were thus a remnant of the children of not only of the Keturah or the Midianite followers of Moses, but were also decendent of From Mazin bin Mansour bin Ikrima were the Khazraj, also in Arabian tradition the descendants of Jephuneh and Caleb brother of Kenaz who fathered Othniel the first Judge of Israel – the Kenizzites were, descendants of Eliphaz in the Bible.Josephus replaces the word Jokshan with Jazar which is Arabic for Gezer or the Khazraj who are also called Khazara, Hazraj, Gazras in various translations. This is also directly related to:

   "From Mazin bin Mansour bin Ikrima were the Khazraj and Aus or Awza children of Tha'laba Muzaikiya or Salebiyya and Jafna Muzaikiya.__Phinehas in one part of the Bible the brother of Hophni. Hophni and Phinehas or Phineas were the two sons of Eli. Another Phinehas is son of Eleazar the priest. Phinehas is also said to be son of Eleazar the priest a son of Harun or Amran brother of Moses who is linked in Arabian genealogy to the ancestral Azd people of MaribPhinehas, like Moses and Nun lived in Egypt during the captivity and their names were shared by the dominant culture there.

Mansoor otherwise Manasse'ir is undoubtedly Manasseh son of Joseph.

El Nas and Ghatafan are mentioned as the Bible as the families of the Judaeans, Neziah and Hatipha in the Biblical book of Ezra 2:54 and Nehemiah 7:56. El Yas, brother of El Nas, was y Elias which is sometimes translated Elijah in the Bible.

"Then Elijah said to them, Seize the prophets of Baal; do not let one of them escape." So they seized them; and Elijah brought them down to the brook Kishon, and slew them there." This is the brook from which the **"Ghusan Khasafa, brother of Ghatafan is apparently Hasupha or Chasupha of Ezra 2:43. They are classified as Levites or priests.**

The brother of Khasafa in Arabian tradition is Ghatafan who gave birth to the tribes of Assiyeh (whom Tabari 9th c. calls "the Israelite woman") and Rahil/Rukhayla (Rachel) and Ghatafan or Ghutayf (Hatepha). **Their South Arabian Azd ancestors were said to have fought against the people already in control of Misrah i.e. "the Amalekites" near Mecca under Moses (Muzaikiya) and Aaron.**

Historically the Rulers had married the daughters of priests who served them. As we saw Joseph, Jacob's first-born son by Rachel had married Asenath who was the daughter of a priest of the Egyptian shrine at Heliopolis. Our Law giver Moses had done the very same with Zipporah. Zipporah was **Moses'** wife and a daughter of Jethro, Priest of Midian. **Moses** met her **at a well and as the Bible says** where she and the other women near the well were being harassed. **Zipporah was Moses half sister or cousin bride in Horite Priest fashion.**

The children of Amram's children: And the Mariban prophet was Zeripha (Zipporah) These Israeli leaders were the children of Amram's children who were saved by Mariban. Moses addresses God using the title Adon/Aten (Exodus 4:10,13; 5:22; 34:9; Numbers 14:17; Deuteronomy 3:23; 7:26; 10:17); Moses, himself, is addressed both by Aaron (Ex.32:22; Num.12:11) and by Joshua (Numbers 11:28) using the title Adon/Aten; and Joshua also addresses God using the title Adon/Aten (Joshua 5:14 b; 7:7).

There was a Prince Tuthmose who was the eldest son of pharaoh Amenhotep III, and who mysteriously disappears from all records. There are very many facts pointing to that he have been the factual origin of the Biblical Moses? The name of this prince - Thutmose - is very similar to Moses

Since Crown Prince Tuthmose and Kiya as well as 3 chidren all disapered, are there any possible traces of any of this very important history? Let's futher consider one piece of evidence of Kiyas children we do have and who she was: *Kiya Ta-sherit*

Mery-khiba or **Mery-Amon (Kiya) - (Miriam)-*Kiya Ta-sherit was the* daughter of Mery-khiba or Mery-Amon (Kiya)**

EGYPT TO MOSES-KIYA LINE TO DAVID – Ahmose-Sipairi, Thutmose I & Mutnefert, Thutmose II & Iset, Tutmose III & Meryetre, Amenhotep II & Tyo, Tuthmosis IV & Mutemwiy, Amenhotep III & Gilukhipa, Kiya (wife of Mose), Kiya-Tasharenti & Aram/Ram, Amminadab & Tora/Thehora, Naason/Nahshon & Simar, Salmon & Rahab (repentant prostitute), Boaz & Ruth (of Moab), Obed, Jesse/Abinadah Nahash & Habliar, King David.

The hero is Amr, the son of Amir, the son of Thalabah (Thutmose, the son of Amenhotep III, the son of Thutmoses IV), surnamed Mozaikiya.

"Moses, a son of the tribe of Levi, educated in Egypt and initiated at Heliopolis, became a High Priest of the Brotherhood under the reign of Pharaoh Amenhotep. He was elected by the Hebrews as their chief and he adapted to the ideas of his people the science and philosophy which he had obtained in the Egyptian mysteries; proofs of this are to be found in the symbols, in the Initiations, and in his precepts and commandments....The dogma of an 'only god' which he taught was the Egyptian Brotherhood interpretation and teaching of the Pharaoh who established the first monotheistic religion known to man." - Egyptian High Priest Manetho (3rd Century BC)

Historically the Rulers had married the daughters of priests who served them. As we saw Joseph, Jacob's first-born son by Rachel had married Asenath who was the daughter of a priest of the Egyptian shrine at Heliopolis. Our Law giver Moses had done the very same with Zipporah. Zipporah was Moses' wife and a daughter of Jethro, Priest of Midian. Moses met her at a well and as the Bible says where she and the other women near the well were being harassed. Zipporah was Moses half sister or cousin bride in Horite Priest fashion.

Since Crown Prince Tuthmose and Kiya as well as 3 chidren all disapered, are there any possible traces of any of this very important history? Let's futher consider one piece of evidence of Kiyas children we do have and who she was: Kiya Ta-sherit Mery-khiba or Mery-Amon (Kiya) - (Miriam)-Kiya Ta-sherit was the daughter of Mery-khiba or Mery-Amon (Kiya)

"Moses, a son of the tribe of Levi, educated in Egypt and initiated at Heliopolis, became a High Priest of the Brotherhood under the reign of Pharaoh Amenhotep. He was elected by the Hebrews as their chief and he adapted to the ideas of his people the science and philosophy which he had obtained in the Egyptian mysteries; proofs of this are to be found in the symbols, in the Initiations, and in his precepts and commandments....The dogma of an 'only god' which he taught was the Egyptian Brotherhood interpretation and teaching of the Pharaoh who established the first monotheistic religion known to man."
- Egyptian High Priest Manetho (3rd Century BC)

Moses of the Bible was an Israelite, a Hebrew, born into the tribe of Levi.

14 And he said, Who made thee a prince and a judge over us? Thinkest thou to kill me, as thou killedst the Egyptian? And Moses feared, and said, Surely the thing is known.15 Now when Pharaoh heard this thing, he sought to slay Moses. But Moses fled from the face of Pharaoh, and dwelt in the land of Midian: and he sat down by a well.

Some great catastrophe in the area of Arim/Yarim (Aram) in ancient Saba forced the tribes of Azd to go scattering over the peninsula, some entering Africa. Hence the phrases "divided as the Sabaeans" and "wandering Aramaeans". Among these tribes were the Canaani and the Israelites under their leaders Muzaikiya of Marib (the Meriba of Exodus), the prophetess Zarifa (Ziphorah),Jafna (Jephunneh) and Caleb. ."Num. 10:29-32 Northern Hedjaz and the land of Midian. Zipporah who was the half sister or cousin bride of Moses is mentioned in Exodus 2:15-16 and in Exodus 18:1-6. Zipporah was the daughter of "the priest of Midian"

This three-person family was the head of the nation: two men and a woman - a ruler, to his holy brother and his wife, who was a prophet. According to the Bible the children of Israel from slavery in Egypt led to the family, which consisted of three people: the Director, in his holy brother and his sister, who was a prophet .**These Israeli leaders were children of Amram's children.** AI-Masudin cited by the leaders of the tribe, who were saved by Mariban, Amir had children. Moses was a holy brother of Aaron, the brother of a sacred tribal chief was Amran. **Moses' sister was Miriam, his wife was Sipora; Mariban prophet was Zeripha.** AI-Masudin report of these three persons and their doings to remind a lot of astonishingly similar report on biblical Moses, Aaron and Miriam and the children of Israel. His report is one of the few, whose origin is not from the Bible or the traditions of the Jews. All current place names in the Sinai and the Negev, that link Israeli scientists are set by David Ben Gurion's request.

The Egyptian language provides an etymology.4 The name Moses is related to common Egyptian names like Amenmose, Ramose and Thutmose,* which are formed of a god's name followed by mose.5 These compound names mean something like "Amen is born" or "Born of Amen" or "The offspring of Ra" or "The child of Thoth." **When the name Mose appears by itself, as it occasionally does in Egyptian, it simply means "the Child" or "the Offspring."6 But in Egyptian, Mose most frequently appears along with the name of a god as part of a compound name.**

The Egyptian root in 'ms' meaning to be born. **The linguistic root of the name Moses is shows itself in the Egyptian word Mos which means "child." But this word also had a much broader legal meaning—"the rightful son and heir."**

Remember the Tale of Two Brothers

The name Mozaikiya does not appear to have been Arabic, but Egyptian origin. Mose-ika-Ya may have a name, which is shaped in the same manner as, for example potassium Smenkh-Re, with reference to the last byte of god - Smenkaren case, Re-Allah, Mosaikayan Ya-Allah event (such as Isa IAH JereM words IAD), a byte national marking the Egyptian language the word "soul". If this is an ancient Arabic word really means Mosaikiya Moses, then in that case we have before us at last, Moses, Semitic, and at the same time an Egyptian name. The name "Jehovah's soul" perfectly suits the man who according to the Bible was the first to whom God revealed his name. Also translated as **The last syllable is the name of a divinity, the 'ya' as in Isaiah and Jeremiah, means Yahweh. The second syllable, 'ka', is Egyptian for soul. So the name means, the soul of Yahweh as well as soul of Jehovah.**

Remember these are The children of Amram's children: And the Mariban prophet was Zeripha (Zipporah) These Israeli leaders were the children of Amram's children who were saved by Mariban.

12:07   **And there-occurred a-War in Heaven ... The Michael and**
       the Angels of-him made-War with the *Dragon* **... and**

      The Dragon **and The Angels of-him Warred.**

12:09 And was-cast ... *The Dragon* ... The Great ... The Serpent
... The Ancient ... The-One being-called a Slanderer ...
and The Satan ... The-One deceiving ... the Whole Inhabited
-Earth ... he-was-cast to the Earth ...

The Sons of Light, consisting of the sons of Levi, the sons of

Judah, and the sons of Benjamin
The Messiah Jesus fulfilled the eternal promise to the line of
Moses as the King of Jeshurun. Jesus being a descendant
of David verifies David's descent from Moses.

Judah had never hitherto possessed it; for **Moses, who was *"king***
in Jeshurun," was of the tribe of Levi; and Joshua, who succeeded
him, was of the tribe of Ephraim: and while the tabernacle was still
at Shiloh, though the ark was not, Samuel anointed Saul of the tribe
of Benjamin, to be king over all Israel. The ark never returned
to Shiloh, and the tabernacle there was destroyed. "So God forsook
the tabernacle of Shiloh;" and did not choose Judah for the staff-
bearing ruler over Israel until the departure *from* Shiloh; and David
became king over alwal Israel, two years after the death of Saul.
But, ***"until he cometh to Shiloh"*** is not the translation of *ad ki yahvo*
Shiloh. There is no word in the text answering to the particle *"to;"*
and furthermore, the verb *yahvo* is not the present tense,
"he cometh**," but is the future** *"shall come;"* nor is
Yehudah the nominative to the verb; it is *Shiloh*, which they
put in the dative, or in the accusative governed by a preposition,

which is not in the text.

In _The War of the Sons of Light Against the Sons of Darkness,_
one of the Dead Sea scrolls, Belial is the leader of the Sons of
Darkness: Edom, Moab, the sons of Ammon, the Amalekites,
Philistia, and the Kittim of Asshur .
But for corruption thou hast made Belial, an angel
of hostility. All his dominions are in darkness, and his purpose
is to bring about wickedness and guilt. All the spirits that are
associated with him are but angels of destruction.

Again: These scrolls contain an apocalyptic prophecy of a war between the Sons of
Light and the Sons of Darkness. **The war is first described as an attack by the**
Sons of Light, consisting of the sons of Levi, the sons of Judah, and the sons of
Benjamin, and the exiled of the desert, against Edom, Moab, the sons of Ammon,
the Amalekites, Philistia, and the Kittim of Asshur (referred to as the army of
Belial), and [those who assist them from among the wicked] who "violate the
covenant." In the end, all of Darkness is to be destroyed and Light will live in peace
for all eternity. The war is then described again as a conflict between the
congregation of God and the congregation of men. The rest of the document is a
detailed description of the events of the war and the ways in which it should be
conducted.. **Kittim** in the genealogy of Genesis 10 in the Hebrew Bible, is the son of
Javan, the grandson of Japheth, and Noah's great-grandson.

1QM consists of 19 columns, of which the first 14-19 lines of each have been
preserved.

> **i**. Summarizes the war between the "Sons of Light" and "Sons of Darkness."

> **ii-ix**. Deals with the battles between the tribes in greater detail, telling of a
> total forty years of combat. Columns iii-iv deal almost exclusively with the
> inscriptions meant to be displays on banners, trumpets, darts, etc.

> **x-xiv**. A number of liturgical pieces.

> **xv-xix**. Describes the seven-stage battle, led by the priests, between Light
> and Darkness. The battle is finally won by divine intervention.

Again: **The Sons of Light, consisting of the sons of Levi, the sons of Judah, and the sons of**
Benjamin Also in _The Dead Sea Scrolls_ is a recounting of a dream of Amram, the father of Moses,
who finds two 'watchers' contesting over him. One is Belial who is described as the King of Evil
and Prince of Darkness

"the great hand of God shall overcome [Belial and al]l the angels of his dominion, and all the men of [his forces shall be destroyed forever]" (IQM 1:14-15).

Sea Scrolls (4Q535, Manuscript B) was written from Amram's point of view,

I saw Watchers in my vision, the dream-vision. Two men were fighting over me...holding a great contest over me. I asked them, 'Who are you, that you are thus empowered over me?' They answered, 'We have been empowered and rule over all mankind.' They said to me, 'Which of us do you choose to rule you?' I raised my eyes and looked. One of them was terrifying in his appearance, like a serpent, his cloak, many-colored yet very dark....And I looked again, and in his appearance, his visage like a viper....I replied to him, 'This Watcher, who is he?' He answered, 'This Watcher...his three names are Belial and Prince of Darkness and King of Evil.' I said (to the other Watcher), 'My lord, what dominion (have you?)' He answered, 'You saw (the viper), and he is empowered over all Darkness, while I (am empowered over all Light.)...My three names are Michael, Prince of Light and King of Righteousness. In Hebrew, *Michael* means "who is like God" (*mi*-who, *ke*-as or like, *El*-deity), which is traditionally interpreted as a rhetorical question: "3Who is like God?" (which expects an answer in the negative) to imply that *no one* is like God. In this way, Michael is reinterpreted as a symbol of humility before God.

Remember in the New Testament Michael leads God's armies against Satan's forces in the Book of Revelation, where during the war in heaven he defeats Satan. In the Epistle of Jude Michael is specifically referred to as an "archangel". Christian sanctuaries to Michael appeared in the 4th century, when he was first seen as a healing angel, and then over time as a protector and the leader of the army of God against the forces of evil.

On the Trumpets of the Battle formation they shall write: Formations of the divisions of God to avenge his Anger on All Sons of Darkness

On the Trumpets for assembling the infantry when the gates of war open that they might go out against the battle line of the enemy, they shall write:

"A rememberance of requital at the appointed time of God."

"Mysteries of God to wipe out Wickedness" on the trumpets of persuit they shall write "God has struck all sons of Darkness, He shall not abate his anger until they are annihilated.

But Belial, the Angel of Malevolence, Thou hast created for the Pit; his [rule] is in Darkness and his purpose is to bring about wickedness and iniquity. All the spirits of his company, the Angels of Destruction, walk according to the precepts of Darkness; towards them is their [inclination].

But let us, the company of Thy truth, rejoice in Thy mighty hand and be glad for Thy salvation, and exult because of Thy suc[cour and] peace. O God of Israel, who can compare with Thee in might? Thy mighty hand is with the poor. Which angel or prince can compare with Thy [redeeming] succour? [For Thou hast appointed] the day of battle from ancient times ... [to come to the aid] of truth and to destroy iniquity, to bring Darkness low and to magnify Light ... to stand for ever, and to destroy all the sons of Darkness ... – 1QM 11-15

Q1-(5) I[srael. Then the]re shall be a time of salvation for the People of God, and a time of dominion for all the men of His forces, and eternal annihilation for all the forces of Belial. There

shall be g[reat] panic [among] (6) the sons of Japheth, Assyria shall fall with no one to come to his aid, and the supremacy of the Kittim shall cease that wickedness be overcome without a remnant. There shall be no survivors of (7) [all the Sons of] Darkness

---

There is no need to appeal to examples in the Bible: There are plenty of

---

references to show that the son of an Israelite father,
like Moses and Tsipora from Midian, was an Israelite.

"Birthright" was the firstborn son's right to a special share, when an inheritance was divided. The Scriptures do not contain any "footnote" where the right of the firstborn son is especially clarified; that was not necessary, because people of old times knew what that right was. Deuteronomy 21:17 gives us an example of how this with "birthright" affected the division of an inheritance. (Again, traditionally a man's firstborn son had the birthright, a right to a special share when the father's property was divided between his sons, either after his death or already before that.) We read:

Jacob and his family had arrived in Egypt in the pre-Hyksos period when the name of the town was Rowaty, "the door of the two roads" (Bietak 1996: 9, 19).

Recently David Rohl has found such names as Yaqub - Hor, Nakhi and Sheshi among the Hyksos scarabs - seemingly the same names as the rulers Jacob, Anak and Sheshai whom Genesis calls early kings of Canaan and Israel. According to Arabian tradition during the time of the Amalekite kings "Qabus" and "Rayan" - Asaf(Josef) was placed on the throne of Misra. His wife being Asiyah or Washiya who is Asenath.

The ruler Asaf, according to Arabian tradition corresponding to the Bible story of Joseph was put in control of Misrah by the Hyksos or Amalekite rulers Raian (El Riyan) and Walid, who ruled in Egypt. Misrah, however, also include Musra or Musran a region or village and people synonymous with the Meluhha or Amalekites living next to and controlling the Egypt of the Hyksos period. In the Bible, Joseph is called a son of Jacob who is identified by some archeologists as the Hyksos ruler who figures on Egyptian scarabs as Yaqub Hor or Yaqub El. In the Bible, Jacob is, of course, also called "Israel".

Jada'ah - Gad (of the **Ka'b bin Amer bin** Za'za'a) **Ka'b - Jacob (Ka'b bin Amer bin Sa'sa'a)**

The Ancient Egyptians blamed the Hyksos for conquering their country. The truth may have been a gradual process of integration.[4]

Amo Isreal Gods people, a view of tribe afiliations

Ka'b - Jacob (Ka'b bin Amer bin Sa'sa'a)

Rachel - (**Masruh/Hawazin/Sulaym**)

Manassir/ Mansur - Manasseh (**Qays Ailan**)

The main branches of the Qais tribes were the Banu Sulaym, Hawazin and the Banu Ghatafan. These three main groups remained in the Eastern Hejaz until the 7th century.

Joseph (Asaf) was an man of who rose to power over the Musri. Assiyah the Arab Djurham woman also ancestral to the Sulaym (Solymi) is Asenath.

As the first was Isaac, thus making Jacob and Esau Patrilineal, and their sons Patrilineal and the sons of Judah and Joseph Patrilineal as well as Levi.

One must understand that the term Horite does not designate a race or ethnicity. It designates a very important caste or rulers and priests. Their brides were the daughters of ruler-priests. They contributed the mtDNA and their ruler husbands contributed the Y chromosome since males who share a common patrilineal ancestor also share a Y chromosome. After years of studying descent systems, Claude Levi-Strauss noted that in patrilineal systems mother and child belong to different tribes. In the case of Abraham's ancestors, the cousin bride belongs to her husband's house while her first-born son belongs to her father's house. .Horite men married only Horite women and according to a pattern which was tied to ancient tradition. It is not any coincidence that Joseph married Asenath, the daughter of "the priest of On" (Gen. 41:45). The exclusive intermarriage between Horite lines requires that we take these words quite literally: **"For me you shall be a kingdom of priests, a holy nation." (Ex. 19:6)**

It is not a coincidence that Siavus in the Persian or Central Asian story is tempted or seduced by Sudabeh in the same manner as Joseph or Yusef also called Asaf in Arabian tradition was tempted many times by the wife of Potiphar. They were both falsely accused of trying to seduce powerful women. Genesis 39:7-8 "And it came to pass after these things, that his master's wife cast her eyes upon Joseph; and she said , lie with me , but he refused… and while Joseph (also called Zafnath - Genesis xli. 45) son of Jacob or Yacov

Others have found a connection between the name of Ziph and Cepheus, in which case Cassiopeia would appear to be the Arabian queen Assiyeh whom is the Biblical Asenath married to Zafnath (Josef).

If as Hashem Moses did indeed prophesies, that if they would turn and repent, Jehovah God would hear from heaven and restore them to their inheritance. It is Jacob's seed that must be preserved. We find this symbolic form used again in Jeremiah 30:9 when after the time of Jacob's trouble in Babylon, The specific seed of King David was Jehoachim that lead to Hashem Jesus Christ Kind David Kingdom was sais was Forever including in our own times the Revelation 12 Rod (Root of David) of Iron that will rule all nations is a direct decedent of Jehoachim the line of David that was chosen as there were many lines of David that we not chosen By Seth Ben Adam Ben Jehovah God.

To further explain, when a man's DNA is tested, we are testing the DNA of his father, his father's father, his father's father an unbroken chain etc. We can go back thousand's of years in this fashion because Y-DNA changes very slowly over time. Only men inherit the Y chromosome. It cannot pass to a female.

This is the seed of a man. It is this seed that passes from father to son. It is the Y-chromosome of King David that is inherited along with the rest of the DNA by Moshiach ben David that will uniquely qualify him as the messiah The Salic law was a body of traditional law codified for governing the Salian Franks in the early Middle Ages during the reign of King Clovis I in the 6th century. Although Salic Law reflects very ancient usage and practices, the Lex Salica likely was first compiled only sometime between 507 and 511.[1]

Revelation 12:9. which states : And the great dragon was cast out, that old serpent called the devil and Satan, which deceive the whole world. The whole world is deceived not only about the right way to worship YHWH, but they are deceived about who are the true Israelites a people near and dear unto YHWH (psalms 148:14).

God must Glorify himself in the face of Belial God must Glorify himself in the face of Belial the Prince of Darkness and King of Evil, and this is the War in Heaven,In Daniel 12:4, the instruction is given: "But thou, O Daniel, shut up the words, and seal the book, even to the time of the end: many shall run to and fro, and knowledge shall be increased."
The Book of Revelation, which consists principally of eschatological visions[3] and opens with the words: "The revelation of Jesus Christ, which God gave him to show to his servants the things that must soon take place"" includes" in those Events a War in Heaven

A "war in heaven" is an expression used in the Book of Revelation in reference to a combat it recounts between angels led respectively by the archangel Michael and by "the dragon", identified with "the devil and Satan", who is defeated and thrown down to the earth.[1][2]

In my historical research I found that the Nasrid Dynasty did indeed trace all the way back to Seth Ben Adam Ben Jehovah God, and I will prove this later in this work. Being a Mother of all Prophets Hashem is a Special thing as other Mothers of all Prophets Hashem included Zipporah the Wife of Hashem Moses, and well as the Mother Mary as Hashem Jesus Christ was the Direct Descendent of Hashem Moses. I found that the Real Line of Hashem Moses did indeed marry Zipporah and the Tribe of Hashem Moses was the tribe of AZD as recalled by many African tribes.

Seir was the Ancestor of the "dukes of the Horites" in the land of Seir, only later did it become Edom (Gen. 36:20-30). [20] These are the sons of Seir the Horite, the inhabitants of the land: Lotan and Shobal and Zibeon and Anah,

[21] and Dishon and Ezer and Dishan: these are the chiefs that came of the Horites, the children of Seir in the land of Edom.

Stop Check

A critical fact to be understood is that true Arabs, like true Jews, are both descendents of Abraham with the mixture of other peoples, both Semitic and non-Semitic. But the important truth is that **only people who might rightfully claim to be "pure blood" descendents of Abraham are those who stand in the /royal priestly lines as these were the lines that became the Biblical patriarchs and the Israelites of the Bible. These lines are found among both Jews and Arabs, as /the priests of Shem and Ham intermarried. By looking at the lineage with an understanding of the pattern in which they**

married, The evidence of the kinship pattern appears to be consistent throughout the generations from Gen. 4 and 5 to well past the time of Moses.

Why are the Israelite's God's chosen people? Because of Abraham's superior faith, God made him a promise. He promised to cause his descendant's to greatly multiply into a great nation, and they would become "his chosen people". It was not individuality based on faith and works, but as a nation, chosen by God, and for God. Even though the fact is that:
A true Israelite must be identified based on the biblical law I Chronicle 9:1 "All Israel were reckoned by genealogies." (on the father's side only) Nachash is the Hebrew word for SERPENT from which nashak the word for usury is derived.

The Sons of Light are the patrilineal decents of Jacob/Israel. The sons of Light were Levi, Judah and Benjamin. Moses himself was of the Sons Levi.

Though it seems quite out of place there is much evidence that Horus was regarded as King of the universe in ancient mythology. He was the only figure portrayed as a Man in ancient Egypt." A caste of priests served him and they were called Horites. The rulers of Abraham's people were the Horite Kings or more accurately Horite ruler-priests that began the priesthood that went on for thousands of years. Who was this priesthood, and was it important to understanding the Bible? **According to the Book of Jubilees (9:5,6), the inheritance of the Earth to be bequeathed to the descendants of Aram included all of the land between the Tigris and Euphrates rivers "to the north of the Chaldees to the border of the mountains of Asshur and the land of 'Arara."[21** Abraham's two wives were Sara and Ketura as they are both are named for well-established Kushitic tribes and were the daughters of established Horite rulers, Sara who was the daughter of Terah. Terah controlled the Euphrates between Ur and Haran. Sarah was born a princess of the house of Aram (Syria). Her mother had been an Aramaean princess who likely raised Sarah to enjoy the noble life. . After Abraham settled in Canaan, she resided at Hebron. She was Abraham's wife and his half-sister. They had the same father, but different mothers (Gen. 20:12). as their father Terah had two wives.

Keturah is specifically referred to as "Abraham's concubine" at 1 Chronicles 1:32, and quite apparently she and Hagar are meant at Genesis 25:6, where reference is made to the sons of Abraham's "concubines." Keturah was therefore a secondary wife who never attained the same position as Sarah the mother of Isaac, through whom the promised Seed came. (Ge 17:19-21; 21:2, 3, 12; Heb 11:17, 18) While "Abraham gave everything he had to Isaac," the patriarch gave gifts to the sons of his concubines and then "sent them away from Isaac his son, while he was still alive, eastward, to the land of the East."—Ge 25:5, 6. One wife was a half-sister and the other was a patrilineal cousin. Terah, his father, had 2 wives, and Nahor his grandfather also had 2 wives. Moses had 2 wives, as did Jacob.1 Chronicles 1:32 was written long after and apparently seeks to reinforce the promise through Sarah's seed exclusively.

Among the ancient Horites the pattern was double descent. The kinship pattern of the rulers listed in the Genesis genealogies shows two lines of descent. One is traced through the cousin/niece bride who named her first-born son after her father. Example: Namaah, Lamech the Elder's daughter,(Gen. 4) married her patrilineal cousin Methuselah (Gen. 5) and named their first-born son Lamech. This pattern, which I call the "cousin bride's naming prerogative," is found with the names Joktan, Sheba and Esau, among others.

The other line of descent is traced through the first-born son of the half-sister bride, as Sarah was to Abraham. The ruler-priest lines of the two first-born sons intermarried, thus preserving the bloodline of those to whom God made the promise that a woman of their people would bring forth the Seed who would crush the serpent's head and restore Paradise.

The term Aramaeans was changed to "Syrian" by late translators. The Aram were originally a southern Arabian people from Arim or Iram where the Sabaean dam was and were similar in appearance to the Aramramma of the Khazraj. As Aws is Biblical Uz and Khazaraj also written Gazara, Jazraj or Khazaras is Gezer. One of the well-known clans of the Khazraj mentioned in Arab texts is the Aramramma. The Hebrew word rammîy is found at 2Chronicles 22:5, also translated Aramaean or Syrian.[15]

These are the names and people of the ancient tribes of the Sabaeans children of Joktan. According to the book The Yemen in Early Islam, published in 1988 the clans Rahawein (Ru'ayn, Rahawiyyin, Rahawi in early Arabia – Reu) belonged to the Madhhij or Madhhaj. Others clans of the Maddhij were the Murad or Amurath also called Qaran, Rualla or Ruwalla bin Anaeza , Ans or Anaeza bin Wa'il, Nakh'l or An-Nakha, Badi'ah, Ghutayf bin Haritha related to the Ghatafan, Nashirah, Sa'ad al Ashirah, Za'afar, Zubayd or Zabeida, al Amluk or Amalek was a clan of the Rahawiyin, as was the tribe of Qataban (Banu Kita'a), and Yafi' (Ephah).

A clear indicator is that almost all of these clans are listed in the Genesis of the Bible. They are Reu, Amorites, Reuel son of Esau, Esau, Hawila, Anoch, Hatepha, Ashira, Zabid, Amalek and Qahit or _Kohath_ and Ephah . It is not improbable, that Madhhij who are listed with the Ma'adei who are mentioned in Syrian inscriptions of the 3rd century B.C. at Nemara are in fact the Madianites especially since the plural of Maadi was Madan who was called brother of Madian.

Kahlan who is called Nakhete Kalnis of Ethiopian/Abyssinian royal genealogy. In addition Qahtan (Joktan brother of Peleg) son of Abir (Eber) or Hud, had kinsmen called Iram (or Aram), Awza or Aus (Uz) (the latter's name said to be derived from "Adah"). These are all closely related individuals in Arabian genealogical tradition who are said to have lived centuries before the time of Moses (Muzaikiya).

It is truly incredible to find that the Biblical record is so reliable that it can literally be used to reconstruct the actual the priestly bloodline that began from Cain and Seth) and this leads to the priesthood of Moses then onto King David then onto Joachim, father of the virgin Mary, Mother of the Promised Son of God.

The Horite Priestly line rightfully believed that the Son of God would become from their bloodline. This is why historically they had taken such pride and great care that their priests very strictly married only their kin that was patrilineal. The bloodline itself which I will give you examples of was traced through the mother and the priesthood itself was traced through the father's patrilineal bloodline.

With Melchizedek as you saw the priesthood of God comes to be associated with the Jebusite settlement of Jerusalem. This distinguishes this greatly important priesthood of God from any other priesthood that did not recognize the many biblical and ancient prophecies concerning Mount Zion and the House of

David. It is here David is shown as a ruler-priest and shepherd the very same roles that characterize the ruler-priests whose patrilineal lines intermarried, bringing us to the House of Joachim, Mary's father.

"The Testament of Qahat" Kohath "Now, my sons, be careful with the heritage which is handed over to you..."Qahat's message was then heeded by his son Amram.

Amran is arabicized to **Imran in the Bible**. In the Qur'an, the name Imran is used for two different people. The first one is Amram the father of Moses and the second one is Joachim the father of Mary, the mother of Jesus. Amram, the father of Moses and Aaron, is a revered patriarch of Islam. The Qur'an says:God did choose Adam and Noah, the family of Abraham, and the family of Amram above all people,——Qur'an, sura 3 (*The House of Imran*), ayah 33Amram, the father of Moses and Aaron. Through him would come many other priests and prophets, including Anne, Elizabeth, Mary, John the Baptist and Jesus. *For instance The House of Imran* is the 3rd chapter of the Qur'an. *Imran* is Arabic for the biblical figure Amram, the father of Moses, and Aaron, the ancestor of Mary and Jesus through his son Moses. the Christian **Joachim** has been attributed the name Imran as well. Muslims distinguish between the two different individuals as 'Imran, ancestor of Mary' and 'Imran, father of Mary'As for the figure of Joachim/Imran, the father of Mary and the grandfather of Jesus and also for being one of the most saintly men present in Jerusalem at the time, along side the priest Zachariah. Imran's wife was **Hannah**, the Christian Saint Anne Jesus, crowned with thorns in a purple robe as the King of the Jews, being mocked and beaten during his Passion, depicted by van Baburen, 1623. In the New Testament, Jesus is referred to as the King of the Jews, both at the beginning of his life and at the end. In the Koine Greek of the New Testament, e.g. in John 19:3 this is written Basileus ton Ioudaion (βασιλεὺς τῶν Ἰουδαίων).[1]Both uses of the title lead to dramatic results in the New Testament accounts. In the account of the Nativity of Jesus in the Gospel of Matthew, the wise men (i.e. Magi) who come from the east call Jesus the "King of the Jews", causing King Herod to order the Massacre of the Innocents. Towards the end of the accounts of all four Canonical Gospels, in the narrative of the Passion of Jesus, the use of the "King of the Jews" title leads to charges against Jesus that result in his Crucifixion.[2][3]The acronym INRI (Iēsus Nazarēnus, Rēx Iūdaeōrum) represents the Latin inscription which in English reads as "Jesus the Nazarene, King of the Jews" and John 19:20 states that this was written in three languages: Hebrew, Latin and Greek during the crucifixion of Jesus. The Greek version reads INBI, representing Ἰησοῦς ὁ Ναζωραῖος ὁ Βασιλεὺς τῶν Ἰουδαίων.[4]In the New testament, the "King of the Jews" title is used only by the gentiles, namely by the Magi, Pontius Pilate and the Roman soldiers. In contrast, the Jewish leaders use the designation "King of Israel".[2] The phrase has also been translated King of the Judeans (see Ioudaioi).

All of these men were ruler-priests, as this pattern pertained only to ruler-priests. There are are 2 main priestly lines from the book of Genesis through the books of Exodus and these lines intermarried exclusively. **The lines are first those of Cain and Seth, Ham and Shem, Sheba and Joktan, Levi and Judah, and Korah and his half-brother's Aaron and Moses.**

The other line of descent is traced through the first-born son of the half-sister bride, as Sarah was to Abraham. **David was also of the priestly line of Ram (Ruth 4:19). Ram is a common name among the priestly lines. One of Shem's sons was named A'ram (Gen. 10:22) and the priestly line of Moses and is traced through their father Am'ram. I will show how the lines intermixed; it was truly an order of great importance**

I found through all my research that my son qualifies as the Revelation 12 Rod of Iron that will Rule all nations As everything got harder on me I identified the Seed of the Woman by working with a Biblical Anthropologist. I traced my sons blood line all the way from Seth Ben Adam Ben Jehovah

The promise made in Eden (Gen. 3:15) about the Woman's Seed This does completely suggest that the tribes had maintained a very high importance to the preservation of the bloodline of these rulers. As they knew the importance of their lineage It is likely that they realized and knew themselves to be heirs of God's promise that the Son of God would come through **their lines.**(Jesus)This strongly suggests that the ruling lines were aware and believed the promise made in Eden (Gen. 3:15) concerning the Woman's Seed who would crush the serpent's head and receive the Father's Kingdom. This line is traced through Jesse and David, but because of the very exclusive intermarriage pattern of the tribes, it is also traced through Sheba and Joktan.

Genesis 3:15 is commonly called the "Protevangelium" — a term that essentially signifies the idea of "first gospel proclamation."
In the American Standard Translation (1901), the text reads as follows:
"and I will put enmity between thee and the woman, and between thy seed and her seed: he shall bruise [crush—NIV] thy head, and thou shalt bruise [strike—NIV] his heel."

Professor William Beck's, *An American Translation* (4th edition), renders the passage:
"And I will put enmity between you and the woman and between your descendants and her Descendant. He will crush your head, and you will bruise His heel."

Ya'rub/Jerah ibn Qahtan/Joktan b. **Eber** b. Shalikh b. Arfakhshad b. **Sam/Shem** b. Nuh/Noah. *Noah ben[11] LAMECH, *Lamech ben[10] METHUSELAH, *Methuselah ben[9] ENOCH, *Enoch ben[8] JARED, *Jared ben[7] MAHALALEEL, *Mahalaleel ben KENAN[6] (CAINAN), *Kenan (Cainan) ben[5] ENOS, *Enos ben[4] SETH, *Seth ben[3] ADAM, *Adam CREATED BY[2] GOD, JEHOVAH[1])

Southern Arabs come from **Qahtan/Joktan**, not **Ishmael**... Pure Arab people were not the **children of Ishmael**.

According to The Bible, Genesis 10:22-31

22 **The children of Shem**: Elam, and Asshur, and Arphaxad and Lud and Aram. 23 And the children of Aram; Uz and Hul, and Gether and Mash. 24 And Arphaxad begat Salah and Salah begat Eber. 25 **And unto Eber were born two sons: the name of one was Peleg; for in his days was the earth divided; and his brother's name was Joktan. 26 And Joktan begat Almodad, and Sheleph, and Hazarmaveth, and Jerah(Ya'rub).** 27 And Hadoram, and Uzal and Diklah, 28 And Obal, and Abimael and Sheba, 29 And Ophir, and Havilah, and Jobab: all these were the sons of Joktan. 30 And their dwelling was from Mesha, as thou goest unto Sephar a mount of the east 31 **These are the sons of Shem, after their families, after their tongues, in their lands, after their nations.**

[Genesis 10:21] Also to Shem, the father of all the Children of Eber

In Biblical tradition it is **Eber** and not Abram who is the eponymous **ancestor** of all Hebrews

Eber (עֵבֶר, ISO 259-3 ʕebr, Standard Hebrew Éver, Tiberian Hebrew ʻĒḇer) is an ancestor of the Israelites, according to the "Table of Nations" in Genesis 10-11 and 1 Chronicles 1. He was a great-grandson of Noah's son Shem and the father of Peleg born when Eber was 34 years old, and of Joktan. He was the son of Shelah a distant ancestor of Abraham.George Bury writes in 1915 in Arabia infelix, or The Turks in Yamen ,"The first concrete fact in the history of the Yaman is the birth of Joktan son of Eber, B.C. 2246. Joktans son Yarab (Jerah of Genesis) was the progenitor of Yamen Arabic and first separated the Yamen tongue from ancient Hebrew. It was who founded the Sabaean Kingdom in Yemen. I will continue tracing the line in the next chapters of this work.

Tribal affiliation and family genealogy can only be traced through the person's father (the patrilineal in accordance with Exodus 28:4, 29:9-30, 30:30, and 40:15 [Priesthood Lineage]; Numbers 36 [Tribal Lineage]; Genesis 49:10, I Kings 11:4, and I Chronicles 17:11-19 [Kingship Lineage].).

Tribal descent, such as whether one is a kohen or a Levite, is still inherited patrilineally in Judaism,[1] Y-DNA" is passed solely along the patrilineal line, from father to son.

EXODUS 19:6 "AND YOU SHALL BE UNTO ME A KINGDOM OF PRIEST AND AN HOLY NATION. THESE ARE THE WORDS WHICH YOU SHALL SPEAK UNTO THE CHILDREN OF ISRAEL."

Tribal descent, such as whether one is a kohen or a Levite, is still inherited patrilineally in Judaism,[13]

It is a fact that Y-chromosome DNA (Y-DNA) is only passed on or paternally inherited enables patrilines of men to be traced through genetic analysis.

Patrilineal Descent ... that in the Bible the line always followed the father, including the cases of Joseph and Moses.

1. ^ This has led to the idea of a single male ancestor of all males members of these groups. In the Bible this individual is identified as Aaron, brother of Moses, so the hypothetical figure is known as the Y-chromosomal Aaron.

We must demand that the line of Joseph, Moses and the Davidic line are all patrilineal. We must no longer disregard this as important fact to history and demand it of our leaders if they are going to claim it as do the children of the line of Queen Victoria until this day and age. Unknown patrilineal lines will no longer be accepted as substitutes, we must demand this, as they simply cannot make themselves something they are not.

In Hebrew law the inheritance of land was passed along patrilineal lines. The Succession by the eldest son, or also called Primogeniture, it was the preferred rule as told in the Biblical passage (Deuteronomy 21:15-17), and numerous other individual accounts. In the biblical terms primogeniture often occurs when and where the rule is broken as was the situations for Isaac, Jacob, Joseph, and David.

The Jews have been expecting a future and the time is now of a Jewish Messiah and he is completely expected to be from the patrilineal (male only) "Davidic line

It is necessary that Moshiach ben David be a male line descendant of King David through Solomon or Nathan. The answer among almost all Hebrew royal genealogists is "yes." By definition alone, the name Son of David that has been designated to identify the messiah, indicates a male line descendant, **with no female breaks in the chain.** **Scripture tells us that Moshiach ben David will be a male line descendant of King David.**

The fact that the Y chromosome is paternally inherited enables patrilines, and agnatic kinships, of individuals to be traced through genetic analysis. The line of descent for monarchs and main personalities is exclusively through the main male personalities which is considered an unbroken paternal line.

Again Case in point: For instance, in **Numbers, chapter 1, verse 18**, we're told that the Jewish people historically and Biblically had declared their **pedigrees according to their fathers' houses.** When Queen Athaliah wanted to eliminate the Royal Line of David, she only killed the males **knowing full well that a female descendant of David couldn't pass on the right to the throne** (II Kings 11; II Chronicles 22).

I will show this history again in complete Context of history and of the Exodus later in this work. We must begin to understand that as the Bible states the father of Moses name was *Amram* which is designated a ruler among Abraham's Horite people. This is the origin of the word Aramean, which also refers to the language spoken by the Asiatic Horites who lived in the territory of Aram, the son of Shem (Gen. 10:22).As we have seen he was the first Aram mentioned in the Bible. And as we can see his throne continued is quite evident from the fact that he had a descendant named Aram as well. Aram the Younger was the son of Kemuel who was Abraham's nephew (Gen. 22:21).As we have also seen Rebecca was Aram's niece and Milkah was Aram's daughter.

The Priesthood was a Fixed Order

The priesthood was a fixed order and it is quite evident that the very priesthood that points to Jesus Christ, the Son of God, pertains exclusively to ruling men. It is an amazing order as it appears to be fixed by God from the beginning. The 3order of creation is fixed and has been since the earliest times.

"For God so loved the world, that he gave his only Son, that whoever believes in him should not perish but have eternal life.

It is this very misunderstanding of history that both Arabs and Jews possess the J System and that many Jews had converted to Islam that has brought us near to the brink of destruction, has caused a deep amount of resentment and has placed us under a mountain of debt for ourselves and our children based on Usery that goes directly against the word of the Bible itself.

Litterally thousands of well meaning Christians use Biblical terms they do not yet understand well enough. Terms like "Jew," and "Israeilite," "The House of Judah,," The House of Israel "" While using these similar words and phrases as if historically the terms always referred to the same people. But according to the flow of Biblical history, there were no "Jews" known as this until near 1500 years after Abraham was born, and several centuries after the death of Moses.

So again, who are the Semites?

The Semites are, according to the highly authoritative Oxford Universal Dictionary, 1944 (p. 1838) the people belonging to the race of mankind which includes most of the peoples mentioned in Genesis 10 as descended from Shem, son of Noah, as the Arabs, Hebrews, Assyrians and Arameans, and speaking a Semitic language as their native tongue.

The Bible mentions two Havilahs in the Table of Nations: Havilah the son of Cush (Gen. 10:7) and Havilah the son of Joktan (Gen. 10:29). The "land of Havilah" has been interpreted by many biblical scholars to be Arabia, and Joktan is considered to be the head of the tribes of Arabia, as most of his sons can be traced to places and districts within what is now Saudi Arabia and Yemen. Apparently the "land of Havilah" referred to a whole region rather than one particular place, since there appears to have been more than one tribe by that name. (Quoted from the American Scientific Affiliation web page)

The separation of the two groups in the time of Peleg and Joktan was territorial only, as the ruling lines continued to intermarry.

These are the sons of Shem, after their families, after their tongues, in their lands, after their nations.

Only the purest Arabs, it is still maintained, are those Semitic Arabs descended from Joktan.

George Bury wrote in 1915 in Arabia infelix, or The Turks in Yamen ,"The first concrete fact in the history of the Yaman is the birth of Joktan son of Eber, B.C., 2246. I identify Eber with Heber the prophet, or Hud as the Arabs call him, who preached to the Adites and warned them of the Divine vengeance...This is said to have overtaken them in the form of a raging simoom along the western margin of what is now called the Rub al Khali or the Empty Quarter...**But to return to Joktan or Kahtan as the Arabs call him. He was a native of Hadramaut valley but settled in Yemen and introduced architecture and agriculture among the pastoral and ten dwelling tribes. His son Yarab (Jerah of Genesis) was the progenitor of Yamen Arabic and first separated the Yamen tongue from ancient Hebrew. He it was who founded the Sabaean Kingdom in Yemen on the ruins of the old Minaean dynasty which had dwindled to a mere tribal confederation in the southern Jauf and was known then and since as Maan – the Arab title for the dynasty itself.(From Arabia infelix or The Turks in Yamen Georg Wyman Bury, 1915. pp. 2-3.)**

Also the Mayans of the Yucatan Peninsula who Rabbi Mattityahu Glazerson (an eminent scholar of the Torah Codes) believes were some of the descendants of Joktan (pronounced Y'katan in Hebrew) the son of Eber (Genesis 10:26).

Many scholars have suggested a link between the **Sabaeans** and the Biblical **land** of Sheba. The ancient Sabaean Kingdom established power in the early 1st millennium BC. In the 1st century BC it was conquered by the Himyarites, but historically after the disintegration of the first Himyarite empire of the Kings of Saba' the Middle Sabaean Kingdom reappeared in the early 2nd century **Its capital was Ma'rib.**

Jeremiah 51:19-20 – "The Portion of **Jacob is not like them (Babylonians),** for **He is the Maker** of all things; and **Israel is the tribe** of His inheritance. **The Lord of** hosts is His name. You are My battle-axe and weapons of war: For with you** I will **break the nation in pieces; with you I will destroy kingdoms."**

Only the beginning of your understanding starts here: The marriage for those of the Davidic line was ritualized to the extent of making redundant any necessity for romanticism. The necessity of continuing the survival of the line in such a rural and, at the same time, persecuted community was paramou nt to all. The Merovingian Anglo-Saxon dynasty came from this line and were the Counts of Toulouse and Narbonne and the Princes of Septimania Midi in what is now south-west France. Middle Ages, the southern part of the town was ruled by the The Counts of Toulouse as Dukes of Narbonne. The word *dux* is usually translated by the Old English word ealdorman. Historian Alan Thacker estimates that there were about eight men holding the title of *dux* in late Northumbria.** The title *patricius* is usually translated as patrician, which ultimately means noble, but in the latter days of the Roman Empire represented a high ranking position, second only to the emperor. The meaning of the title in Northumbria is unclear, but it appears that there was only one *patricius*. While it may be simply an alternative to *dux*, it might represent a position approximating to that of the mayor of the palace in late Merovingian France

For instance one of the eight Dux's of Northumbria was Wada Dux, and others all from the same Patrilineal Anglo-Saxon heritage. A Dynasty is a series of Related Rulers, and they folowed the Salic law. Prophecy has been and is being fulfilled in **Israelites**; **Anglo-Saxon Israelites**, a true race of Israel the line of Ephraim.

The *Anglo-Saxon Chronicle*, written around 800ad, traces the origins of the Saxon peoples to the region of Armenia (*ibid.*, p. 209).

The *Anglo-Saxon Chronicle,* written around 800ad, traces the origins of the Saxon peoples to the region of Armenia (*ibid.*, p. 209).

Archeologist George Rawlinson stated, "We have reasonable grounds for regarding the *Gimirri,* or *Cimmerians*... and the *Sacae* of the Behistun Rock... as identical with the Beth-Khumree of Samaria, or the Ten Tribes of the House of Israel" (*The Story of Celto-Saxon Israel,* Bennett, p. 151).

The Monarchs from the line of David were recorded in Scythian Sakastan in Ancient Persia as Seistan and sakastan were named after them. the Scythians latter migrated southwards and joined their cousins in what is today Afghanistan. In so much that Zabulistan (the land of the children of Zabol or Zebulon son of Yaqoob Jacob) came to be synonyms with Sakastan or the land of Scyths, or children of Ishaq Isaac who came from the north**. From this region came part of the Anglo-Saxon monarchs: The Covenant was always with the Bloodline of Isaac**

Elohim The Creator

El Elyon The God Most High

EL Roi GOD who sees

El Shaddai The all Sufficent one

Adonai Lord Master

Yahweh Lord (Jehovah)

Jehovah Jireh The Lord will provide

Jehovah Rapha The Lord that healeth

Jehjovah Nissi The Lord my banner

Jehovah Mekoddishkem The Lord who Santifies you

Jehovah Shalom The Lord is peace

Jehovah Sabaoth The Lord of Host

Jehovah Raah The Lord my shepard

Jehovah Tsidkenu The Lord our Righteousness

Jehovah Shammah The Lord is there

EL Olam The Everlasting God

It's easier to fool people that to convince them that they have been fooled –Mark Twain

God (Jehovah) Made the promise that the Seed of the Woman "Adam" would crush the Serpent Seed of Cain and Inherite the Fathers Kingdom Seth Ben Adam Ben Jehovah's End Days Kingdom. The Seed of the Woman "Adam" Must crush the serpent seed of Cain to Inherite the Father's Kindom Jehovahs Kindom has always existed within the Bloodline decendents of "Adam" Seth Ben Adam Ben Jehovah to this day. All the Tribes of Israel were decendents of Seth Ben Adam Ben Jehovahs and are the Heirs of Seth Ben Adam Ben Jehovahs End Days Kingdom. One Million dollars has to be raised to rescue 144,000 decendents of Seth Ben Adam Ben Jehovah! As listed in Revleation 7:5

_God's People will Be Preserved

1After this I saw four angels standing at the four corners of the earth, holding the four winds of the earth, that no wind should blow on the earth, or on the sea, or upon any tree. 2And I saw another angel ascend from the sunrising, having the seal of the living God: and he cried with a great voice to the four angels to whom it was given to hurt the earth and the sea, 3saying, Hurt not the earth, neither the sea, nor the trees, till we shall have sealed the servants of our God on their foreheads.

144,000 Sealed

4And I heard the number of them that were sealed, a hundred and forty and four thousand, sealed out of every tribe of the children of Israel:

5Of the tribe of Judah were'sealed twelve thousand: Of the tribe of Reuben twelve thousand; Of the tribe of Gad twelve thousand; 6Of the tribe of Asher twelve thousand; Of the tribe of Naphtali twelve thousand; Of the tribe of Manasseh twelve thousand; 7Of the tribe of Simeon twelve thousand; Of the tribe of Levi twelve thousand; Of the tribe of Issachar twelve thousand; 8Of the tribe of Zebulun twelve thousand; Of the tribe of Joseph twelve thousand; Of the tribe of Benjamin were'sealed twelve thousand.

Praise from the Great Multitude

9After these things I saw, and behold, a great multitude, which no man could number, out of every nation and of all tribes and peoples and tongues, standing before the throne and before the Lamb, arrayed in white robes, and palms in their hands; 10and they cry with a great voice, saying, Salvation unto our God who sitteth on the throne, and unto the Lamb. 11And all the angels were standing round about the throne, and about the elders and the four living creatures; and they fell before the throne on their faces, and worshipped God, 12saying, Amen: Blessing, and glory, and wisdom, and thanksgiving, and honor, and power, and might, be unto our God for ever and ever. Amen.

13And one of the elders answered, saying unto me, These that are arrayed in white robes, who are they, and whence came they? 14And I say unto him, My lord, thou knowest. And he said to me, These are they that come of the great tribulation, and they washed their robes, and made them white in the blood of the Lamb. 15Therefore are they before the throne of God; and they serve him day and night in his temple: and he that sitteth on the throne shall spread his tabernacle over them. 16They shall hunger no more, neither thirst any more; neither shall the sun strike upon them, nor any heat: 17for the Lamb that is in the midst of the throne shall be their shepherd, and shall guide them unto fountains of waters of life: and God shall wipe away every tear from their eyes.

"In theology and Biblical studies, the word **"covenant" refers to any of a number of the solemn agreements that were made between God and the children of Israel** in the Hebrew Bible, as well as to the New Covenant, Likewise, some Christians use the term Old Covenant to collectively refer to the covenants described in their "Old Testament"."

Of whose line in the Bible did the line of patriarchs stem from according to genesis? Seth was born when Adam was 130 years old "a son in his likeness and image." The genealogy is repeated at 1 Chronicles 1:1-3. Genesis 5:4-5 states that Adam fathered "sons and daughters" before his death, aged 930 years. In Genesis 4:25, there is a folk etymology for Seth's name, which derives it from the Hebrew word for "plant" as in "plant a seed" (*syt*). Eve says, "God has planted another seed, under/replacing Abel's". Seth lived to the age of 912 Seth is also included in the Genealogy of Jesus, according to Luke 3:23–38.

Of whose line in the Bible did the line of patriarchs stem from according to genesis? Seth was born when Adam was 130 years old The genealogy is repeated at 1 Chronicles 1:1-3. Genesis 5:4-5 states that Adam fathered "sons and daughters" before his death, aged 930 years. In Genesis 4:25, there is a folk etymology for Seth's name, which derives it from the Hebrew word for "plant" as in "plant a seed" (*syt*). Eve says, "God has planted another seed, under/replacing Abel's". Seth lived to the age of 912. Seth is also included in the Genealogy of Jesus, according to Luke 3:23–38.

Each ruler-priest has been seen historically to have two wives. One was a half-sister and the other, married later in life, was a patrilineal cousin or niece. The firstborn son of the sister wife ascended to the throne of his biological father. The firstborn son of the cousin wife or the niece wife ascended to the throne of his maternal grandfather, after whom he was named. This is important to history as the lines at that time were traced Patrilineal, and they only married their sister or half sister and then a cousin or niece. Sometimes they would marry the cousin or neice wife even first.

It has been found by many researchers that many of the Bible's greatest patriarchs were also sons that were sent-away. This very important marriage and /ascendency pattern had driven the historical Kushite expansion and all of this has been /confirmed by DNA studies.
How it all began is one of the major conundrums of history. It was upon the shores of the Nile a mysterious group began to emerge and they were called the followers of Horus. These Horus Kings began what would become the Pharaohs of Egypt. What sparked Egyptian history and who were these followers of Horus? How did this history interrelate with our Biblical history? You cannot look at the history of Egypt without seeing the Biblical history that was related. **The ancient kings had sprung from Ancient Sumer**

"The [original] people of Sumer were designated 'Sumerians' after **Shem**

Yemeni history timeframe

2500 BC Ancient Arab tribes move North and South in Yemen. Qahtan and A'ad settle South Arabia. The Akkadians and Amalek settle the North.

c. 2500 BCE: Valley Temple of Khafra, Giza, is built.

c. 2500 BCE: Khafra from Giza Valley, Temple of Khafra is made. Fourth dynasty of Egypt. Discovered by Auguste Mariette. It is now kept in Egyptian Museum, Cairo.

Shelah (ben CAINAN) of CHALDEA

aka Shaleh (Shelach Sala Sale Salah) ibn ARPHECKSHAD

Born: abt. 2307 BC Died: abt. 1874 BC

The first biblical ruler of this name is Ar-pacshad, who lived four generations after Noah. He was a descendant of both Ham and Shem

11Q13

(11QMelch) is a fragment (that can be dated to the end of the 2nd or start of the 1st century BC) of a text about Melchizedek found in Cave 11 at Qumran in the Israeli Dead Sea area and which comprises part of the Dead Sea Scrolls. In this eschatological text, Melchizedek is seen as a divine being and Hebrew titles as Elohim are applied to him. According to this text Melchizedek will proclaim the **"Day of Atonement" and he will atone for the people who are predestined to him. He also will judge the peoples**

Shem is traditionally held to be the ancestor of the Semitic peopleThe word "Semitic" is an adjective derived from Shem, one of the three sons of Noah in the Bible (Genesis 5.32, 6.10, 10.21),

or more precisely from the Greek derivative of that name, namely Σημ (Sēm); the noun form referring to a person is *Semite*.

The birthright was passed to Shem, the youngest son of Noah, as priest of God in the order of Melchisedek. <u>The descendants of Shem carried the priesthood down to Abraham and on into the lines of the descendants of Abraham. Shem produced a number of children and from them sprung a number of important nations of the world.</u>

The descendants of Shem.

Here is a genealogy, or list of names, ending in Abram, the friend of God, and thus leading towards Christ, the promised Seed, who was the son of Abram. Nothing is left upon record but their names and ages; the Holy Ghost seeming to hasten through them to the history of Abram. How little do we know of those that are gone before us in this world, even of those that lived in the same places where we live, as we likewise know little of those who now live in distant places! We have

enough to do to mind our own work. When the earth began to be peopled, men's lives began to shorten; this was the wise disposal of Providence. (Ge 11:27-32)

We must look more closely at the genealogical information.

Indeed the oldest tradition appears to be the King Lists of Genesis 4 and 5 in which we discover the marriage and ascendency pattern of Abraham's Kushite ancestors.

Genesis 9:25-27 Cursed be Canaan: a servant of servants shall he be unto his brethren And he said Blessed be Yahweh the Elohim of Shem: and Canaan shall be his servant. Elohim shall enlarge (Heb: yapth 'persuade') <u>Japheth and he shall dwell in the tents of Shem</u>: and Canaan shall be his servant.

<u>**The birthright was passed to Shem, and this birthright was passed down patrilineal historically.**</u>

21And unto Shem, the father of all the children of Eber, the elder brother of Japheth, to him also were children born. <u>22The sons of Shem: Elam, and Asshur, and Arpachshad, and Lud, and Aram. 23And the sons of Aram: Uz, and Hul, and Gether, and Mash. 24And Arpachshad begat Shelah; and Shelah begat Eber. 25And unto Eber were born two sons: The name of the one was Peleg. For in his days was the earth divided. And his brother's name was Joktan.</u> 26And Joktan begat Almodad, and Sheleph, and Hazarmaveth, and Jerah, 27and Hadoram, and Uzal, and Diklah, 28and Obal, and Abimael, and Sheba, 29and Ophir, and Havilah, and Jobab: all these were the sons of Joktan. 30And their dwelling was from Mesha, as thou goest toward Sephar, the mountain of the east. 31

Aram is a son of Shem, according to the Table of Nations in Genesis 10 of the Hebrew Bible, and the father of Uz, Hul, Gether and Mash.[3] The Book of Chronicles confirms Aram as one of Shem's sons, confirming Uz, Hul, Gether and Mash, as also on the list of Shem's descendants.[4]

^ Genesis 10:23

2445–2160 BC: 9th -10th Dynasties Nimrod, Arpachshad, Salah, Eber and Peleg and Joktan

[Genesis 10:21] Also to Shem, the father of all the Children of Eber

In Biblical tradition it is **Eber** and not Abram who is the eponymous **ancestor** of all Hebrews

Eber (עֵבֶר, ISO 259-3 ʕebr, Standard Hebrew Éver, Tiberian Hebrew ʻĒḇer) is an ancestor of the **Israelites, according to the "Table of Nations" in Genesis 10-11 and 1 Chronicles 1. He was a great-grandson of Noah's son Shem and the father of Peleg born when Eber was 34 years old, and of Joktan. He was the son of Shelah a distant ancestor of Abraham.George Bury writes in 1915 in Arabia infelix, or The Turks in Yamen ,"The first concrete fact in the history of the Yaman is the birth of Joktan son of Eber, B.C. 2246. Joktans son Yarab (Jerah of Genesis) was the progenitor of Yamen Arabic and first separated the Yamen tongue from ancient Hebrew. It was who founded the Sabaean Kingdom in Yemen. I will continue tracing the line in the next chapters of this work.**

Eber's first-born son Joktan the Elder, after whom one of Abraham's sons by Keturah named Jockshan received his throne name (Gen. 25:1).

Genesis 10:21 lists Shem as Eber's ancestor, but Eber was also a descendant of Kush as evidence shows that the royal descendants of Ham and Shem intermarried. The fact that Eber was indeed a great ruler was attested to in the pre-canonical /Girgam (Diwan) there can be found his name appears as *Abir* and also within this text he is designated ***Amir, which is*** the Arabic word for ruler.

Y-Chromosomal Haplogroup T.

Joktan was the great-grandson of Arpachshad, and son of Eber. His brother was Peleg (he had many brothers and sisters whose descendants lived in Paliga, on the Euphrates, just above the mouth of the Khabur River. Concerning Joktan or *Yoktan,* himself, the southern Arabs of the 1Arabian peninsula claim descent from him, calling him *Qahtan* in Arabic.

We are told that Joktan's descendant's *"dwelling was from Mesha as thou goest towards Sephar, a mount of the east"* 1Mesha has been identified as Mousa, a city of note on the western shore of Arabia, and Arab tradition identifies 1Sephar with 1Dhofar in Oman. Joktan's blood is infused with all Arabian tribes, and is held in high esteem. According to the Arab tradition, Joktan's sons are the fathers of various tribes such as the Banu Lakhm, the Shammar, the tribes of Nejd, Ajman in the United Arab Emirates, Jiddat al Harasis region in Oman, as well as the Janibia, Al Kathir, and Al Murrah tribes.

Joktan's name is preserved in the modern tribal federation called Kahtan or Among the sons of Qahtan are noteworthy figures like A'zaal (Uzal, believed by Arabs to have been the original name of 1Sana'a) and 1Hadhramaut. Another son is Ya'rub or Yarab (Jerah), and his son Yashjub is the father of 'Abd Shams, who is also called Saba. All Yemeni tribes trace their ancestry back to this "Saba" (Sheba) either through Himyar or Kahlan, his two sons. The Qahtani people are divided into the two sub-groups of Himyar and Kahlan, who represent the settled Arabs of the south and their nomadic kinsmen (nomads). The Kahlan division of Qahtan consists of 4 subgroups: the Ta' or Tayy, the Azd group which invaded Oman, the 'Amila-Judham group ofPalestine, and the Hamdan-Madhhij group who mostly remain in Yemen The Kahlan branch includes the following tribes: Aus and Khazraj, Barig, 1Ghassan, Azd, Hamdan, Khath'am, Bajflah, Madhhij, Murad, Zubaid and Nakh', Ash'ar, Lakhm and Kindah

Kush was the father of Nimrod. In the Bible you see Nimrod's descendents later in the persons of Noah and Nahor and Terah who was Abraham's father. Ramaah settled in the Arabian Peninsula, south of Dedan. We meet Ramaah's descendents later in the lineage of Seir the Horite.[4] Rohl identified another deified person by Mesopotamians and Egyptians as the flood hero Noah whose title "The Far Distant One" was associated with Horus.

Kush was the father of Nimrod. In the Bible you see Nimrod's descendants later in the persons of Noah and Nahor and Terah who was Abraham's father. Ramaah settled in the Arabian Peninsula, south of Dedan. We meet Ramaah's descendants later in the lineage of Seir the Horite.[4] **You see Nimrods and Ramaahs decedent's began as well with historical persons as Zayd (ibn KAHLAN) of al-HIRAH who is called Nakhete Kalnis of Ethiopian/Abyssinian royal genealogy , and how they all intermarried in very specific patterns.**

All historical accounts clearly state that the near descendant (great grandson) of Qahtan/Joktan was Saba (Seba) whose two sons according to most accounts were Himyar (or Humayr) and Kahlan (Nakhete Kalnis of Ethiopian genealogy).lines became many of the bloodlines of the Biblical Patriarchs. They went on to populate the whole of Arabia and to rule a great part of the ancient world under leaders such as Numayr ibn Qassit (Nimrod)

Joktan's name is preserved in the modern tribal federation called Kahtan or Among the sons of Qahtan are noteworthy figures like A'zaal (Uzal, believed by Arabs to have been the original name of 1Sana'a) and 1Hadhramaut. Another son is Ya'rub or Yarab (Jerah), and his son Yashjub is the father of 'Abd Shams, who is also called Saba. All Yemeni tribes trace their ancestry back to this "Saba" (Sheba) either through Himyar or Kahlan, his two sons. The Qahtani people are divided into the two sub-groups of Himyar and Kahlan, who represent the settled Arabs of the south and their nomadic kinsmen (nomads). The Kahlan division of Qahtan consists of 4 subgroups: the Ta' or Tayy, the Azd group which invaded Oman, the 'Amila-Judham group of Palestine, and the Hamdan-Madhhij group who mostly remain in YemenThe Kahlan branch includes the following tribes: Aus and Khazraj, Barig, 1Ghassan, Azd, Hamdan, Khath'am, Bajflah, Madhhij, Murad, Zubaid and Nakh', Ash'ar, Lakhm and Kindah.

Kush was the father of Nimrod. In the Bible you see Nimrod's descendents later in the persons of Noah and Nahor and Terah who was Abraham's father. Ramaah settled in the Arabian Peninsula, south of Dedan. We meet Ramaah's descendents later in the lineage of Seir the Horite.[4] Rohl identified another deified person by Mesopotamians and Egyptians as the flood hero Noah whose title "The Far Distant One" was associated with Horus.

Kush was the father of Nimrod. In the Bible you see Nimrod's descendents later in the persons of Noah and Nahor and Terah who was Abraham's father. Ramaah settled in the Arabian Peninsula, south of Dedan. We meet Ramaah's descendents later in the lineage of Seir the Horite.[4] **You see Nimrods and Ramaahs decedent's began as well with historcal persons as Zayd (ibn KAHLAN) of al-HIRAH who is called Nakhete Kalnis of Ethiopian/Abyssinian royal genealogy , and how they all intermarried in very specific paterns.**

All historical accounts clearly state that the near descendant (great grandson) of Qahtan/Joktan was Saba (Seba) whose two sons according to most accounts were Himyar (or Humayr) and Kahlan (Nakhete Kalnis of Ethiopian genealogy).lines became many of the bloodlines of the Biblical Patriarchs. They went on to populate the whole of Arabia and to rule a great part of the ancient world under leaders such as Numayr ibn Qassit (Nimrod)

Noah's other grandson was Kush who was the father of Nimrod. From ancient Kush Abraham's ancestors spread far and wide as rulers in the ancient Afro-Asiatic Dominion. Genesis itself is actually the most reliable record of showing the ancient Horite kinship and rule.

Cush was the eldest son of Ham, brother of Canaan and the father of Nimrod, and Raamah, mentioned in the "Table of Nations" in the Hebrew Bible (Book of Genesis 10:6, I Chronicles 1:8). The name is usually considered to be the eponym of the people of Kush.

According to Genesis, Cush's other sons were Seba, Havilah, Sabtah, Raamah, and Sabtecah, names identified by modern scholars with Arabian tribes.

Though it seems quite out of place there is much evidence that Horus was regarded as King of the universe in ancient mythology. He was the only figure portrayed as a Man in ancient Egypt." A caste of priests served him and they were called Horites. The rulers of Abraham's people were the Horite Kings or more accurately Horite ruler-priests that began the priesthood that went on for thousands of years. Who was this priesthood, and was it important to understanding the Bible?

Cush was the eldest son of Ham, brother of Canaan and the father of Nimrod, and Raamah, mentioned in the "Table of Nations" in the Hebrew Bible (Book of Genesis 10:6, I Chronicles 1:8). The name is usually considered to be the eponym of the people of Kush.

According to Genesis, Cush's other sons were Seba, Havilah, Sabtah, Raamah, and Sabtecah, names identified by modern scholars with Arabian tribes.

Though it seems quite out of place there is much evidence that Horus was regarded as King of the universe in ancient mythology. He was the only figure portrayed as a Man in ancient Egypt." A caste of priests served him and they were called Horites. The rulers of Abraham's people were the Horite Kings or more accurately Horite ruler-priests that began the priesthood that went on for thousands of years. Who was this priesthood, and was it important to understanding the Bible?

1Now these are the generations of the sons of Noah, namely, of Shem,

Ham, and Japheth: and unto them were sons born after the flood.

2The sons of Japheth: Gomer, and Magog, and Madai, and Javan,

and Tubal, and Meshech, and Tiras. -3%223"3And the sons of Gomer:

Ashkenaz, and Riphath, and Togarmah. -4%224"4And the sons of Javan:
Elishah, and Tarshish, Kittim, and Dodanim. -5%225"5Of these were
the isles of the nations divided in their lands, every one after his tongue,
after their families, in their nations.
6And the sons of Ham: Cush, and Mizraim, and Put, and Canaan.
-7%227"7And the sons of Cush: Seba, and Havilah, and Sabtah,
and Raamah, and Sabteca; and the sons of Raamah: Sheba, and Dedan.
-8%228"8And Cush begat Nimrod: he began to be a mighty one in the earth.
-9%229"9He was a mighty hunter before Jehovah: wherefore it is said,
Like Nimrod a mighty hunter before Jehovah. -10And the beginning of
his kingdom was Babel, and Erech, and Accad, and Calneh, in the land of
Shinar. -11Out of that land he went forth into Assyria, and builded Nineveh,
and Rehoboth-ir, and Calah, -12and Resen between Nineveh and Calah
(the same is the great city). -13And Mizraim begat Ludim, and Anamim,
and Lehabim, and Naphtuhim, -14and Pathrusim, and Casluhim
(whence went forth the Philistines), and Caphtorim.
15And Canaan begat Sidon his first-born, and Heth, -16
and the Jebusite, and the Amorite, and the Girgashite, -17
and the Hivite, and the Arkite, and the Sinite, -18and the
Arvadite, and the Zemarite, and the Hamathite: and afterward
were the families of the Canaanite spread abroad. -19And the
border of the Canaanite was from Sidon, as thou goest toward
Gerar, unto Gaza; as thou goest toward Sodom and Gomorrah
and Admah and Zeboiim, unto Lasha. -20These are the sons of
Ham, after their families, after their tongues, in their lands, in their
nations. 21And unto Shem, the father of all the children of Eber,
the elder brother of Japheth, to him also were children born.
-22The sons of Shem: Elam, and Asshur, and Arpachshad, and Lud,

and Aram. -23And the sons of Aram: Uz, and Hul, and Gether, and Mash. -24And Arpachshad begat Shelah; and Shelah begat Eber. -25And unto Eber were born two sons: The name of the one was Peleg. **For in his days was the earth divided. And his brother's name was Joktan. -26And Joktan begat Almodad, and Sheleph, and Hazarmaveth, and Jerah, -27and Hadoram, and Uzal, and Diklah, -28and Obal, and Abimael, and Sheba, -29and Ophir, and Havilah, and Jobab: all these were the sons of Joktan.** -30And their dwelling was from Mesha, as thou goest toward Sephar, the mountain of the east. -31These are the sons of Shem, after their families, after their tongues, in their lands, after their nations.

32These are the families of the sons of Noah, after their generations, in their nations: and of these were the nations divided in the earth after the flood.

Qahtan's also known as Joktan grandson (Yarrob bin Yashjub bin Qahtan) and holds that he is the forefather of al-'Arab al-'Ariba "pure arabs"), who are identified with the Qahtanites and its two main tribes are the Himyar and the Kahlan.[3] .[2][4] Shams-i Qais Razi, writing in the 12-13th century CE, traced the origins of Arabic poetry to Ya'rab and he is also credited with having invented the Kufic script.[5][6]

Notice there were no children of Peleg are mentioned in the passage above.

It is not until Gen 11.18, shows that Peleg had descendants Reu, Serug, Nahor, Terah, and Abram.

The lines of Eber and Sheba continued to intermarry, which means that wives were chosen from kin of distant territories (as did Jacob when he married his patrilineal cousin

The significance is that science is now beginning to hold and accept that I and J were once the same group and that all I Hg. people came from the same ancestry as the Jews and Arabs that possess the J system. Thus we have a clear acceptance in biblical terms that the Bible record that Hebrew peoples came from the one ancestor, Arphaxad, is correct. This is also an important point to history I wish to emphasize.

It has been found by many researchers that many of the Bible's greatest patriarchs were also sent-away sons. This very important marriage and /ascendency pattern had driven the historical Kushite expansion **and all of this has been** /confirmed by DNA studies.

How it all began is one of the major conundrums of history. It was upon the shores of the Nile a mysterious group began to emerge and they were called the followers of Horus. These Horus Kings began what would become the Pharaohs of Egypt. What sparked Egyptian history and who were these followers of Horus? How did this history interrelate with our Biblical history? You cannot look at the history of Egypt without seeing the Biblical history that was related. **The ancient kings had sprung from Ancient Sumer**

"The [original] people of Sumer were designated 'Sumerians' after **Shem**

Upon the shores of the Nile a mysterious clan began to emerge called the followers of Horus. These Horus Kings began what would become the Pharoes of Egypt. What sparked Egyptian history and who were these followers of Horus? How did this history interrelate with our Biblical history. You cannot look at the history of Egypt witout seeing the Biblical history that was related. The ancient kings had sprung from Ancient Suma

The original settlement on the Nekhen site dates from the culture known as Naqada I of 4400 BC At its height from about 3400 BC Nekhen had at least 5,000 inhabitants. Nekhen was the center of the cult of a hawk deity Horus of Nekhen, which raised in this city one of the most ancient temples in Egypt, and it retained its importance as the cult center of this divine patron of the kings long after it had otherwise declined. The quality of the gold work at Nekhen is shown by the discovery of this gold plumed falcon that represented Horus.

The oldest known site of Horite religion at Nehken dates to about 4000 B.C. and reflects a high level of technological and cultural achievement. **A marriage and ascendancy pattern was already clearly well established among powerful rulers this strongly indicates that they had been in power even long before the time of the patriarch Noah.**

Kush, the native name of the Kingdom was likely *kaš*, recorded in Egyptian as *k š*. This name *Kash* is probably connected to Cush in the Hebrew Bible (Hebrew: כוש), son of Ham (Genesis 10:6). The conventional name "kingdom of Kush" was introduced in 19th-century Egyptology. In Genesis 10 it speaks of this migration of the Kushites into Mesopotamia. Of one of the many migrations out of Africa, this is one of the later migrations out of Africa that occured between 3500 and 1500 BC. The mighty Nimrod (2290 and 2215 BC.) is noted in Genesis as one of the Kushite kingdom builders. Both he and his brother Ramah were the sons of Kush and they both moved out of the Nile Valley and establish vast territories; Ramah in Arabia and Nimrod in Mesopotamia.

All historical accounts state that the near descendant (great grandson) of Qahtan was Saba (Seba) whose two sons according to most accounts were Himyar (or Humayr) and Kahlan (Nakhete Kalnis of Ethiopian genealogy). These went on to populate the whole of Arabia and to rule a great part of the ancient world under leaders such as Numayr ibn Qassit (Nimrod)

Noah's other grandson was Kush who was the father of Nimrod. From ancient Kush Abraham's ancestors spread far and wide as rulers in the ancient Afro-Asiatic Dominion. Genesis itself is actually the most reliable record of showing the ancient Horite kinship and rule.

Cush was the eldest son of Ham, brother of Canaan and the father of Nimrod, and Raamah, mentioned in the "Table of Nations" in the Hebrew Bible (Book of Genesis 10:6, I Chronicles 1:8). The name is usually considered to be the eponym of the people of Kush.

Seba, son of Cush. Has been connected with both Yemen and Eritrea, with much confusion with Sheba (The Shibboleth-like division amongst the Sabaeans into Sheba and Seba is acknowledged elsewhere, for example in Psalm 72, leading scholars to suspect that this is not a mistaken duplication of the same name, but a genuine historical division. The significance of this division is not yet completely understood, though it may simply reflect which side of the sea each was on.)

According to Genesis, Cush's other sons were Seba, Havilah, Sabtah, Raamah, and Sabtecah, names identified by modern scholars with Arabian tribes.

Eber) is an ancestor of the Israelites, according to the "Table of Nations" in Genesis 10-11 and 1 Chronicles 1. He was a great-grandson of Noah's son Shem and the father of Peleg born when Eber was 34 years old, and of Joktan. He was the son of Shelah a distant ancestor of Abraham. According to the Hebrew Bible, Eber died at the age of 464 (Genesis 11:14-17) when Jacob was 20.

Joktan was the brother of Peleg and their father was Eber (B.C. 2196-2121). It was during this period that the linguistic division between Old Arabic (Dedanite) and Aramaic first emerged. "Shad" (as in Arpac-shad) is an Arabic word. Ar-pacshad, who lived four generations after Noah was a descendant of both Ham and Shem.

The ancient Kushite rulers had spread themselves quickly across the ancient Afro-Asiatic Dominion. Raamah and Nimrod had ruled separate territories that had been united under their father Kush. We can find historically that Asshur and **Arpachshad ruled separate territories that had once been united under their father Shem. As well, both Peleg and Joktan ruled separate territories that had once been unified under their father Eber.**

The clans of Joktan, Sheba and Jebu became became separated in the time of Peleg, but their rulers continued to intermarry as it was a deep tradition. The two lines then continued to intermarry according to a pattern that is traceable, using the Biblical genealogies, to Jesus Christ.

Chapter 5 The Nasrid Dynasty I Donated in this book was Seth Ben Adam Ben Jehovah's kingdom and the Anglo Saxon Dynasty I Donated in this book

For instance the Top Ancestors for the following two Dynasties are:

Nasrid Dynasty - Seth ben[3] ADAM Ben Jehovah and much more will be shown

Anglo-Saxon: Were related historically as well

Enos is the first son of Seth

Of the 60 YDNA lines tested only eight were actual Semites. F and I comprise 25% of the Semitic Levite YDNA tested.

The original DNA of the Semites including the Joktan Hebrews was not J but F and the primary Semitic derivative is I and the secondary derivatives are J, and then H and G. All the Eastern Semites of Elam and Joktan were Hg. I, rather than J. Thus these mutations occurred over the second Millennium BCE.

The sons of Arphaxad are: Salah and Eber (from where the name Hebrews is derived. His sons Peleg and Joktan saw the split in the Hebrews.

Seth was the son of Adam and Eve born when Adam was 130 years old.

Eve named him Seth because, as she said, "God has appointed another seed in place of Abel, because Cain killed him."

According to Genesis 5:4, Adam had "sons and daughters," some of whom may have been born before Seth.

Seth is worthy of note because Noah ---and through him the present-day race of mankind---descended from him, not from the murderous Cain.

At the age of 105 years Seth became father to Enosh.

Seth died at the age of 912 years (3896-2984 B.C.E.)

—Ge 4:17, 25, 26; 5:3-8; 1Ch 1:1-4; Lu 3:38.

My Anglo-Saxon Brothers are the ones I am most worried about as the Angl-Saxon dynasty is realated to the Nasrid dynasty and have comman ancestors. My Grandfather was decendent from and Anglo-Saxon Dux so I traces both Dynastie. My son is decendent through the Nasrid Dynasty. The Anglo-Saxons are the Tribes of Josph. Epraim is double stuff and that means both land and Gold. The tribes of Joseph Aka Epraim his son do not know who they are today but they are the Anglo-Saxon are the Celts and the Jutes.   Salic law is an all male law and yet the Anglo Saxon's Gold Hords were stolen by one marriage to Poppa of Bavaria and that was historically illegal. The Tribes of Joseph and all other tribes are all heirs to Seth Ben Adam Ben Jehovah's End days Kingdom! Thr Tribes are all quualifed as the Seed of the Woman Adam that must crush the Serpent seed of Cain and inherit the Fathers Kingdom Seth Ben Adam Ben Jehovahs End days Kingdom.   The Seed of the Woman Adam is 100% traced in the Royal Nasrid Bloodline as shown clearly below.   Seek ye first the Kingdom of God (Jehovah God) when Jehovah's God makes a promise don't ignore it.

Anglo-Saxon

Ecglaf, Eadgils, Eomaer, *Eormenric, Frod(a), Hereric, *Hoc, *Hrothmund,

Ingeld, **Offa**, Oslaf, Sigemund, *Aehha, Sigeferth, Aetla, *Hagena, Theodric,

Waldhere, Becca, Witta, **Wada**, Oswine, Sigehere, *Sceafthere, Alewih, Aelfwine, Eadwine, Wulfhere, Frithuric ; perhaps also Herebald. The asterisk denotes names limited to persons of the sixth and seventh centuries.

3 Eadgils, Eanmund, Heardred, Hygelac, Ingeld, **Offa**, Wermund, Weohstan,

Wiglaf, **Wada**, *Scilling, Oswine, Sigehere, *Gislhere (perhaps Eomaer).

4 *Aelfhere, Ecglaf, Eanmund, Heremod, **Offa**, Sigemund, Wermund, Weohstan,

Wiglaf, Wulfgar, Garwulf, *Ordlaf, Sigeferth, Waldhere, Becca, **Wada**, *Hun, *Hringwald, Aelfwine, Eadwine, Wulfhere, Frithuric (possibly also Deor).

This genetic invasion continued in 1492 the with the fall of the Kingdom of Granada, they grabbed the line of the Jews and Moors of Granada, of no right of their own to do so, this was all based upon the crusades that upset the balance. I am not stating that anyone can stop them now, but understanding truth of things is always better than accepting deception. They systematically either killed or kicked out (deported) anyone of these family lines so they could take them for themselves. It was their plan to not leave anyone alive that could make any claim to the families own God given lineage that has been stolen from them matrilinealy. Instead of just accepting the events of 1492, and looking down on the peoples of Spain at that time, lets take a look at what this line was and represented **and why** the European monarchies dogpiled and took over its heritage, lineage and lands **Matrilinealy without right as the Nasrid line is a Patrilineal line only as will be shown.**

The **Nasrid dynasty** or **Banū Naṣr** The Nasrid dynasty rose to power after the defeat of the Almohad dynasty in 1212 at the Battle of Las Navas de Tolosa. Twenty-three different emirs ruled Granada from the founding of the dynasty in 1232 by Muhammed I ibn Nasr until January 2, 1492.

Yusuf al-Ahmar ibn Muhammad ibn Ahmad ibn Muhammad ibn (Khamees ibn)[2] Nasr ibn Muhammad ibn Nusair ibn Ali ibn Yahya ibn Sa'd ibn Qais ibn Sa'd ibn Ubadah[3] ibn Dulaym ibn Harithah ibn Abi Hazima ibn Tha'labah ibn Tarif ibn al-Khazraj ibn Sa'ida ibn Ka'b ibn al-Khazraj[4] ibn Harithah ibn **Tha'labah ibn Amr ibn Amir** ibn Harithah ibn **Imri' al-Qays** ibn Tha'labah ibn Mazin ibn **al-Azd** ibn al-Ghawth ibn Nabt ibn Malik ibn **Zayd ibn Kahlan** ibn **Saba'** ibn Yashjub ibn **Ya'rub ibn Qahtan/Joktan** b. Aybar b. Shalikh b. Arfakhshad b. **Sam/Shem** b. Nuh/Noah. *Noah ben[11] LAMECH, *Lamech ben[10] METHUSELAH, *Methuselah ben[9] ENOCH, *Enoch ben[8] JARED, *Jared ben[7] MAHALALEEL, *Mahalaleel ben KENAN[6] (CAINAN), *Kenan (Cainan) ben[5] ENOS, *Enos ben[4] SETH, *Seth ben[3] ADAM, *Adam CREATED BY[2] GOD, JEHOVAH[1])

0.

The family tree below shows the genealogical relationship between each sultan of the Nasrid dynasty.[1] It starts with their common ancestor, Yusuf al-Ahmar.

Imran bin Amr was no doubt Aaron the brother of Moses. Amr his father is thus Amram the father of Aaron and Moses. "And at the end of forty days they came to Moses and Aaron, and they brought him word as it was in their hearts, and ten of the men brought up an evil report to the children of Israel, of the land which they had explored, saying, It is better for us to return to Misraim than to go to this land, a land that consumes its inhabitants. But Joshua the son of Nun, and the son of Jephuneh, who were of those that explored the land, said, The land is exceedingly good."

The story of Jafna, **Muzaikiya** and Tha'labah is unmistakably too similar to that of Jephuneh and his father Caleb in the Bible to be coincidental as well.

The line of Muzaikiya is this:
Al-Aus and al-Khazraj. Al-Aus and al-Khazraj are the sons of Harithah ibn-Tha'labah ibn-'Amr Muzaikiya ibn- 'Amir, and their mother was Kailah, daughter of al-Arkam. Moses was Amr Ibn Amir, Then came Tha'labah ibn-'Amr Muzaikiya with his son The people of Amr bin Amir the soothsayer after being expelled by Akk bin Adnan disengaged and dispersed in idifferent directions. Jafna bin Amr bin Amir settled in Syria, Aus and Khazraj settled in Yathrib and Khuza'a went to Marra.

The Direct male line Descendents of 3 Morrish princes names Cici Haya, Cad, and Nazar who in the vicinity of Granada Spain received Catholic religion and received baptism in the names Pierre Ferdinand De Grenade, and Jean De Grenade. In "Trophees Du Brabant, 1724" by R.P Burkens it is mentioned that among the Lords admitted to the court of Charlequint (Charles V) at Brussells in 1546-1547 is found Jean De Grenade. In this family were also mentioned were Jean and Bernadine-Jerome De Grenade with the spouses, and children. likewise the facts concerning the arms granted to Pierre De Grenade (Cici Haya) are also confirmed "d 'azure A Cinq Grenades d' or translated 5 Golden Pomegranates on a field of blue which as also adopted by Nicholas de Grenade 9de0 family notice of 12/6/1548.

Remember The Khazraj of Medina the Harrah who were the same as the Kush or Ghassan were thus a remnant of the children of not only of the Keturah or the Midianite followers of Moses, but were also decendent of From Mazin bin Mansour bin Ikrima were the Khazraj, also in Arabian tradition the descendants of Jephuneh and Caleb brother of Kenaz who fathered Othniel the first Judge of Israel – the Kenizzites were, descendants of Eliphaz in the Bible.Josephus replaces the word Jokshan with Jazar which is Arabic for Gezer or the Khazraj who are also called Khazara, Hazraj, Gazras in various translations. This is also directly related to:

Hawazin, Sulaym and Mazin, three sons of Mansour, son of Ikrima, son of Khasafa, son of Al Nas or Qays Ailan. "From Mazin bin Mansour bin Ikrima were the Khazraj and Aus or Awza children of Tha'laba Muzaikiya or Salebiyya and Jafna Muzaikiya. " The tribes of Mansour or Manasse'ir had branched off from the Ma'adi who appear to have been the origin of the Ma'adi'ah a family of priests (Levites) named in (Nehemiah 12). It will be shown that Mansour or Manasse'ir is the same as Manasseh, child of Joseph and that in genealogy of Arabia most of Mansour's descendants figure among the **children of Levi** in the Bible who had been captured by Bukht al Nasir (Nebuchadnezzar) the Chaldean in charge of Babylon centuries before the Christian era.

The Oxford Guide to the Bible and Brown-Driver-Briggs' Hebrew and English Lexicon identify it as a variant of the Egyptian name Pa-nehasi. According to the former, "The Bible also uses Egyptian and Nubian names for the land and its people... For the Egyptians used to these color variations, the term for their southern neighbors was Nehesi, "southerner", which eventually also came to mean "the Nubian". This Egyptian root (nhsj, with the preformative p' as a definite article) appears in Exodus 6.25 as the personal name of Aaron's grandson Phinehas (=pa-nehas)"[1] The Theological Wordbook of the Old Testament interprets the name to mean "the bronze-colored one".

Phinehas in one part of the Bible the brother of Hophni. Hophni and Phinehas or Phineas were the two sons of Eli

Another Phinehas is son of Eleazar the priest. Phinehas is also said to be son of Eleazar the priest a son of Harun or Amran brother of Moses who is linked in Arabian genealogy to the ancestral Azd people of Marib,[2] Phinehas, like Moses and Nun lived in Egypt during the captivity and their names were shared by the dominant culture there.

My son is indeed a direct male line of the Nasrid Dynasty created by Seth Ben Adam Ben Jehovahs Thousands of years ago. The Boodline was traced though the Princely Royal line for thousands of years historically. My son is not the only one that is the Seed of the Woman Adam decended though Seth Ben Adam Ben Jehovah all the Tribes of Israel were decended though Seth Ben Adam Ben Jehovah too!

It has been my burdon and my pleasure to prove that Seth Ben Adam Ben Jehvovah's Kindom has always existed in the Seed of the Woman "Adam" to this day and divide his heritage away from the Little Horn of Danial, the Cain Monarchies of Europe so Seth Ben Adam Ben Jehovah 's Kingdom can knock down and Crush the Little Horn of Danial and Crush the Serpent Seed of Cain that is sittling on Seth Ben Adam Ben Jehovahs Kingdom historically with no right to do so.

Gensis 3:15 is the same as Revleaion 12 is the only way any human can Susrvie Revleaion 13. My son is the Revelation 12 Rod of Iron that will Rule all nations and he is a direct patrilineal decendent of the Nasrid Dynasty and the Kingdom of Seth Ben Adam Ben Jehovahs created tho9usands of years ago and it has been %100 traced. I have historically divided Seth Ben Adam Ben Jehovahs patrilineal decent away in their own family Bloodline via the Nastrid Dynasty. This way the Nasrid Dynasty can be its own Kingdom again because the Nasrid Dynasty Originated with Seth Ben Adam Ben Jehovahs and was traced deliberately for thousands of years to our current days and that is why Genesis 3:15 is the same as Revleaion 12 final Judgment.

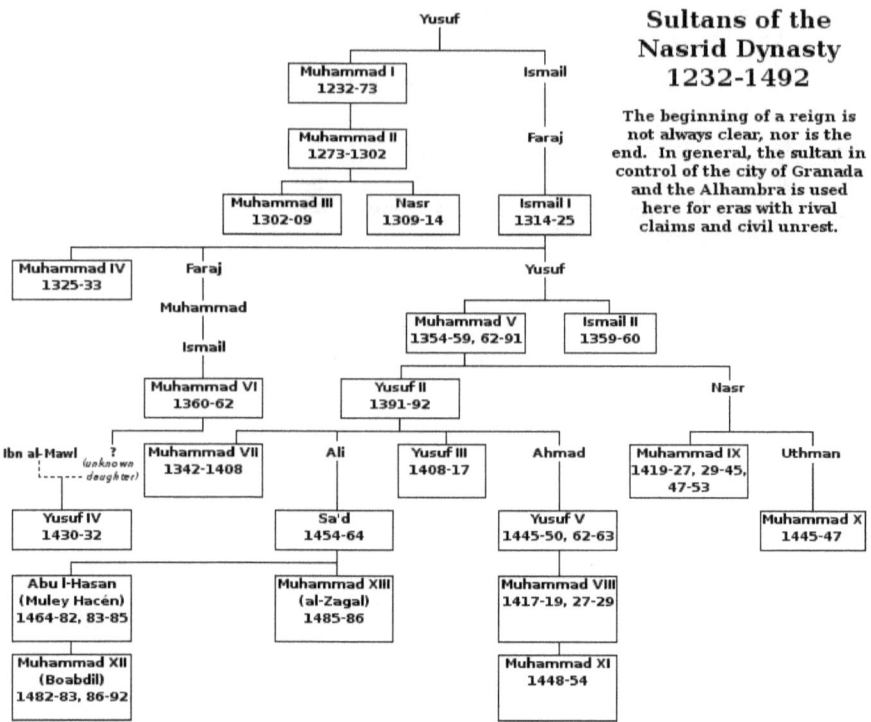

Sultans of the Nasrid Dynasty 1232-1492

The beginning of a reign is not always clear, nor is the end. In general, the sultan in control of the city of Granada and the Alhambra is used here for eras with rival claims and civil unrest.

21:25 And thou, profane wicked prince of Israel, whose day is come, when inequity shall have an end,

21:26 Thus saith the Lord God; Remove the diadem (sovereignty), and take off the crown: this shall not be the same: exalt him that is low, and abase him that is high.

21:27 I will overturn (1st), overturn (2nd), overturn (3rd), it: and it shall be no more, overturned (4th) UNTIL he come whose Right it is; and I will give it him - Shiloh (Gen. 49:10).

God (Seth Ben Adam Ben Jehovah God made the promise that the Seed of the Woman Adam must Crush the Serpent seed of Cain and inherit the Fathers Kingdom, Seth Ben Adam Ben Jehovah's End Days Kingdom. Genesis 3:15 is the same as Revlelation 12 Final Judgment. No one can say that Seth Ben Adam Ben Jehovha's Kindom did not exist because HERE IS PROOF THAT IT DID INDEED EXIST, AND ALL THE Tribes of Israel Decendend from Seth Ben Adam Ben Jehovah too, their decendents still exist till this day as well, though they are unaware. This book is to prove that Jehovahs End days Kindom is the the Most valuable Kindom in the Seth Ben Adam Ben Jehovahs End days Kingdom is being terribly abused right now currently because no one realizes His Kindom still exist to this day. There are many decendents of Seth Ben Adam Ben Jehovah's kingdom both the Nasrid and

Anglo- Saxon dynasty were decended from Seth Ben Adam Ben Jehovah. These Dynasties are both Heirs of Seth Ben Adam Ben Jehovahs End days Kindom but they are unaware. That is what this book is written for is to change everyone currect understanding. It is now Seth Ben Adam Ben Jehovahs End Days Kingdom as fortold by Nebuchanezzars dream.

The purpose of this book is to prove that the Royal Bloodlines were traced though thousands of years as well as to prove that there are really decendents of Seth Ben Adam Ben Jehovahs still today. My son the Revleaion 12 Rod of Iron is a direct makle line decendent of the Nasrid Dynasty so I know his bloodline traces from Seth Ben Adam Ben Jehovahs and he is qualified as the Seed of the Woman Adam that muyst crush the Serpent seed of Cain and inherit that Fathers Kingdom Seth Ben Adam Ben Jehovahs End Days Kingdom.

I no longer waqnt to be persecuted for the Fathers Kingdom and now you have your very own proof that the Fathers Kingdom has always exited and that there are still heirs to Seth Ben Adam Ben Jehovahs End ays kindom they are the Seed of the Woman Adam That carry the Seed of Seth Ben Adam Ben Jehovah to this very day.

Seth Ben Adam Ben Jehovah's End days Kindom is the most Valuable Kindom in the World but is so persecuted because the tribes did not remember that the Fathers Kingdom actually exist both Historically and currently. Denying the Fathers kindom will only make it to where the Tribes will not Inherit the Fathers Kingdom and that is tragic to history since these dynasties are to inherit the Fathers Kingdom. It is for the Seed of the Woman Adam to Crush the Serpent seed of Cain and inherit the Fathers Kindom because the Seed of the Woman Adam has biirthrights and the Seed of the Serpent Cain Does not. All there Tribes of Israel decend from Seth as well Seth Ben Adam Ben Jehovah too and are also heirs to the Father's kingdom as well. If we continue to persecute Seth Ben Adam Ben Jehovahs end days kingdom we will not ever inherit Seth Ben Adam Ben Jehovahs End Days Kingdom and shown in Nebuchanezzars dream in the Book of Danial.

Seth ben Adam (3630 BC-2718 BC)

Luke 3:38
38 Enos is the son of Seth and Set is the son of Adam and Adam is the **son of God**.
We read in the Appendix 23 From *The Companion Bible:*
It is only by the Divine specific act of creation that any created being can be called "**a son of God**". For that which is "born of the flesh is flesh". God is spirit, and that which is "born of the Spirit is spirit" (John 3:6). Hence Adam is called a "**son of God**" in Luke 3:38. Those "in Christ" having "the new nature" which is by the direct creation of God (2 Corinthians 5:17. Ephesians 2:10) can be, and are called "**sons of God**" (John 1:13. Romans 8:14,15. 1John 3:1).

Now this is a little complex, because the tribes were complex, yet simple as well to understand. My challenge is to show you litterally thousands of years of history, yet in a shortend understandable way that will keep your interest as long as you the reader keeps an open heart and mind.

Lamech is the eighth generation descendant of Seth (Genesis 5:25), the son of Methuselah and the father of Noah (Genesis 5:29), in the genealogy of Seth in Genesis 5. In Genesis 5:12-25, Lamech was a son of

Methuselah who was a grandson of Jared who was a grandson of Kenan descended from Adam. According to Genesis 5:9-14, Kenan/Cainan was a son of Enos and an unnamed woman, and a grandson of Seth. Born when Enos was ninety years old, Kenan had his only named son, Mahalalel, when he was seventy. Other sons and daughters were born to Kenan before he died at 910 years of age. We begin with the history of ancient Mesopotamia and it begins with the emergence of urban societies during the Ubaid period (ca. 5300 BC). The history of the Ancient Near East begins in the Lower Paleolithic period.

Kenan (Cainan), was the son of Enos (and thus the grandson of Seth and the great-grandson of Adam), Kenan, from the Hebrew name pronounced kay-nawn, as listed in the ancient records Cainan was the son of Enos and this also appears in the newer Strong's Concordance. The Kenites according to the Hebrew Bible, were a nomadic clan in the ancient Levant, they were sent under Jethro who was a priest in the land of Midian. The Kenites played a very important role in the history of ancient Israel and this will be explored much further later in this work as it is very important to history as well as the future for the important history it fully played a role in called the Exodus.

Moses' father-in-law, Jethro, was a shepherd and a priest in the land of Midian. Judges 1:16 identifies that Moses had a father-in-law who was a Kenite. Certain groups of Kenites settled among the Israelite population, including the descendants of Moses' brother-in-law, [ ] though the Kenites descended from Rechab, maintained a distinct, nomadic lifestyle for some time. Moses apparently identified Jethro's concept of God, El Shaddai, with Yahweh, the Israelites' God.[ ] According to the Kenite hypothesis, Yahweh was originally the tribal god of Jethro, borrowed and adapted by the Hebrews. Then there was Cush which is also called *Kush who* was the eldest son of Ham and a brother of Mizraim (Egypt), Canaan and the father of Nimrod, and Raamah who are mentioned in the "Table of Nations" in the Genesis 10:6 and I Chronicles 1:8. He was traditionally considered the eponymous ancestor of the people of Cush.

Kush, the native name of the Kingdom was likely *kaš*, recorded in Egyptian as *k š*. This name *Kash* is probably connected to Cush in the Hebrew Bible (Hebrew: כוש), son of Ham (Genesis 10:6). The conventional name "kingdom of Kush" was introduced in 19th-century Egyptology. In Genesis 10 it speaks of this migration of the Kushites into Mesopotamia. Of one of the many migrations out of Africa, this is one of the later migrations out of Africa that occured between 3500 and 1500 BC. The mighty Nimrod (2290 and 2215 BC.) is noted in Genesis as one of the Kushite kingdom builders. Both he and his brother Ramah were the sons of Kush and they both moved out of the Nile Valley and establish vast territories; Ramah in Arabia and Nimrod in Mesopotamia.

When God makes a promise he cannot lie. So since God (Jehovah) made the promise that the seed of the Woman Adam would crush the Serpent seed of Cain and inherit the Fathers Kingdom Seth Ben Adam Ben Jehovahs End Days Kingdom.The Seed of the Woman Adam will inherit the Most Valuable Kingdom in the World.

Cain and Abel

(Romans 2:1-16; Jude 1:3-16)

1And the man knew Eve his wife; and she conceived, and bare Cain, and said, I have gotten a man with the help of Jehovah. 2And again she bare his brother Abel. And Abel was a keeper of sheep, but Cain was a tiller of the ground. 3And in process of time it came to pass, that Cain brought of the fruit of the ground an offering unto Jehovah.4And Abel, he also brought of the firstlings of his flock and of the fat thereof. And Jehovah had respect unto Abel and to his offering: 5but unto Cain and to his offering he had not respect. And Cain was very wroth, and his countenance fell. 6And Jehovah said unto Cain, Why art thou wroth? and why is thy countenance fallen? 7If thou doest well, shall it not be lifted up? and if thou doest not well, sin coucheth at the door: and unto thee shall be its desire, but do thou rule over it.

Cain Murders Abel

8And Cain told Abel his brother. And it came to pass, when they were in the field, that Cain rose up against Abel his brother, and slew him.

9And Jehovah said unto Cain, Where is Abel thy brother? And he said, I know not: am I my brother's keeper? 10And he said, What hast thou done? the voice of thy brother's blood crieth unto me from the ground. 11And now cursed art thou from the ground, which hath opened its mouth to receive thy brother's blood from thy hand; 12when thou tillest the ground, it shall not henceforth yield unto thee its strength; a fugitive and a wanderer shalt thou be in the earth. 13And Cain said unto Jehovah, My punishment is greater than I can bear. 14Behold, thou hast driven me out this day from the face of the ground; and from thy face shall I be hid; and I shall be a fugitive and a wanderer in the earth; and it will come to pass, that whosoever findeth me will slay me. 15And Jehovah said unto him, Therefore whosoever slayeth Cain, vengeance shall be taken on him sevenfold. And Jehovah appointed a sign for Cain, lest any finding him should smite him.

16And Cain went out from the presence of Jehovah, and dwelt in the land of Nod, on the east of Eden.

The Descendants of Cain

17And Cain knew his wife; and she conceived, and bare Enoch: and he builded a city, and called the name of the city, after the name of his son, Enoch. 18And unto Enoch was born Irad: and Irad begat Mehujael: and Mehujael begat Methushael; and Methushael begat Lamech. 19And Lamech took unto him two wives: the name of the one was Adah, and the name of the other Zillah. 20And Adah bare Jabal: he was the father of such as dwell in tents and have cattle. 21And his brother's name was Jubal: he was the father of all such as handle the harp and pipe. 22And Zillah, she also bare Tubal-cain, the forger of every cutting instrument of brass and iron: and the sister of Tubal-cain was Naamah.

23And Lamech said unto his wives: Adah and Zillah, hear my voice; Ye wives of Lamech, hearken unto my speech: For I have slain a man for wounding me, And a young man for bruising me: 24If Cain shall be avenged sevenfold, Truly Lamech seventy and sevenfold.

Seth and Enosh

25And Adam knew his wife again; and she bare a son, and called his name Seth. For,'said she , God hath appointed me another seed instead of Abel; for Cain slew him.26And to Seth, to him also there was born a son; and he called his name Enosh. Then began men to call upon the name of Jehovah.

"Book of the Generations of Adam." This is not a list of all his posterity, but only of his decedents through the lineage of Seth. This is called the "royal" line because the decedents of Seth believed and followed God. Through them God's promise of the coming Messiah, the Lord Jesus Christ, would be accomplished. The Gospel of Luke, Christ's genealogy begins with Adam and Seth. (Luke 3:23-38) The posterity of Cain, Adam's son who rejected God is not included here. Eve named the third son Seth, which she explained meant, "For God has appointed another seed instead of Abel, who Cain shew." (Gen. 4:25) Abel believed and followed the Lord. Until the birth of Seth, Cain and his children did not trust God. Genesis 4:26, states that after the birth of Seth men began to call on the name of God again.

Here's what the prophet Isaiah records: "Then a shoot will grow from the stump of Jesse, and a branch from his roots will bear fruit" (Isa. 11:1). But then Isaiah calls this coming Redeemer the root of Jesse: "On that day the root of Jesse will stand as a banner for the peoples. The nations will seek Him, and His resting place will be glorious" (Isa. 11:10). KING OF JESHURUN."The Lord Jesus Christ is the KI of Jeshurun"(Deut 33:5)."Jesus Christ is the KING of kings and LORD of Lords"(Rev 19:16).

25 Therefore thus saith the Lord Jehovah: Now will I bring back the captivity of Jacob, and have mercy upon the whole house of Israel; and I will be jealous for my holy name.26..The Messiah Jesus fulfilled the eternal promise to the line of Moses as the King of Jeshurun. Jesus being a descendant of David verifies David's descent from Moses. KING OF JESHURUN." .For the Torah shall go forth from Tzyion and the word of HaShem from Yerushalyim: Yeshayahu 2:3 Jeremiah 23:7 "So then, the days are coming - it is HaShem Who speaks - when people will no longer say, 'As HaShem lives, Who brought the sons of Israel (12 tribes) out of the land of Egypt', but, 'As HaShem lives, Who led back and brought home the descendants of the House of Israel out of the land of the North, and from all the countries to which He had dispersed them, to live on their own soil ." To Orthodox Jews, Moses is called Moshe Rabbenu, `Eved HaShem, Avi haNeviim zya"a. He is defined "Our Leader Moshe", "Servant of God", and "Father of all the Prophets".Hebrew Shema', "Hear O Israel: The Lord our God, the Lord is One." (Deut. 6:4) The Shema' comes from the hand of Moses about 1400 BC.EL MELEKH NE'EMAN (Heb. "God, faithful King"), an affirmation of faith pronounced before the recital of the *Shema

The Lord Jesus Christ is the KI of Jeshurun"(Deut 33:5).

24 No man can serve two masters; for either he will hate the one, and love the other; or else he will hold to one, and despise the other. Ye cannot serve God and mammon.25 Therefore I say unto you, be not anxious for your life, what ye shall eat, or what ye shall drink; nor yet for your body, what ye shall put on. Is not the life more than the food, and the body than the raiment?26 Behold the birds of the heaven, that they sow not, neither do they reap, nor gather into barns; and your heavenly Father feedeth them.

Are not ye of much more value then they?27 And which of you by being anxious can add one cubit unto the measure of his life?28 And why are ye anxious concerning raiment? Consider the lilies of the field, how they grow; they toil not, neither do they spin:29 yet I say unto you, that even Solomon in all his glory was not arrayed like one of these.0 But if God doth so clothe the grass of the field, which to-day is, and to-morrow is cast into the oven, shall he not much more clothe you, O ye of little faith?31 Be not therefore anxious, saying, What shall we eat? or, What shall we drink? or, Wherewithal shall we be clothed?32 For after all these things do the Gentiles seek; for your heavenly Father knoweth that ye have need of all these things.33 But seek ye first his kingdom, and his righteousness; and all these things shall be added unto you.34 Be not therefore anxious for the morrow: for the morrow will be anxious for itself. Sufficient unto the day is the evil thereof.

The Man of Sin 1Now we beseech you, brethren, touching the coming of our Lord Jesus Christ, and our gathering together unto him; 2to the end that ye be not quickly shaken from your mind, nor yet be troubled, either by spirit, or by word, or by epistle as from us, as that the day of the Lord is just at hand; 3let no man beguile you in any wise: for it will not be, except the falling away come first, and the man of sin be revealed, the son of perdition, 4he that opposeth and exalteth himself against all that is called God or that is worshipped; so that he sitteth in the temple of God, setting himself forth as God. 5Remember ye not, that, when I was yet with you, I told you these things? 6And now ye know that which restraineth, to the end that he may be revealed in his own season. 7For the mystery of lawlessness doth already work: only there is one that restraineth now, until he be taken out of the way. 8And then shall be revealed the lawless one, whom the Lord Jesus shall slay with the breath of his mouth, and bring to nought by the manifestation of his coming; 9even he , whose coming is according to the working of Satan with all power and signs and lying wonders, 10and with all deceit of unrighteousness for them that perish; because they received not the love of the truth, that they might be saved. 11And for this cause God sendeth them a working of error, that they should believe a lie: 12that they all might be judged who believed not the truth, but had pleasure in unrighteousness.Stand Firm 13But we are bound to give thanks to God always for you, brethren beloved of the Lord, for that God chose you from the beginning unto salvation in sanctification of the Spirit and belief of the truth: 14whereunto he called you through our gospel, to the obtaining of the glory of our Lord Jesus Christ. 15So then, brethren, stand fast, and hold the traditions which ye were taught, whether by word, or by epistle of ours.16Now our Lord Jesus Christ himself, and God our Father who loved us and gave us eternal comfort and good hope through grace, 17comfort your hearts and establish them in every good work and word.

"The Lord Jesus Christ is the KI of Jeshurun"(Deut 33:5)."Jesus Christ is the KING of kings and LORD of Lords"(Rev 19:16).The Messiah Jesus fulfilled the eternal promise to the line of Moses as the King of Jeshurun. Jesus being a descendant of David verifies David's descent from Moses.King David's kingdom will be established forever. The operative term is "seed. The Fruition of the Priestly lines: To me this says it all because: Holy Holy is the Lord, Holy is the Lord: Who Was AND Who IS to Come : Ah Amen and Amen!!!! The Contents of a Masada Dead Sea Scroll Revealed "There is no one like the God of JeshurunThis does suggest that the tribes maintained a very high importance to the preservation of the bloodline of these rulers. As they knew the importance of their lineage It is likely that they realized and knew themselves to be heirs of God's promise that the Son of God would come through their lines.(Jesus)!!The assembly of Jacob comes into its inheritance; there was a king (then he became king*) in Jeshurun when the heads of the people foregathered and the tribes of Israel were all assembled! Moses the King of Jeshrun is the Shiloh mentioned by Jacob. Moses himself had the scepter when the people gathered to him from Egypt as a Levi."Moses commanded us a law, the inheritance of the congregation of Jacob. And he was king in Jeshurun, when the heads of the people and the tribes of Israel were gathered together." KING OF JESHURUN.

Ezekiel 37:1,11, 19, 21-22 - "The hand of the Lord came upon me and brought me out in the Spirit of the Lord, and set me down in the midst of the valley'; and it was full of bones…Then He said to me, 'Son of man, these bones are the whole house of Israel. They indeed say, 'our bones are dry, our hope is lost, and we ourselves are cut off!...Surely I will take the stick of Joseph, which is in the hand of Ephraim, and the tribes of Israel, his companions; and I will join them with it, with the stick of Judah, and make them one stick…Surely I will take the children of Israel from among the nations, wherever they have gone, and will gather them from every side and bring them into their own land; and I will make them one nation in the land, on the mountains of Israel; and one king shall be king over them all; they shall no longer be two nations, nor shall they ever be divided into two kingdoms again."The belief is that during the 'War of the Sons of Light Against the Sons of Darkness', Archangel Michael, described as the "Prince of Light", leads the forces of God The name Michael has an important meaning, it means: "(one) who is like God. The computer lexicon describes Michael as: "one of, the chief, or the first archangel who is described as the one who stands in time of conflict for the children of Israel".

(Matt. 5:35). His throne shall be established there, and it shall be the gathering point for all nations (Zech. 8:23; 14:16-21). Then shall the despised descendants of Jacob be "the head" of the nations, and no longer the tail (Deut. 28:13); then shall the people of Jehovah's ancient choice be the center of His earthly government; then shall the Fig Tree, so long barren, "blossom and bud, and fill the face of the world with fruit" (Isa. 27:6)

Seth Ben Adam Ben Jejhovahs End days Kingdom had to raise at least One Million dollars to be able to Rescue 144,000 Tribes of Israel. All the Tribes of Israel are decendents of Seth Ben Adam Ben Jehovah too. So they are all the Seed of the Woman "Adam" that must crush the Seed of the Serpent Cain and Inherite Seth Ben Adam Ben Jehovahs End Days Kingdom. This cannot be don't alone by one Mother of all prophets Hashem as I have already lost my Home, my Car when I was trying to defend the Fathers Kingdom Seth Ben Adam Ben Jehovah's Kingdom but I know to defend it because it has always been here in the Seed of the Woman Adam! And it is as God promised the Seed of the Woman Adam that will inherit Seth Ben Adam Ben Jehovahs End a Days Kingdom.

Again: To further explain, when a man's DNA is tested, we are testing the DNA of his father, his father's father, his father's father an unbroken chain etc. We can go back thousand's of years in this fashion because Y-DNA changes very slowly over time. Only men inherit the Y chromosome. It cannot pass to a female. This is the seed of a man. It is this seed that passes from father to son. It is the Y-chromosome of King David that is inherited along with the rest of the DNA by Moshiach ben David that will uniquely qualify him as the messiah

Prophecy to the Mountains of Israel

1And thou, son of man, prophesy unto the mountains of Israel, and say, Ye mountains of Israel, hear the word of Jehovah. 2Thus saith the Lord Jehovah: Because the enemy hath said against you, Aha! and, The ancient high places are ours in possession;3therefore prophesy, and say, Thus saith the Lord Jehovah: Because, even because they have made you desolate, and swallowed you up on every side, that ye might be a possession unto the residue of the nations, and ye are taken up in the lips of talkers, and the evil report of the people; 4therefore, ye mountains of Israel, hear the word of the Lord Jehovah: Thus saith the Lord Jehovah to the mountains and to the hills, to the watercourses and to the valleys, to the desolate wastes and to the cities that are forsaken, which are become a prey and derision to the residue of the nations that are round about; 5therefore thus saith the Lord Jehovah: Surely in the fire of my jealousy have I spoken against the residue of the nations, and against all Edom, that have appointed my land unto themselves for a possession with the joy of all their heart, with despite of soul, to cast it out for a prey. 6Therefore prophesy concerning the land of Israel, and say unto the mountains and to the hills, to the watercourses and to the valleys, Thus saith the Lord Jehovah: Behold, I have spoken in my jealousy and in my wrath, because ye have borne the shame of the nations: 7therefore thus saith the Lord Jehovah: I have sworn,'saying , Surely the nations that are round about you, they shall bear their shame. 8But ye, O mountains of Israel, ye shall shoot forth your branches, and yield your fruit to my people Israel; for they are at hand to come. 9For, behold, I am for you, and I will turn into you, and ye shall be tilled and sown; 10and I will multiply men upon you, all the house of Israel, even all of it; and the cities shall be inhabited, and the waste places shall be builded; 11and I will multiply upon you man and beast; and they shall increase and be fruitful; and I will cause you to be inhabited after your former estate, and will do better unto you than at your beginnings: and ye shall know that I am Jehovah. 12Yea, I will cause men to walk upon you, even my people Israel; and they shall possess thee, and thou shalt be their inheritance, and thou shalt no more henceforth bereave them of children.

13Thus saith the Lord Jehovah: Because they say unto you, Thou land art a devourer of men, and hast been a bereaver of thy nation; 14therefore thou shalt devour men no more, neither bereave thy nation any more, saith the Lord Jehovah; 15neither will I let thee hear any more the shame of the nations, neither shalt thou bear the reproach of the peoples any more, neither shalt thou cause thy nation to stumble any more, saith the Lord Jehovah.

The Lord's Holy Name

16Moreover the word of Jehovah came unto me, saying, 17Son of man, when the house of Israel dwelt in their own land, they defiled it by their way and by their doings: their way before me was as the uncleanness of a woman in her impurity. 18Wherefore I poured out my wrath upon them for the blood which they had poured out upon the land, and because they had defiled it with their idols; 19and I scattered them among the nations, and they were dispersed through the countries: according to their way and according to their doings I judged them. 20And when they came unto the nations, whither they went, they profaned my holy name; in that men said of them, These are the people of Jehovah, and are gone forth out of his land. 21But I had regard for my holy name, which the house of Israel had profaned among the nations, whither they went.

A New Heart and Spirit

22Therefore say unto the house of Israel, Thus saith the Lord Jehovah: I do not this for your sake, O house of Israel, but for my holy name, which ye have profaned among the nations, whither ye went. 23And I will sanctify my great name, which hath been profaned among the nations, which ye have profaned in the midst of them; and the nations shall know that I am Jehovah, saith the Lord Jehovah, when I shall be sanctified in you before their eyes. 24For I will take you from among the nations, and gather you out of all the countries, and will bring you into your own land. 25And I will sprinkle clean water upon you, and ye shall be clean: from all your filthiness, and from all your idols, will I cleanse you. 26A new heart also will I give you, and a new spirit will I put within you; and I will take away the stony heart out of your flesh, and I will give you a heart of flesh. 27And I will put my Spirit within you, and cause you to walk in my statutes, and ye shall keep mine ordinances, and do them. 28And ye shall dwell in the land that I gave to your fathers; and ye shall be my people, and I will be your God.29And I will save you from all your uncleannesses: and I will call for the grain, and will multiply it, and lay no famine upon you. 30And I will multiply the fruit of the tree, and the increase of the field, that ye may receive no more the reproach of famine among the nations. 31Then shall ye remember your evil ways, and your doings that were not good; and ye shall loathe yourselves in your own sight for your iniquities and for your abominations. 32Nor for your sake do I this , saith the Lord Jehovah, be it known unto you: be ashamed and confounded for your ways, O house of Israel.

33Thus saith the Lord Jehovah: In the day that I cleanse you from all your iniquities, I will cause the cities to be inhabited, and the waste places shall be builded. 34And the land that was desolate shall be tilled, whereas it was a desolation in the sight of all that passed by. 35And they shall say, This land that was desolate is become like the garden of Eden; and the waste and desolate and ruined cities are fortified and inhabited.36Then the nations that are left round about you shall know that I, Jehovah, have builded the ruined places, and planted that which was desolate: I, Jehovah, have spoken it, and I will do it.

37Thus saith the Lord Jehovah: For this, moreover, will I be inquired of by the house of Israel, to do it for them: I will increase them with men like a flock. 38As the flock for sacrifice, as the flock of Jerusalem in her appointed feasts, so shall the waste cities be filled with flocks of men; and they shall know that I am Jehovah.

Daniel 2American Standard Version (ASV)
2 And in the second year of the reign of Nebuchadnezzar, Nebuchadnezzar dreamed dreams; and his spirit was troubled, and his sleep went from him.[2] Then the king commanded to call the magicians, and the enchanters, and the sorcerers, and the Chaldeans, to tell the king his dreams. So they came in and stood before the king.
[3] And the king said unto them, I have dreamed a dream, and my spirit is troubled to know the dream.[4] Then spake the Chaldeans to the king in the Syrian language, O king, live for ever: tell thy servants the dream, and we will show the interpretation.
[5] The king answered and said to the Chaldeans, The thing is gone from me: if ye make not known unto me the dream and the interpretation thereof, ye shall be cut in pieces, and your houses shall be made a dunghill. [6] But if ye show the dream and the interpretation thereof, ye shall receive of me gifts and rewards and great honor: therefore show me the dream and the interpretation thereof. [7] They answered the second time and said, Let the king tell his servants the dream, and we will show the interpretation.
[8] The king answered and said, I know of a certainty that ye would gain time, because ye see the thing is gone from me. [9] But if ye make not known unto me the dream, there is but one law for you; for ye have prepared lying and corrupt words to speak before me, till the time be changed: therefore tell me the dream, and I shall know that ye can show me the interpretation thereof.

¹⁰ The Chaldeans answered before the king, and said, There is not a man upon the earth that can show the king's matter, forasmuch as no king, lord, or ruler, hath asked such a thing of any magician, or enchanter, or Chaldean. ¹¹ And it is a rare thing that the king requireth, and there is no other that can show it before the king, except the gods, whose dwelling is not with flesh. ¹² For this cause the king was angry and very furious, and commanded to destroy all the wise men of Babylon. ¹³ So the decree went forth, and the wise men were to be slain; and they sought Daniel and his companions to be slain.

¹⁴ Then Daniel returned answer with counsel and prudence to Arioch the captain of the king's guard, who was gone forth to slay the wise men of Babylon;

¹⁵ he answered and said to Arioch the king's captain, Wherefore is the decree so urgent from the king? Then Arioch made the thing known to Daniel.

¹⁶ And Daniel went in, and desired of the king that he would appoint him a time, and he would show the king the interpretation.

¹⁷ Then Daniel went to his house, and made the thing known to Hananiah, Mishael, and Azariah, his companions:

¹⁸ that they would desire mercies of the God of heaven concerning this secret; that Daniel and his companions should nor perish with the rest of the wise men of Babylon.

¹⁹ Then was the secret revealed unto Daniel in a vision of the night. Then Daniel blessed the God of heaven.

²⁰ Daniel answered and said, Blessed be the name of God for ever and ever; for wisdom and might are his.

²¹ And he changeth the times and the seasons; he removeth kings, and setteth up kings; he giveth wisdom unto the wise, and knowledge to them that have understanding;

²² he revealeth the deep and secret things; he knoweth what is in the darkness, and the light dwelleth with him.

²³ I thank thee, and praise thee, O thou God of my fathers, who hast given me wisdom and might, and hast now made known unto me what we desired of thee; for thou hast made known unto us the king's matter.

²⁴ Therefore Daniel went in unto Arioch, whom the king had appointed to destroy the wise men of Babylon; he went and said thus unto him: Destroy not the wise men of Babylon; bring me in before the king, and I will show unto the king the interpretation.

²⁵ Then Arioch brought in Daniel before the king in haste, and said thus unto him, I have found a man of the children of the captivity of Judah, that will make known unto the king the interpretation.

²⁶ The king answered and said to Daniel, whose name was Belteshazzar, Art thou able to make known unto me the dream which I have seen, and the interpretation thereof?

²⁷ Daniel answered before the king, and said, The secret which the king hath demanded can neither wise men, enchanters, magicians, nor soothsayers, show unto the king;

²⁸ but there is a God in heaven that revealeth secrets, and he hath made known to the king Nebuchadnezzar what shall be in the latter days. Thy dream, and the visions of thy head upon thy bed, are these:

²⁹ as for thee, O king, thy thoughts came into thy mind upon thy bed, what should come to pass hereafter; and he that revealeth secrets hath made known to thee what shall come to pass.

³⁰ But as for me, this secret is not revealed to me for any wisdom that I have more than any living, but to the intent that the interpretation may be made known to the king, and that thou mayest know the thoughts of thy heart.

[31] Thou, O king, sawest, and, behold, a great image. This image, which was mighty, and whose brightness was excellent, stood before thee; and the aspect thereof was terrible.

[32] As for this image, its head was of fine gold, its breast and its arms of silver, its belly and its thighs of brass,

[33] its legs of iron, its feet part of iron, and part of clay.

[34] Thou sawest till that a stone was cut out without hands, which smote the image upon its feet that were of iron and clay, and brake them in pieces.

[35] Then was the iron, the clay, the brass, the silver, and the gold, broken in pieces together, and became like the chaff of the summer threshing-floors; and the wind carried them away, so that no place was found for them: and the stone that smote the image became a great mountain, and filled the whole earth.

[36] This is the dream; and we will tell the interpretation thereof before the king.

[37] Thou, O king, art king of kings, unto whom the God of heaven hath given the kingdom, the power, and the strength, and the glory;

[38] and wheresoever the children of men dwell, the beasts of the field and the birds of the heavens hath he given into thy hand, and hath made thee to rule over them all: thou art the head of gold.

[39] And after thee shall arise another kingdom inferior to thee; and another third kingdom of brass, which shall bear rule over all the earth.

[40] And the fourth kingdom shall be strong as iron, forasmuch as iron breaketh in pieces and subdueth all things; and as iron that crusheth all these, shall it break in pieces and crush.

[41] And whereas thou sawest the feet and toes, part of potters' clay, and part of iron, it shall be a divided kingdom; but there shall be in it of the strength of the iron, forasmuch as thou sawest the iron mixed with miry clay.

[42] And as the toes of the feet were part of iron, and part of clay, so the kingdom shall be partly strong, and partly broken.

[43] And whereas thou sawest the iron mixed with miry clay, they shall mingle themselves with the seed of men; but they shall not cleave one to another, even as iron doth not mingle with clay.

[44] And in the days of those kings shall the God of heaven set up a kingdom which shall never be destroyed, nor shall the sovereignty thereof be left to another people; but it shall break in pieces and consume all these kingdoms, and it shall stand for ever.

[45] Forasmuch as thou sawest that a stone was cut out of the mountain without hands, and that it brake in pieces the iron, the brass, the clay, the silver, and the gold; the great God hath made known to the king what shall come to pass hereafter: and the dream is certain, and the interpretation thereof sure.

[46] Then the king Nebuchadnezzar fell upon his face, and worshipped Daniel, and commanded that they should offer an oblation and sweet odors unto him.

[47] The king answered unto Daniel, and said, Of a truth your God is the God of gods, and the Lord of kings, and a revealer of secrets, seeing thou hast been able to reveal this secret.

[48] Then the king made Daniel great, and gave him many great gifts, and made him to rule over the whole province of Babylon, and to be chief governor over all the wise men of Babylon.

[49] And Daniel requested of the king, and he appointed Shadrach, Meshach, and Abed-nego, over the affairs of the province of Babylon: but Daniel was in the gate of the king.

Calling on the name (having a prayer service[12]) of HaShem began with Seth:

> **Bereshit (Genesis) 4:26** *Seth also had a son, and he named him Enosh. At that time men began to call on the name of HaShem.*

David commanded us to call on the name of HaShem:

> **I Divrei HaYamim (Chronicles) 16:8** *Give thanks to HaShem, call on his name; make known among the nations what he has done.*

> **Tehillim** (Psalms) *116:13 I will lift up the cup of salvation and call on the name of HaShem.*

> **Tehillim (Psalms) 116:17** *I will sacrifice a thank offering to you and call on the name of HaShem.*

We will be calling on the name of HaShem in the future:

> **Yeshayahu (Isaiah) 12:4** *In that day you will say: "Give thanks to HaShem, call on his name; make known among the nations what he has done, and proclaim that his name is exalted.*

> **Yiremeyahu (Jeremiah) 3:17** *At that time they will call Jerusalem The Throne of HaShem, and all nations will gather in Jerusalem to honor thename of HaShem. No longer will they follow the stubbornness of their evil hearts.*

Hashem Moses was also a decendent of Seth Ben Adam Ben Jehovah too he was of the tribe of AZD This three-person family was the head of the nation: two men and a woman - a ruler, to his holy brother and his wife, who was a prophet. According to the Bible the children of Israel from slavery in Egypt led to the family, which consisted of three people: the Director, in his holy brother and his sister, who was a prophet .These Israeli leaders were children of Amram's children. AI-Masudin cited by the leaders of the tribe, who were saved by Mariban, Amir had children. Moses was a holy brother of Aaron, the brother of a sacred tribal chief was Amran. **Moses' sister was Miriam, his wife was Sipora; Mariban prophet was Zeripha.** AI-Masudin report of these three persons and their doings to remind a lot of astonishingly similar report on biblical Moses, Aaron and Miriam and the children of Israel. His report is one of the few, whose origin is not from the Bible or the traditions of the Jews. All current place names in the Sinai and the Negev, that link Israeli scientists are set by David Ben Gurion's request.

The Anglo Saxons came in from the Middle East as part of the horde at the fall of the Parthian Empire from what is now the area of Iraq and the area north of it.

"Franklin was in full accord except that he thought the Israelites should be shown emerging in the distance from the Red Sea which had been miraculously divided, and show the Egyptians in the foreground all being drowned."

I cannot yet validate with complete certaintly that the Merovingian line is an unbroken patrilineal chain to the line of David. Due to the Patrilineal Salic law though I see it may be possible.

(Minister, fl. 1005-1012)

Anglo-Saxon - <u>In Widsith, there is a long recital of people, clans and tribes who were known in the Germanic world of the 6th century</u>

Widsið maðolade,

wordhord onleac,

Widsith spake,

se þe monna mæst

he unlocked his treasure of words.

mægþa ofer eorþan,

He who among men

folca geondferde;

had travelled most in the world,

oft he on flette geþah

through peoples and nations;

mynelicne maþþum.

he had often in the hall

earned valuable treasures.

Him from Myrgingum

He was one of the Myrgings

æþele onwocon.

of noble blood.

He mid Ealhhilde,

He together with Ealhhilde,

fælre freoþuwebban,

the friendly weaver of peace

forman siþe

went for the home

Hreðcyninges

of the king of the Goths (3000 g

ham gesohte

he was searching

eastan of Ongle,

east of the Angles,

Eormanrices,

Ermanaric,

wraþes wærlogan.

wrathful against traitors.

Ongon þa worn sprecan:

He began to speak:

...ond Alexandreas

and Alexander's

ealra ricost	whole kingdom
monna cynnes,	together with the men of his clan
ond he mæst geþah	and he prospered most
þara þe ic ofer foldan	of which I all over the world
gefrægen hæbbe.	have heard the reports.
ætla weold Hunum,	ruled the Attila,
Eormanric Gotum,	Ermanaric ruled the Goths,
Becca Baningum,	Becca the 1Banings,
Burgendum Gifica.	Gebicca the Burgundians,
Casere weold Creacum	Caesar ruled the Greeks
ond Cælic Finnum,	and 1Caelic the Finns,
Hagena Holmrygum	Hagena the Rugians
ond Heoden Glommum.	and Heoden the Gloms.
Witta weold Swæfum,	Witta ruled the Suebi,
Wada Hælsingum,	Wada the 3444lsings"Hälsings,
Meaca Myrgingum,	Meaca the Myrgings,
Mearchealf Hundingum.	Mearchealf the Hundings.
þeodric weold Froncum,	Theuderic ruled the Franks,
þyle Rondingum,	Thyle the Rondings,

Revelation 10:11 And they said to me, "You must prophesy again concerning many peoples and nations and tongues and kings."

The genetic invasion started with the Anglo-Saxon dynasty then continued with the Nasrid Dynasty. Both Dynasties are patrilineal lines.

Da. Magdalena de Granada married into the house of Aviz, and then the lineage of the Kingdom of Granada was genetically invaded Matrilineal, and the houses of Europe tried, and still to this day try to make Gods of themselves with this female line. It was not their genetics at all, one

marriage, and the whole of the dynasty was absorbed just as they had absorebed the Anglo-Saxon Dynasty many hundreds of years before. These two dynasties though are Related historically. Please do not be prejudice as that is the history the illuminati hide, is the history they do not want for you to understand.

The Nasrid lineage is very deep indeed and related as will be shown, what the Victorian/Stuart Monarchies stole was immeasurable. It was Hebrew, Israelite, Levite then Jewish then after it was kidnapped it was turned Muslim. But then a very special branch became Christian once again, they were the Infants of Granada who also have true Castile line from their mother Zoraya, then however, under the influence of Queen Isabella, returned to the Christian faith, the religion of her infancy, and resumed her Spanish name of Isabella. Her two sons, Cad and Nazar, were baptized under the names of Don Fernando and Don Juan de Granada, and were permitted to take the titles of infantas or princes.

The Patrilineal line escaped Europe during the days of religious persecution when many palentines migrated to America to be free from the persecution of Europe. How the Nasrid dynasty and the Anglo-Saxons are related in history is a very special time in history that must be finally understood as this understanding brings us much closer to what the Bible says in that the Truth will Set you free. This you will find is a beautiful understanding of the flow of history.

To be honest I came to this understanding after researching my heritage of Wadsworth, and my son's heritage of the Nasrid. I knew already several years ago that the Victorian/ Stuart monarchies had Matrilinealy taken over the complete Anglo-Saxon heritage, and in fact have been proven to be barely Anglo-Saxon themselves at all. I thought ouch but I guess let bygones be bygones until the British monarchy overturned the Salic law illegally, and I realized the Truth that they Never had Right to the Anglo-Saxon heritage at all.

I then studied the actual lineage and heritage of the Nasrid Dynasty and saw the same history in that Both Dynasties had been taken over Matrilinealy by one marriage by theVictorian/Stuart monarchies and the Illuminati. Then as I dug deeper I realized completely that Both Dynasties are Patrilineal Dynasties for very sound and just reasons and are Related Historically, and they these Monarchies and their bankers never did and still don't have any right to use the hertage and lands based on a Matrilineal claim that you will see more proof on why both dynasties were Patrlineal and by all rights including Birthrights.

I will to my very best ability prove I am speaking truth, Should we continue to disregard this line of Queen Victoria for so long just so they can be rich beyond our wildest dreams while people live in Cardboard boxes, and at the same time forced to support the future War of Gog and Magog against our own Patrilineal lines. I have already shown how the Monarchies absorbed the Anglo-Saxon heritage and lands. The following is how they took the Nasrid heritage and lands as well . The Matrilineal line of Da.Magdalena de Granada was absorbed into the Victoria line in the following way:

- The Kings of the House of Aviz, or Joannine Dynasty (1385–ca. 1580)

- The Kings of the Portuguese House of Habsburg, or Philippine Dynasty (1580–1640)

- The Kings of the House of Braganza, (1640–1834) and

- The Kings of the House of Braganza-Saxe-Coburg and Gotha, or Braganza-Coburg (1834–1910)

Chapter7: The Ties that Bind

The Words of King Lemuel

1The words of king Lemuel; the oracle which his mother taught him.

2What, my son? and what, O son of my womb? And what, O son of my vows?

3Give not thy strength unto women, Nor thy ways to that which destroyeth kings.

4It is not for kings, O Lemuel, it is not for kings to drink wine; Nor for princes to say , Where is strong drink?

5Lest they drink, and forget the law, And pervert the justice due to any that is afflicted.

6Give strong drink unto him that is ready to perish, And wine unto the bitter in soul:

7Let him drink, and forget his poverty, And remember his misery no more.

8Open thy mouth for the dumb, In the cause of all such as are left desolate.

9Open thy mouth, judge righteously, And minister justice to the poor and needy.

The Virtues of Noble Woman

א

10A worthy woman who can find? For her price is far above rubies.

ב

11The heart of her husband trusteth in her, And he shall have no lack of gain.

ג

12She doeth him good and not evil All the days of her life.

ד

13She seeketh wool and flax, And worketh willingly with her hands.

ה

14She is like the merchant-ships; She bringeth her bread from afar.

ו

15She riseth also while it is yet night, And giveth food to her household, And their task to her maidens.

ז

16She considereth a field, and buyeth it; With the fruit of her hands she planteth a vineyard.

ח

17She girdeth her loins with strength, And maketh strong her arms.

ט

18She perceiveth that her merchandise is profitable: Her lamp goeth not out by night.

י

19She layeth her hands to the distaff, And her hands hold the spindle.

20 She stretcheth out her hand to the poor; Yea, she reacheth forth her hands to the needy.

21 She is not afraid of the snow for her household; For all her household are clothed with scarlet.

22 She maketh for herself carpets of tapestry; Her clothing is fine linen and purple.

23 Her husband is known in the gates, When he sitteth among the elders of the land.

24 She maketh linen garments and selleth them, And delivereth girdles unto the merchant.

25 Strength and dignity are her clothing; And she laugheth at the time to come.

26 She openeth her mouth with wisdom; And the law of kindness is on her tongue.

27 She looketh well to the ways of her household, And eateth not the bread of idleness.

28 Her children rise up, and call her blessed; Her husband also , and he praiseth her,'saying :

29 Many daughters have done worthily, But thou excellest them all.

30 Grace is deceitful, and beauty is vain; But a woman that feareth Jehovah, she shall be praised.

31 Give her of the fruit of her hands; And let her works praise her in the gates.

The Law of Moses strictly prohibited usury

"If thou lend money to any of my people that	"Thou shalt not give him thy money upon usury,	"Thou shalt not lend upon usury to thy	"He that putteth not out his money to

is poor by thee, thou shalt not be to him as an usurer, neither shalt thou lay upon him usury "(Exodus 22:25).	nor lend him thy victuals for increase" (Lev. 25:37).	brother; usury of money, usury of victuals, usury of any thing that is lent upon usury "(Deut. 23:19).	usury, nor taketh reward against the innocent. He that doeth these things shall never be moved" (PS. 15:5).

Moses did state only _one_ case in which usury was allowed in Deuteronomy 23:19-20 "Thou shalt not lend upon usury to thy brother; usury of money, usury of victuals, usury of anything that is lent upon usury: Unto a stranger _(Nokri_y) thou mayest lend upon usury; but unto thy brother thou shalt not lend upon usury: that the LORD thy God may bless thee in all that thou settest thine hand to in the land whither thou goest to possess it "(Deuteronomy 23:19-20).The **Law of Moses** is a term that is first found in in the Bible in Joshua 8:31-32 when Joshua writes the words of "**the Law of Moses**" on the altar at **Mount Ebal**. The text continues "And afterward he read all the words of thef law, the blessings and cursings, according to all that is written in the book of the law." (Joshua 8:34). The term occurs 15 times in the Hebrew Bible and then another 7 times in the New Testament.

In the words of Frank Herbert "The Sleeper must awaken" Jacob did try and make amends with Esau, and their lines even intermarried with Kenaz as will be shown. But as time went on certan branches of Esau went on to be the Pharisees that Jesus spoke much of. Again I say Deliverance, for I fear the Lord, and I pray for those who listen, and fear the Lord as well, for he alone is our grace._ **Remember the Lord gave a default button, a re-set button called The Truth will set us Free.** Deuteronomy 9:5 "Not for thy righteousness, or for the righteousness of thine heart, dost thou go to possess their land: but for the wickedness of these nations the "I AM" thy God doth drive them out from before thee, and that He may perform the Word which the "I AM" sware unto thy fathers, Abraham, Isaac, and Jacob/Israel."You will know the Truth; and the Truth will set you free." -- John 8:33.Paul said in Romans 9:6-8, _"Not as though God's Word had failed, for they are not all elect Israelites, who are of born of Jacob: Neither, because they are the seed of Abraham, are they all heirs of the Promise: because It was to come through the line of Isaac. So the heirs of the Promise are not children from Abraham's loins, but an election from Isaac through Jacob"._Law one of an Israeilite: **among ancient Israelites, the inheritance is patrilineal**. It comes from the father, who bequeaths only to his male descendants (daughters don't inherit). The eldest son received twice as much as the other sons. The father gives his name to his children; for example: the sons of **Israel are called Israelites, because the land belonged to the father, and every one of his twelve sons gave his name to his descendants.**

Now in an effort to bring the 12 tribes together there are factions that are trying to influence and sway the many. Understanding the truth is your best defence in surviving the days to come.

What does this tell us of our current times? Must Esau once again reconcile with Jacob? Is much of the danger and dispute with see both Biblically and in our current world? What does histories

tell us, what does scripture tell us? Are there any clues Ah clue number 2, Matrilinealy lines are sitting on the line of Jacob and Levi. There is a clue number 3 and 4 that will also be revealed later in this work.

Genesis 32–33 tells of **Jacob** and **Esau's** eventual reconciliation.

I thank the Moses of the Bible for everything I understand. One day we will sing the Song of Moses no doubt!!!!!!! Seed of Moses: Crown Prince Thutmose The king's son the sem-priest Djhutmose;eldest son of pharaoh Amenhotep III and Queen Tiye, as the successor to the Egyptian throne I am the servant of this noble god, his miller; Incense for the Ennead of the western necropolis. The 10.5 centimetres (4 in) schist recumbent mummiform bier has Thutmose prone with the Ba, Soul Bird upon his lower breast. The sides of the small statuette contain the following hieroglyphs, recording him as 'S-M Thoth-MS-S ', "True of Voice" '–SM (priest?) Tutmosis, "True of Voice"-("deserving", worthy, or "venerable").[7] **As the first was Isaac, thus making Jacob and Esau Patrilineal, and their sons Patrilineal and the sons of Judah and Joseph Patrilineal as well as Levi.**

"Then Joseph told his brothers. 'Listen,' he said, 'I had another dream, and this time the sun and moon and eleven stars were bowing down to me.' When he told his father as well as his brothers, his father rebuked him and said, 'What is this dream you had? Will your mother and I and your brothers actually come and bow down to the ground before you?" Genesis 37:9-11

Wetjes-ren-en-Aten

Wetjes-khau-em-Iunu-Shemay

According to Biblical chronology, Moses fled Egypt 40 years after his birth

Exodus 2:15 The Egyptian root in 'ms' meaning to be born. The linguistic root of the name Moses is shows itself in the Egyptian word Mos which means "child." But this word also had a much broader legal meaning—"the rightful son and heir." Crown Prince Thutmose/Tutmosis' The king's son the sem-priest Djhutmose;eldest son of pharaoh Amenhotep III and Queen Tiye, as the successor to the Egyptian throne I am the servant of this noble god, his miller; Incense for the Ennead of the western necropolis. A religious reformation was occurring, that reached its pinnacle under the reign of Akhenaton, Thutmose's brother.**Israelites were to be ruled by a Priest or "Levitical King ". Crown Prince Tuthmose, the eldest son of pharaoh Amenhotep III, who mysteriously disappears from all records. Could he have been the factual origin of the Biblical character Moses? The name of this prince - Thutmose - is very similar to Moses and The Key for its heritage and our understanding of the True Moses of the Bible, "The Moses that was married to Zipporrah. "**Zipporah (zĭp`ərə), in the Bible, daughter of Jethro and wife of **Moses**.

Yahya is usually understood to mean "he shall live", spiritually meaning that John will forever be remembered as a great prophet.Yahya (John the Baptist) was the son of Prophet Zakariyya The duties at the temple in Jerusalem alternated between each of the family lines that had descended from those appointed by king David (1st Chronicles 24:1–19).[2] Luke states that during the week when it was the duty of Zechariah's family line to serve at "the temple of the Lord", the lot for performing the incense offering had fallen to Zechariah (Luke 1:8–11).(Luke 1:8–11).:"Now we begin the story of Jesus .

As a prelude we have the birth of Mary and the parallel story of John the Baptist, Yahya, the son of Zakariya. Yahya's mother, Elizabeth, was a cousin of Mary, the mother of Jesus, (Luke 1:36) and therefore John and Jesus were cousins by blood. And there was a spiritual cousinhood in their birth and career. Elizabeth was of the daughters of Aaron (Luke 1:5) of a priestly family which went back to Aaron, the brother of Moses and son of Imran. John the Baptist is described in the Gospel of Luke as a relative of Jesus[13]

The Egyptian root in 'ms' meaning to be born. The linguistic root of the name Moses is shows itself in the Egyptian word Mos which means "child." But this word also had a much broader legal meaning—"the rightful son and heir. Nachash is the Hebrew word for SERPENT from which nashak the word for usury is derived. There was no specific Hebrew word for money as silver was considered money. The Law of Moses strictly prohibited usury"Until Shiloh Come" The passage in Jacob's prophecy I translate thus, ... for Moses, who was "king in Jeshurun," was of the tribe of Levi I thank Moses who was married to Zipporah (KETURAH (meaning incense, perfume), the second legal wife of Abraham, married after the death of Sarah ... Likewise Zipporah (Exodus 4:24-26) .Moses also had his brother and sister, the Moses of the Bible for everything I understand at this critical time. One day we will sing the Song of Moses no doubt!!!!!!! Grandfather of the Moses of the Bible: the king's son the sem-priest Djhutmose;eldest son of pharaoh Amenhotep III and Queen Tiye, as the successor to the Egyptian throne I am the servant of this noble god, his miller; Incense for the Ennead of the western necropolis./Imran
The 10.5 centimetres (4 in) schist recumbent mummiform bier has Thutmose prone with the Ba, Soul Bird upon his lower breast. The sides of the small statuette contain the following hieroglyphs, recording him as 'S-M Thoth-MS-S ', "True of Voice" '–SM (priest?) Tutmosis, "True of Voice"-("deserving", worthy, or "venerable").[7] "But this is the covenant which I will make with the house of Israel after those days," declares the Lord. "I will put My Law within them, and on their heart I will write it; and I will be their God, and they shall be My people. And they shall not teach again, each man his neighbor and each man his brother, saying 'know the Lord,' for they shall all know Me, from the least of them to the greatest of them," declares the Lord, "for I will forgive their iniquity, and their sin I will remember no more.Messiah Text (4Q285)This six-line fragment, commonly referred to as the "Pierced Messiah" text, is written in a Herodian script of the first half of the 1st Century and refers to a Messiah from the Branch of David, to a judgement The War of the Messiah Jesus:"Naz Seir". This hawk symbol represents the star Sirius in Canis Major. In Egyptian, "Naz" means "Sent," while "Seir" means "Prince" or "Chief." Therefore, the title "Naz Seir" can mean "Sent Prince." Since "Naz" and "Zar" both mean "Prince" in Hebrew. Hear Jesus and what he says about himself and the Biblical Moses he was an decendent himself of,The War of the Messiah is a series of Dead Sea scroll fragments describing the conclusion of a battle led by the Leader of the Congregation. The fragments that make up this document include 4Q285, also known as The Pierced Messiah Text, and 11Q14 with which it was found to coincide. It is possible that it also represents the conclusion of the War Scroll.[1] [edit]The Pierced Messiah Text (4Q285)This six-line fragment, commonly referred to as the "Pierced Messiah" text, is written in a Herodian script of the first half of the 1st Century and refers to a Messiah from the Branch of David, to a judgement The War of the

Messiah (4Q285)(4Q285) The Roman Ruler Herod Antipas was the ruler of Galilee. He had an adulterous relations with Herodias, the wife of his brother Herod Philip. John the Baptist reproached him for this grave sin. Herod Antipas got annoyed and imprisoned him till his execution.The Sons of Light, consising of the sons of Levi, the sons of Judah, and the sons Joseph

The roots of so much of the dispute are truly found in many places in the Holy Scriptures and therefore it should greatly remind the Many that the ultimate resolution of the matter may also very well reside with the Holy One of Israel/Jacob. This may very well be the long lost Key to the end of so much of the conflict and usury we see today, and the end of the Victorian age we are currently so very plagued by.

Oh Holy one of Israel Jacob, the words of the father:

Therefore say unto the house of Israel, Thus saith the Lord GOD;

I do not this for your sakes, O house of Israel, but for mine holy name's sake, which ye have profaned among the heathen, whither ye went.

And I will sanctify my great name, which was profaned among the heathen,

which ye have profaned in the midst of them;

and the heathen shall know

that I am the LORD, saith the Lord GOD,

when I shall be sanctified in you before their eyes.

Ezekiel 36:22,23

"For the children of Israel shall abide many days without a king, and without a prince and without a sacrifice, and without an image, and without an ephod and without teraphim, Afterward shall the children of Israel return, and seek YHWH their POWER, and David their king; and shall fear YHWH and his goodness in the latter days." Hosea 3:4,5.

The religion and laws of Judaism and Muslim such as Matrilineal laws do not apply to a True Israelite of Jacob, as the laws of Judaism as well as Islam in this regard are in direct contrast with the Patrilineal laws of an Israelite. **In early biblical history, descent was clearly patrilineal (Exodus 31:2). Abraham was the first Hebrew (Genesis 14:13). Abraham and Sarah would have a son, Isaac, which would establish the line. Isaac and Rebecca would then have a son, Jacob, which would further that line, and Jacob would then have twelve sons, establishing tribal authority.**

*Charge some that they teach no other doctrine, neither give heed to legends and endless genealogies, which minister questions. For the time will come when they will not endure sound doctrine; but after their own lusts shall they heap to themselves teachers, and they shall turn away their ears from the Truth, and instead shall be turned unto legends. **1Timothy 1:3-4 and 2Timothy 4:3-4***

("Hebrew")

As is shown clearly in the Hebrew Bible, (or the Tanakh) which is called the "Old Testament" by Christians, the "Treasured People" is the exact phrase used in the text, referring to the Hebrews/Israelites. We also find that in the Book of Deuteronomy, YHWH proclaims the Nation of Israel, known originally as the Children of Israel, as his "treasured people out of all the people on the face of the earth" (Deuteronomy 7:6). As mentioned in the Book of Exodus, the Hebrew people are God's chosen people, and from them shall come the Messiah, or redeemer of the world. The Israelites also possess the "Word of God" and/or the "Law of God" in the form of the Torah as communicated by God to Moses.

"Now therefore, if you will obey my voice indeed, and keep my covenant, then you shall be a peculiar treasure unto me above all people" (Exodus 19:5), God promises that He will never exchange His people with any other. "And I will establish My covenant between Me and you and your descendants after you in their generations, for an everlasting covenant, to be God to you and your descendants after you." (Genesis 17:7).

The actual word Jew only first appeared in the Bible in books, 1st Kings, 2 Kings, and Jeremiah in the Old Testament and was an incorrect translation of the Hebrew word for Yehudah and is often pronounced Judah in English. The history of the Old Testament reveles that the "chosen people" of the Bible were descendants of a man named Jacob and he was named Israel. As a result of this his descendants were called Israelites not Jews, not to exclude that any Israelite's did not later become a Jew/Judiah, but that is a small fraction of the current Jewish population. The religion and laws of Judaism and Muslim such as Matrilineal laws do not apply to a True Israelite of Jacob, as the laws of Judaism as well as Muslim in this regard are in direct contrast with the Patrlineal laws of an Israelite.

The fact is that Y-chromosome DNA (Y-DNA) is paternally inherited enables patrilines, and agnatic kinships, of men to be traced through genetic analysis.

Y-chromosomal Adam (Y-MRCA) is the patrilineal human most recent common ancestor, from whom all Y-DNA in living men is descended. Y-chromosomal Adam probably lived between 60,000 and 90,000 years ago, judging from molecular clock and genetic marker studies. A man's genetic Y-DNA and his family name (in most cultures) have descended down this same line from father to son. In a patrilineal descent system Patrilineal Descent ... that in the Bible the line always followed the father, including the cases of Joseph and Moses.

The Original Israelite's lost their footprint, and are in our current times are in a very dangerous and vulnerable position. All of this is due to our lack of understanding, and it is critical for our understanding to catch up and protect the Israelites. This is why the First law of an Israelite is so very important, and the persecution of the Israelites must stop. This persecution is what has allowed Evil to march on, and take over in the first place, as now the Israelite remnant are in more danger than ever before, and is fast reaching critical mass . These are very dangerous times, but you cannot even begin to fathom how and why unless you understand many pieces of history, then a picture begins to form of the tragic truth, and the dangers we face. I emphasize the extreme importance of what I call the First Law of an Israelite, and what the laws were among the ancient Israelite's, and how this is critical for our current times, and always was important but was forgotten, and history then took a path of the Evil we see in our own times. We must start from the beginning to see with much more clarity the Hebrews that became the Israelites.

Again :Law one of an Israelite: **among ancient Israelites, the inheritance is patrilineal**. **It comes from the father, who bequeaths only to his male descendants (daughters don't inherit)**. The eldest son received twice as much as the other sons. The father gives his name to his children; for example: the sons of Israel are called Israelites, because the land belonged to the father, and every one of his twelve sons gave his name to his descendants.

"Thus says the Lord God: 'Although I have cast them far off among the Gentiles, and although I have scattered them among the countries, yet I shall be a little sanctuary for them in the countries where they have gone.' Therefore say, 'Thus says the Lord God: I will gather you from the peoples, assemble you from the countries where you have been scattered, and I will give you the land of Israel'"

For thus saith the Lord; Sing with gladness for Jacob, and shout among the chief of the nations: publish ye, praise ye, and say, O Lord, save thy people, the remnant of Israel.

History as you have seen has been hijacked in many ways, and it began its tracks long ago. The results has been what is truly a war against Shem, and the order the lord had put in place long before man took control, and tried to make its own World order that is way out of line of what the Bible clearly tells us. The tracks of truth, and <u>bread crumbs that were in place were tossed aside, and the Evil began its trek through history.</u>

We can fight back in such ways as taking our money out of the bank. And you can maintain an account for monthly payments; just keep its balance at almost zero. Pay your bills and take out the rest. There are ideas at least of what can be done. <u>**Our love though for the True Israelites and the promise from God though should become our top priority.**</u> We should finally hear the Lord when he tells us the truth will set us free, and even how this is accomplished. <u>**The Patrilineal lines of Jacob, as the Birthrights and true Y-DNA are found in the their Patrilineal decedents only.**</u>

Again :Law one of an Israelite: **among ancient Israelites, the inheritance is patrilineal**. **It comes from the father, who bequeaths only to his male descendants (daughters don't inherit)**. The eldest son received twice as much as the other sons. The father gives his name to his children; for example: the sons of Israel are called Israelites, because the land belonged to the father, and every one of his twelve sons gave his name to his descendants.

The Words of King Lemuel: 1The words of king Lemuel; the oracle which his mother taught him.2What, my son?f and what, O son of my womb? And what, O son of my vows? 3Give not thy strength unto women, Nor thy ways to that which destroyeth kings.4It is not for kings, O Lemuel, it is not for kings to drink wine; Nor for princes to say , Where is strong drink? 5Lest they drink, and forget the law, And pervert the justice due to any that is afflicted.6Give strong drink unto him that is ready to perish, And wine unto the bitter in soul:7Let him drink, and forget his poverty, And remember his misery no more.8Open thy mouth for the dumb, In the cause of all such as are left desolate. 9Open thy mouth, judge righteously, And minister justice to the poor and needy.The Virtues of Noble Woman א

10A worthy woman who can find? For her price is far above rubies. ב11The heart of her husband trusteth in her, And he shall have no lack of gain. ג12She doeth him good and not evil All the days of her life. ד13She seeketh wool and flax, And worketh willingly with her hands. ה14She is like the merchant-ships; She bringeth her bread from afar. ו15She riseth also while it is yet night, And giveth food to her household, And their task to her maidens. ז16 She considereth a field, and buyeth it; With the fruit of her hands she planteth a vineyard. ח17She girdeth her loins with strength, And maketh strong her arms. ט18She perceiveth that her merchandise is profitable: Her lamp goeth not out by night. י 19She layeth her hands to the distaff, And her hands hold the spindle. כ20She stretcheth out her hand to the poor; Yea, she reacheth forth her hands to the needy. ל21 She is not afraid of the snow for her household; For all her household are clothed with scarlet. מ22She maketh for herself carpets of tapestry; Her clothing is fine linen and purple. נ23Her husband is known in the gates, When he sitteth among the elders of the land. ס24 She maketh linen garments and selleth them, And delivereth girdles unto the merchant. ע25Strength and dignity are her clothing; And she laugheth at the time to come. פ26She openeth her mouth with wisdom; And the law of kindness is on her tongue. צ27She looketh well to the ways of her household, And eateth not the bread of idleness. ק28Her children rise up, and call her blessed; Her husband also , and he praiseth her,'saying : ר29Many daughters have done worthily, But thou excellest them all. ש30Grace is deceitful, and beauty is vain; But a woman that feareth Jehovah, she shall be praised. ת31Give her of the fruit of her hands; And let her works praise her in the gates. Psalm 112:1 Praise the LORD. Blessed are those who fear the LORD, who find great delight in his commands. Proverbs 11:16 A kindhearted woman gains honor, but ruthless men gain only wealth.Proverbs 22:4 Humility is the fear of the LORD; its wages are riches and honor and life.Proverbs 31:29 "Many women do noble things, but you surpass them all."Proverbs 31:31 Honor her for all that her hands have done, and let her works bring her praise at the city gate. The whole emphasis is on the LORD God! Greatness, power, glory, victory and majesty – all are yours O God – throughout the earth and the heavens! Yours is the kingdom! Not ours, but yours, O King! For they are attributes of a king! God's greatness is vast, incomparable and unfathomable. God's power is that of a warrior: almighty, overwhelming yet alluring; and all power comes from Him to every dependent creature. God's glory is the exuberant and ecstatic magnificence of His very being! Victory shows God as an all-conquering hero: transcendent and supreme, to whom all creatures and creation are subject. His victories are irrefutable and undeniable. His uncompromising majesty symbolises a dignity, regency, splendour and awesome magnificence! These things: greatness, power, glory, victory and majesty are essential attributes of who God is: indelible, immutable, unchangeable and permanent. God is a King in greater splendour than any of the excesses of King Louis XVI. If you don't know about Louis, go look him up and the scale of extravagance! This God is a mighty King to be exalted above all things and He is to be held in His rightful place: high and lifted up! As for the kingdom, whose is it? Is it Israel's? No! Is it David's? No! It is God's and His alone! His Kingdom is of total magnificence and greater than the Roman Empire! Even greater than the British Empire, which was never to see the sun set on it. Jesus is probably quoting here, in what we call the Lord's Prayer. So David's words resonate down through history.

God's purpose and will? (Matt. 26:39; John 5:30; 14:10, 24). Yeshua's prayer to the Father before his crucifixion, recorded in John 17, confirms this understanding of "one":JOHN 17:11 "Now I am no longer in the world, but these are in the world, and I come to You. Holy Father, keep through Your name those whom You have given Me, that they may be one as We areYeshua prayed that the disciples Yah had given him would become one, just as he and the Father were one. How then were the disciples to become one? Were they to become some sort of divine triune being? Or were they to be united through the Holy Spirit to do the will of God, just as Yeshua was united to his Father during his entire life on earth?JOHN 17:20 "I do not pray for these alone, but also for those who will believe in Me through their word; 21 that they all may be one, as You, Father, are in Me, and I in You; that they also may be one in Us, that the world may believe that You sent Me. 22 And the glory which You gave Me I have given them, that they may be one just as We are one: 23 I in them, and You in Me; that they may be made perfect in one, and that the world may know that You have sent Me, and have loved them as You have loved Me." I will Make Music with My Soul (2 Samuel 23:1-7)1My heart is fixed, O God; I will sing, yea, I will sing praises, even with my glory.2Awake, psaltery and harp: I myself will awake right early. 3I will give thanks unto thee, O Jehovah, among the peoples; And I will sing praises unto thee among the nations.4For thy lovingkindness is great above the heavens; And thy truth reacheth unto the skies.5Be thou exalted, O God, above the heavens, And thy glory above all the earth.6That thy beloved may be delivered, Save with thy right hand, and answer us.7God hath spoken in his holiness: I will exult; I will divide Shechem, and mete out the valley of Succoth.8Gilead is mine; Manasseh is mine; Ephraim also is the defence of my head; Judah is my sceptre.9Moab is my washpot; Upon Edom will I cast my shoe; Over Philistia will I shout.10Who will bring me into the fortified city? Who hath led me unto Edom?11Hast not thou cast us off, O God? And thou goest not forth, O God, with our hosts.12Give us help against the adversary; For vain is the help of man.13Through God we shall do valiantly: For he it is that will tread down our adversaries.

"**Thus says the Lord God: 'Although I have cast them far off among the Gentiles, and although I have scattered them among the countries, yet I shall be a little sanctuary for them in the countries where they have gone.' Therefore say, 'Thus says the Lord God: I will gather you from the peoples, assemble you from the countries where you have been scattered, and I will give you the land of Israel'"**

For thus saith the Lord; Sing with gladness for Jacob, and shout among the chief of the nations: publish ye, praise ye, and say, O Lord, save thy people, the remnant of Israel.

English Egyptologist **David Rohl** and other researchers are finding that the time dating of the Pharos of Egypt must be wrong, and with that it distorts our view of Ancient History. The Egyptian Chronology has been artificially extended by over 300 years. And with that much of any archeological footprint of the Israelites was lost.

With correct dating of this time period we are able to see the beginnings of actual evidence of these Biblical times. It is our deep disregard for the Covenants with God that is slowly but surely destroying the very fabric of our core, and allowing for Evil to have its way with us on a massive scale. We must look to the Covenants, and to the Bible deeply in what it tells us clearly. **We must desire this with all our hearts in what the Lord said in that the Truth shall set us free.**

Law one of an Israelite is:

Law one of an Israeilite: <u>among ancient Israelites, the inheritance is patrilineal</u>. It comes from the father, who bequeaths only to his male descendants (daughters don't inherit). The eldest son received twice as much as the other sons. <u>The father gives his name to his children; for example:</u> <u>the sons of Israel are called Israelites, because the land belonged to the father, and every one of his</u> <u>twelve sons gave his name to his descendants.</u>

<u>The great importance to mandate the Y-chromosome to group each man into clans based on</u> <u>patrilineal lines of descent (e.g., Abraham begat Isaac who begat Jacob.</u> Levi (**Levite**) - **Patrilineal** descendant of Levi the son of Jacob, Scholars suggest that the original rule of Jewish descent must have been **patrilineal**. <u>The fact is that Y-chromosome DNA (Y-DNA) is paternally inherited enables</u> <u>patrilines, and agnatic kinships, of men to be traced through genetic analysis.</u>

<u>Exodus 19:3-6 records a promise God made to the children of Israel encamped about Mount Sinai.</u> <u>Speaking to Moses, God says,</u>

Thus you shall say to the house of Jacob, and tell the children of Israel: "You have seen what I did to the Egyptians, and how I bore you on eagles' wings and brought you to Myself. <u>Now therefore,</u> <u>if you will indeed obey My voice and keep My covenant, then you shall be a special treasure to Me</u> <u>above all people; for all the earth is Mine. And you shall be to Me a kingdom of priests and a holy</u> <u>nation."</u>

<u>For thus saith the Lord; Like as I have brought all this great evil upon this people, so will I bring</u> <u>upon them all the good that I have promised them. Jeremiah 32:41,42</u>

Jeremiah 31:10 ASV

[10] Hear the word of the LORD, O nations,
And declare in the coastlands afar off,
And say, "He who scattered Israel will gather him
And keep him as a shepherd keeps his flock."
[11] **For the LORD has ransomed Jacob**
And redeemed him from the hand of him who was stronger than he

<u>For thus saith the Lord; Like as I have brought all this great evil upon this people, so will I bring</u> <u>upon them all the good that I have promised them. Jeremiah 32:41,42</u>

<u>God became "the God of Jacob." (Gen. 25:23)</u>
<u>The Israelites, as described in the Hebrew Bible, were the descendants of the patriarch Jacob,</u> <u>later known as Israel.</u>

<u>These are the words of the covenant that Jehovah commanded Moses to conclude with the sons of</u> <u>Israel in the land of Moab aside from the covenant that he had concluded with them in Horeb.</u> <u>(Deuteronomy 29:1)</u>

<u>12 that thou mayest enter into the covenant of Jehovah thy God, and into his oath, which Jehovah</u> <u>thy God maketh with thee this day;</u>

¹³ that he may establish thee this day for a people unto himself, and [that] he may be to thee a God, as he hath said unto thee, and as he hath sworn unto thy fathers, to Abraham, to Isaac, and to Jacob.

Revelation 5:1-10And I saw in the right hand of him that sat on the throne a scroll written within and on the backside, sealed with seven seals. And I saw a strong angel proclaiming with a loud voice, Who is worthy to open the scroll, and to loose the seals thereof? And no man in heaven, nor in earth, neither under the earth, was able to open the scroll, neither to look thereon. And I wept much, because no man was found worthy to open and to read the scroll, neither to look thereon. And one of the elders saith unto me, Weep not: behold, the Lion of the tribe of Judah, the Root of David, hath prevailed to open the scroll, and to loose the seven seals thereof. And I beheld, and, lo, in the midst of the throne and of the four beasts, and in the midst of the elders, stood a Lamb as it had been slain, having seven horns and seven eyes, which are the seven Spirits of God sent forth into all the earth. And he came and took the scroll out of the right hand of him that sat upon the throne. And when he had taken the scroll, the four beasts and four and twenty elders fell down before the Lamb, having every one of them harps, and golden vials full of odours, which are the prayers of saints. And they sung a new song, saying, Thou art worthy to take the scroll, and to open the seals thereof: for thou wast slain, and hast redeemed us to God by thy blood out of every kindred, and tongue, and people, and nation; And hast made us unto our God kings and priests: and we shall reign on the earth.KING OF JESHURUN."The Lord Jesus Christ is the KI of Jeshurun"(Deut 33:5)."Jesus Christ is the KING of kings and LORD of Lords"(Rev 19:16).The Messiah Jesus fulfilled the eternal promise to the line of Moses as the King of Jeshurun. Jesus being a descendant of David verifies David's descent from Moses. KING OF JESHURUN." 25 Therefore thus saith the Lord Jehovah: Now will I bring back the captivity of Jacob, and have mercy upon the whole house of Israel; and I will be jealous for my holy ame.26...For the Torah shall go forth from Tzyion and the word of HaShem from Yerushalyim: Yeshayahu 2:3 Jeremiah 23:7 "So then, the days are coming - it is HaShem Who speaks - when people will no longer say, 'As HaShem lives, Who brought the sons of Israel (12 tribes) out of the land of Egypt', but, 'As HaShem lives, Who led back and brought home the descendants of the House of Israel out of the land of the North, and from all the countries to which He had dispersed them, to live on their own soil ." To Orthodox Jews, Moses is called Moshe Rabbenu, `Eved HaShem, Avi haNeviim zya"a. He is defined "Our Leader Moshe", "Servant of God", and "Father of all the Prophets".Hebrew Shema', "Hear O Israel: The Lord our God, the Lord is One." (Deut. 6:4) The Shema' comes from the hand of Moses about 1400 BC.EL MELEKH NE'EMAN (Heb. "God, faithful King"), an affirmation of faith pronounced before the recital of the *Shema The Lord Jesus Christ is the KI of Jeshurun"(Deut 33:5)."Jesus Christ is the KING of kings and LORD of Lords"(Rev 19:16).The God of Jeshurun*, who rides the heavens in his power,There is none like the God of Jeshurun, Riding the heavens in thy help, ... extol him who rides on the clouds--his name is the LORD-- and rejoice before him. King David's kingdom will be established forever. Matthew 6:9 -6:15 (ASV)

Our Father who art in heaven. Hallowed be thy name. 10 Thy kingdom come. Thy will be done, as in heaven, so on earth. 11 Give us this day our daily bread. 12 And forgive us our debts, as we also have forgiven our debtors. 13 And bring us not into temptation, but deliver us from the evil one. 14 For if ye forgive men their trespasses, your heavenly Father will also forgive you. 15 But if ye forgive not men their trespasses, neither will your Father forgive your trespassesGod also forbade the Israelites to be involved with various types of magic, familiar spirits, and necromancy."A man also or woman that hath a familiar spirit, or that is a wizard, shall surely be put to death: they shall stone them with stones: their blood [shall be] upon them." Lev 20:27 If you are going to live in my House, you are going to play by My Rules Says: !HALLELUYAH BLESS THE NAME YAHSHUA: Shiloh is calling:"I AM WHO I AM. This is what you are to say to the Israelites: 'I AM has sent me to you.'" God also said to Moses,

"Say to the Israelites, 'The LORD, the God of your fathers—the God of Abraham, the God of Isaac and the God of Jacob—has sent me to you. This is my name forever, the name you shall call me from generation to generation."

And we'll Sing to you "Your My Everything "Oh "Your my master you my Savior, your my Elohim ("Blessed be Yahweh the Elohim of Shem") Your my Abba Father ("'Abba, Father,' he said, 'everything is possible for you. Take this cup from me. Yet not what I will, but what you will.'" (Mark 14:36) "For you did not receive a spirit that makes you a slave again to fear, but you received the Spirit of sonship. And by him we cry, 'Abba, Father.'" (Romans 8:15)"Because you are sons, God sent the Spirit of his Son into our hearts, the Spirit who calls out, 'Abba, Father.'" (Galatians 4:6)) I praise your Kodesh Name (The Foundation Stone under the Dome of the Rock, a possible historical location for the Kodesh Hakodashim: Kodesh Hakodashim, in Hebrew: (Biblical: קֹדֶשׁ הַקֳּדָשִׁים Qṓḏeš HaqQŏḏāšîm), "Holy of Holies",) You are my El Shadi In chapter 2 of Deuteronomy, God the most high ("El 'Aliyon" in the Hebrew version) divided the nations into their inheritance giving Jacob's descendants to the "Lord" (Yahweh in the Hebrew version).

Yeshua always knew God's will because of the indwelling of the Holy Spirit; he remained in the Father by always doing His will. Yeshua's prayer for all believers was that the Father would make them one with both of them; this would be accomplished by God's Spirit flowing through Messiah (the mediator) to dwell within them.Jesus says, "On the Judgment Day the Queen of Sheba will stand up and accuse you, because she traveled all the way from her country to listen to King Solomon's wise teaching." Two accounts in the New Testament describe Jesus as born in Bethlehem. According to the Gospel of Luke,[15] Jesus' parents lived in Nazareth but traveled to Bethlehem for the census of AD 6, and Jesus was born there before the family returned to Nazareth.The Gospel of Matthew account implies that the family already lived in Bethlehem when Jesus was born, and later moved to Nazareth.[19][20] Matthew reports that Herod the Great, told that a 'King of the Jews' has been born in Bethlehem, ordered the killing of all the children aged two and under in the town and surrounding areas. Jesus' earthly father Joseph is warned of this in a dream, and the family escapes this fate by fleeing to Egypt and returning only after Herod has died. But being warned in another dream not to return to Judea, Joseph withdraws the family to Galilee, and goes to live in Nazareth.Early Christians interpreted a verse in the Book of Micah[21] as a prophecy of the birth of the Messiah in Bethlehem.[22] Many modern scholars question whether Jesus was really born in Bethlehem, and suggest that the different Gospel accounts were invented to present the birth of Jesus as fulfillment of prophecy and imply a connection to the lineage of King David.[23][24][25][26] The Gospel of Mark and the Gospel of John do not include a nativity narrative or any hint that Jesus was born in Bethlehem, and refer to him only as being from Nazareth.[27] In a 2005 article in Archaeology magazine, archaeologist Aviram Oshri pointed to the absence of evidence of settlement of the area at the time when Jesus was born, and postulates that Jesus was born in Bethlehem of Galilee.[28] Opposing him, Jerome Murphy-O'Connor argues for the traditional position.[29

John the Baptist, Yahya, the son of Zakariya. Yahya's mother, Elizabeth, was a cousin of Mary, the mother of Jesus, (Luke 1:36) and therefore John and Jesus were cousins by blood. And there was a spiritual cousinhood in their birth and career. Elizabeth was of the daughters of Aaron (Luke 1:5) of a priestly family which went back to Aaron, the brother of Moses and son of Imran. By tradition Mary's mother was called Hannah, and her father was called Imran. Hannah is therefore both a descendant of the priestly house of Imran and the wife of Imran, - 'a woman of Imran' in a double sense."The House of Imran (Arabic: آل عمران) is the 3rd chapter of the Qur'an and contains two hundred verses. Imran is Arabic for the biblical figure Amram who is regarded as being the ancestor of Mary. This chapter is named after the family of Imran (Joachim) which includes; Imran (Arabic: عمران, Joachim), Hanna (Arabic: حنّا, Anne), Maryam (Arabic: مريم, Mary),Haroon(Mary's brother According to Quran)and Jesus (Arabic: عيسى, Jesus). In this chapter the miraculous births of Mary, Yahya ibn Zakariyya and Jesus are mentioned. References ^ Ronald Brownrigg, Canon Brownrigg Who's Who in the New Testament 2001 ISBN 0-415-26036-1 page T-62 ^ Machen Virgin birth^ Doctrina Jacobi, written about 634; similarly in On the Orthodox Faith iv.14: Joachim's father Panther and Eli's father Melchi were brothers, sons of Levi.^ The reference to a temple at Sepphoris seems to contradict the generally held view that at that time no Jewish temple was admitted other than that in Jerusalem: see The Temple at Jerusalem and Its Culture.^ Dom Gaspar LeFebvre, "The Saint Andrew Daily Missal, with Vespers for Sundays and Feasts," Saint Paul, MN: The E. M. Lohmann Co., 1952, p. 1513 ^ "Calendarium Romanum" (Libreria Editrice Vaticana 1969), pp. 98 and 135 Luke 11:31), Nazar as used by Christians, it means "from Nazareth," the town where Jesus Christ was said to have lived. The etymology of Nazareth from as early as Eusebius up until the 20th century has been said to derive from the Hebrew word נצר netser, meaning a "shoot" or "sprout", while the apocryphal Gospel of Phillip derives the name from Nazara meaning "truth".[1]Remember the name John is derived, via Latin and Greek, from the Hebrew name Yochanan (Hebrew: יוחנן) meaning: "Yahweh is gracious". Arab Christians use the name Youhanna for John, coming directly from the Hebrew and Aramaic which was used at the time.The Arabic name Yahya is usually understood to mean "he shall live", spiritually meaning that John will forever be remembered as a great prophet. The names Youhanna and Yahya are, however, likely to be derived from the same base meaning and root

The New Bible Dictionary says this about the "host of heaven":This phrase (tzeva' hashamayim) occurs about 15 times, in most cases implying the object of heathen worship (Dt. 4:19, etc.). The two meanings 'celestial bodies' and 'angelic beings' are inextricably intertwined. The LXX translation, using kosmos, stratia, or dynamis, does not help to resolve this. No doubt to the Heb[rew] mind the distinction was superficial, and the celestial bodies were thought to be closely associated with heavenly beings. . . . The Bible certainly suggests that angels of different ranks have charge of individuals and of nations; no doubt, in the light of modern cosmology this concept, if retained at all (as biblically it must be), ought properly to be extended, as the dual sense of the phrase 'host of heaven' suggests, to the oversight of the elements of the physical universe--planets, stars and nebulae. (p. 495, "Host, Host of Heaven")Regarding the meaning of the related title "Lord of hosts" (Heb. YHVH tzeva'ot), the New Bible Dictionary states:It is thought by some to have arisen as a title of God associated with his lordship over the 'host' of Israel; but its usage, especially in the prophets, clearly implies also a relationship to the 'host of heaven' in its angelic sense; and this could well be the original connotation. (p. 495, "Host, Host of Heaven")The following Scriptures indicate that the "host of heaven" is more than just the stars in the night KING OF JESHURUN."The Lord Jesus Christ is the KI of Jeshurun"(Deut 33:5).

I say Deliverance, for I fear the Lord, and I pray for those who listen, and fear the Lord as well, for he alone is our grace. *Notice in Revelation 15 we sing the song of Moses and the song of the Lamb.

Revelation 15

¹ And I saw another sign in heaven, great and marvellous, seven angels having seven plagues, which are the last, for in them is finished the wrath of God.

² And I saw as it were a sea of glass mingled with fire; and them that come off victorious from the beast, and from his image, and from the number of his name, standing by the sea of glass, having harps of God.

³ And they sing the song of Moses the servant of God, and the song of the Lamb, saying, Great and marvellous are thy works, O Lord God, the Almighty; righteous and true are thy ways, thou King of the ages.

⁴ Who shall not fear, O Lord, and glorify thy name? for thou only art holy; for all the nations shall come and worship before thee; for thy righteous acts have been made manifest.

⁵ And after these things I saw, and the temple of the tabernacle of the testimony in heaven was opened:

⁶ and there came out from the temple the seven angels that had the seven plagues, arrayed with precious stone, pure and bright, and girt about their breasts with golden girdles.

⁷ And one of the four living creatures gave unto the seven angels seven golden bowls full of the wrath of God, who liveth for ever and ever.

⁸ And the temple was filled with smoke from the glory of God, and from his power; and none was able to enter into the temple, till the seven plagues of the seven angels should be finished.

Again I repeat where I began:

Hebrew Shema', "Hear O Israel: The Lord our God, the Lord is One." (Deut. 6:4) The Shema' comes from the hand of Moses about 1400 BC.

EL MELEKH NE'EMAN (Heb. "God, faithful King"), an affirmation of faith pronounced before the recital of the *Shema*

Psalm 25:14 reads, "The Lord confides in those who fear him; he makes his covenant known to them."

There is only about one-quarter of the book of Genesis is the story of God's dealings with Abraham and his ancestors (chapter 1-12). The other chapters deal with Abraham's descendants before the establishment of Israel. It is because this is so, it is imperative that we must recognize that the promise concerning the coming of the Seed of God by the Woman (Gen. 3:15) does not originate with the Jews. It is so much very much older!!!The firstborn son of the cousin/niece wife ascended to the throne of his maternal grandfather, after whom he was named. So Isaac ruled over Abraham's territory by Joktan ruled over the territory of Joktan the Elder, Ketu-rah's father. The two lines continued to intermarry according to a pattern that is traceable, using the Biblical genealogies, to Jesus Christ. Amen and Amen

The Greatest Prophecy And I will put enmity between thee and the woman, and between thy seed and her seed; King David's kingdom will be established forever.And there was a cloud that overshadowed them: and a voice came out of the cloud, saying, This is my beloved Son: hear him. Mark 9:7 ---- God told us to listen to Jesus. Jesus told us and showed us how to love God above all and bless others in His Name. Thank You Jesus! ---- 7. And it happened a cloud overshadowed them and there was a voice from the cloud, "This is My beloved Son, you must habitually listen to Him." 8. Then suddenly, when they looked around, they no longer saw anyone but only Y'shua (Jesus) with them. 9. Then while they were coming down from the mountain He gave orders to them that they should not discuss what they saw, except at the time that the Son of Man would have risen from the dead. 10. And they kept the word to themselves, not discussing what that was until He rose from the dead. (See Luke 9:36)Matthew 6:9 - 6:15 (ASV)

It is likely that Melchizedek was the brother-in-law of Joktan, Abraham's father-in-law. In reality, Melchizedek did have an earthly father, probably Sheba the Elder.:

Worship the Serpent Seed that that ol Dragon Satan and perish eternally: Genesis 3:14-15 14 So the LORD God said to the serpent:" Because you have done this,You are cursed more than all cattle,And more than every beast of the field;On your belly you shall go,And you shall eat dust All the days of your life.Discern for yourselves. Genesis 3:15, "And I will put enmity between thee and the woman, and between thy seed and her seed; it shall bruise thy head, and thou shalt bruise his heel."Satan, his demons, and his offspring have been running the planet's governments and kingdoms since the dawn of time (Matthew 4:8-9). They look human and act human, but unfortunately they deceive humans and eat the flesh of humans (Micah 3:3).Jesus came in the flesh to free us from our sin, as well as the world system that is owned and operated by the Enemy (Ephesians 6:12). Choose to humble yourself before Him today, before Judgment and Wrath is poured out, for then it will be too late.7

For the mystery of lawlessness doth already work: only there is one that restraineth now, until he be taken out of the way. 8And then shall be revealed the lawless one, whom the Lord Jesus shall slay with the breath of his mouth, and bring to nought by the manifestation of his coming: 9even he , whose coming is according to the working of Satan with all power and signs and lying wonders, 10and with all deceit of unrighteousness for them that perish; because they received not the love of the truth, that they might be saved. 11And for this cause God sendeth them a working of error, that they should believe a lie: 12that they all might be judged who believed not the truth, but had pleasure in unrighteousness.Stand Firm 13But we are bound to give thanks to God always for you, brethren beloved of the Lord, for that God chose you from the beginning unto salvation in sanctification of the Spirit and belief of the truth: 14whereunto he called you through our gospel, to the obtaining of the glory of our Lord Jesus Christ. 15So then, brethren, stand fast, and hold the traditions which ye were taught, whether by word, or by epistle of ours.16Now our Lord Jesus Christ himself, and God our Father who loved us and gave us eternal comfort and good hope through grace, 17comfort your hearts and establish them in every good work and word.

And there was a cloud that overshadowed them: and a voice came out of the cloud, saying, This is my beloved Son: hear him. Mark 9:7 ---- God told us to listen to Jesus. Jesus told us and showed us how to love God above all and bless others in His Name. Thank You Jesus! ---- 7. And it happened a cloud overshadowed them and there was a voice from the cloud, "This is My beloved Son, you must habitually listen to Him." 8. Then suddenly, when they looked around, they no longer saw anyone but only Y'shua (Jesus) with them. 9. Then while they were coming down from the mountain He gave orders to them that they should not discuss what they saw, except at the time that the Son of Man would have risen from the dead. 10. And they kept the word to themselves, not discussing what that was until He rose from the dead. (See Luke 9:36)Matthew 6:9 -6:15 (ASV)Worship the Serpent Seed that that ol Dragon Satan and perish eternally: Genesis 3:14-15 14 So the LORD God said to the serpent:" Because you have done this,You are cursed more than all cattle,And more than every beast of the field;On your belly you shall go,And you shall eat dust All the days of your life.

The Greatest Prophecy And I will put enmity between thee and the woman, and between thy seed and her seed; King David's kingdom will be established forever.A hint of it can be seen in this oracle issued in 800 B.C by Isaiah (Is.7, esp 7:10-15), and especially in the symbolic name given to the child in this prophecy: "Immanuel" ('God WITH us'). Both seem to point to a decisive intervention by God Himself in Israel's affairs. Isaiah shows us a Son of David that seems to touch divinity itself.]The Davidic Dynasty - King David, his Royal Lineage and relation to the Messiah, Jesus That relationship can be seen even more clearly a few passages later:"For there is a child born for us, a son given to us and dominion is laid on his shoulders; and this is the name they give him: WonderCounsellor, Mighty-God, Eternal-Father, Princeof-Peace. Wide is his dominion in a peace that has no end, for the throne of David and for his royal power, which he establishes and makes secure in justice and integrity...forever." (Is. 9:5-7).Because all of this seemed to be concentrated in the House of Judah, the Jewish leaders came to the conclusion that since the House of David was a lineage within their own tribe, it made them sole heirs to all the promises of scripture with respect to Israel.Ezekiel bluntly castigated the Judeans for thinking that the disappearance of the ten lost tribes of Israel was permanent, and for being so arrogant to declare that they, the Jews were now singular heirs to the lineage of Moses. Ezekiel warned the Jews that those lost tribes were going to be restored by God and led back to Jerusalem in great glory."Son of man, your brothers, your kinsmen, the whole House of Israel, these are told by the citizens of Jerusalem, "you have been sent away from God; it is to us that the land was given as our domain". Say therefore, "The Lord God says this: Yes, I have sent them far away among the nations and I have dispersed them to foreign countries; and for a while I have been a sanctuary for them in the country to which they have gone", Then say, "The Lord God says this: I will gather you together from the peoples, I will bring you all back from the countries where you have been scattered and I will give you the land of Israel. They will come and purge it of all the horrors and filthy practices. I will give them a single heart and I will put a new spirit in them; I will remove the heart of stone from their bodies and give them a heart of flesh instead, so that they will kieep my laws and respect my observances and put them into practice. Then they shall be my people and I will be their God." (Ez. 11:14-21).

"I mean to raise up one shepherd, my servant David, and to Because Jewish leaders rejected Jesus as the Messiah promised by God, the nation of Israel has remained divided into two spiritual houses, the House of David, those who accept Jesus as the Davidic king forecast by scripture, on one side, and the House of Judah on the other. The Apostle Paul has prophesied that this division will not be reconciled until the very last day when Jewish recognition of Jesus will instantly bring the birth of the new creation.The Man of Sin 1Now we beseech you, brethren, touching the coming of our Lord Jesus Christ, and our gathering together unto him; 2to the end that ye be not quickly shaken from your mind, nor yet be troubled, either by spirit, or by word, or by epistle as from us, as that the day of the Lord is just at hand; 3let no man beguile you in any wise: for it will not be, except the falling away come first, and the man of sin be revealed, the son of perdition, 4he that opposeth and exalteth himself against all that is called God or that is worshipped; so that he sitteth in the temple of God, setting himself forth as God. 5Remember ye not, that, when I was yet with you, I told you these things? 6And now ye know that which restraineth, to the end that he may be revealed in his own season. 7For the mystery of lawlessness doth already work: only there is one that restraineth now, until he be taken out of the way. 8And then shall be revealed the lawless one, whom the Lord Jesus shall slay with the breath of his mouth, and bring to nought by the manifestation of his coming; 9even he , whose coming is according to the working of Satan with all power and signs and lying wonders, 10and with all deceit of unrighteousness for them that perish; because they received not the love of the truth, that they might be saved. 11And for this cause God sendeth them a working of error, that they should believe a lie: 12that they all might be judged who believed not the truth, but had pleasure in unrighteousness.Stand Firm 13But we are bound to give thanks to God always for you, brethren beloved of the Lord, for that God chose you from the beginning unto salvation in sanctification of the Spirit and belief of the truth: 14whereunto he called you through our gospel, to the obtaining of the glory of our Lord Jesus Christ. 15So then, brethren, stand fast, and hold the traditions which ye were taught, whether by word, or by epistle of ours.16Now our Lord Jesus Christ himself, and God our Father who loved us and gave us eternal comfort and good hope through grace, 17comfort your hearts and establish them in every good work and word. Genesis 3:15 Hallowed be thy name The God of Jeshurun*, who rides the heavens in his power,There is none like the God of Jeshurun, Riding the heavens in thy help, ... extol him who rides on the clouds--his name is the LORD-- and rejoice before him.The Greatest Prophecy And I will put enmity between thee and the woman, and between thy seed and her seed; King David's kingdom will be established forever.And there was a cloud that overshadowed them: and a voice came out of the cloud, saying, This is my beloved Son: hear him.

The ruler-priest lines of the two first-born sons intermarried, thus preserving the bloodline of those to whom God made the promise that a woman of their people would bring forth the Seed who would crush the serpent's head and restore Paradise. The firstborn son of the cousin/niece wife ascended to the throne of his maternal grandfather, after whom he was named. So Isaac ruled over Abraham's territory by Joktan ruled over the territory of Joktan the Elder, Ketu-rah's father. The two lines continued to intermarry according to a pattern that is traceable, using the Biblical genealogies, to Jesus Christ. The heirs of God's promise that the Son of God would come through their lines.(Jesus)This strongly suggests that the ruling lines were aware and believed the promise made in Eden (Gen. 3:15) concerning the Woman's Seed who would crush the serpent's head, deliver from death and receive the Father's Kingdom. This line is traced through Jesse and David, but because of the very exclusive intermarriage pattern of the Kushite clans, it is also traced through Sheba and Joktan. The Messiah Jesus fulfilled the eternal promise to the line of Moses as the King of Jeshurun. Jesus being a descendant of David verifies David's descent from Moses.

The word Jerusalem was read as 'Hiero-Solyma' or 'holy place of the Solymi'.

They will **turn** their ears **away from the truth** and turnaside to myths.

In the case of the Law Covenant, this was Moses:

… "Write down for yourself these words, because it is in accordance with these words that I do conclude a covenant with you and Israel." (Exodus 34:27)

To Orthodox **Jews**, **Moses** is called Moshe Rabbenu, `Eved HaShem, Avi haNeviim zya"a. He is defined "Our Leader Moshe", "Servant of God", and "Father of all the Prophets".

Jeremiah 23:7 "So then, the days are coming - it is HaShem Who speaks - when people will no longer say, 'As HaShem lives, Who brought the sons of Israel (12 tribes) out of the land of Egypt', but, 'As HaShem lives, Who led back and brought home the descendants of the House of Israel out of the land of the North, and from all the countries to which He had dispersed them, to live on their own soil ."

In history, four of the most famous divine bloodlines are: Abraham, Moses, David, Jesus

On the night of my night journey I passed by Moses b. 'Imran

"For lo! That day is at hand, burning like an oven. All the arrogant and all the doers of evil shall be straw, and the day that is coming – said HaShem of Hosts – shall burn them to ashes and leave them neither stock nor boughs. But for you who revere My Name the son of righteousness shall rise to bring healing. You shall go forth and stamp like stall fed calves, and you shall trample the wicked to a pulp, for they shall be dust beneath your feet on the day that I am preparing. Be mindful of the Torah of Moshe whom I charged at Horeb with laws and rules for all of Israel.

To Orthodox **Jews**, **Moses** is called Moshe Rabbenu, `Eved HaShem, Avi haNeviim zya"a. He is defined "Our Leader Moshe", "Servant of God", and "Father of all the Prophets".

Jeremiah 23:7 "So then, the days are coming - it is HaShem Who speaks - when people will no longer say, 'As HaShem lives, Who brought the sons of Israel (12 tribes) out of the land of Egypt', but, 'As HaShem lives, Who led back and brought home the descendants of the House of Israel out of the land of the North, and from all the countries to which He had dispersed them, to live on their own soil ."

20And it shall come to pass in that day, that the remnant of Israel, and they that are escaped of the house of Jacob, shall no more again lean upon him that smote them, but shall lean upon Jehovah, the Holy One of Israel, in truth.

21A remnant shall return, even the remnant of Jacob, unto the mighty God.

22For though thy people, Israel, be as the sand of the sea, only a remnant of them shall return: a destruction is determined, overflowing with righteousness.

Now the children of Isaac, Jacob, Levi and Joseph who includes Manassa and Ephraim and Moses are all Israelite's. The Israelite's must protect their patrilineal lines from these current day deceptions. We must follow Law one of an Israelite. Exodus 15 & Revelation 15

A true Israelite must be identified based on the biblical law I Chronicle 9:1 "All Israel were reckoned by genealogies." (on the father's side only)

The Bloodlines of Jacob must be Patrilieal for all sons we must require the First Law of an Israelite.

Again the **Israelites** (or children of Israel) were the "chosen people" of the god Yahweh.

The **Israelites** practiced **patrilineal** descent they had to prove that their "father's house and **descent were Israelite.**"

God Promises to Save the Israelites (Ex 5: 22-23, 6: 1-13)

In the Bible Moses spoke to God as the intermediary for the Israelites telling God that the king of Egypt was treating wrongly the Israelites and they felt like God was doing nothing to help. God let Moses know that he would force the king to set them free. God had reaffirmed His promise of the land of Canaan to Abraham, Isaac, Jacob and that He will save their descendants, the Israelites.

Moses, with God's power, saved the Israelites from slavery in Egypt, from Pharaoh's army at the Red Sea, and from the Amalekites in the wilderness south of Israel.

"Ye are my witnesses, saith the Lord, and my servant whom I have chosen; that ye may know and believe me, and understand that I am he: before me there was no God formed, neither shall there be after me." (Isaiah 43:10)

According to the Book of Genesis, the Midianites were descended from Midian, who was the son of the Hebrew patriarch Abraham by the latter's second wife, Keturah. Jethro, priest-leader of the Midianite sub-tribe known as the Kenites, and his daughter Zipporah (a wife of Moses), influenced early Hebrew thought: it was Yahweh, the lord of the Midianites, who was revealed to Moses as the God of the Hebrews.Some great catastrophe in the area of Arim/Yarim (Aram) in ancient Saba forced the tribes of Azd to go scattering over the peninsula, some entering Africa. Hence the phrases "divided as the Sabaeans" and "wandering Aramaeans". Among these tribes were the Canaani and the Israelites under their leaders Muzaikiya of Marib (the Meriba of Exodus), the prophetess Zarifa (Ziphorah),Jafna (Jephunneh) and Caleb. ."Num. 10:29-32 Northern Hedjaz and the land of Midian. Zipporah who was the half sister or cousin bride of Moses is mentioned in Exodus 2:15-16 and in Exodus 18:1-6. Zipporah was the daughter of "the priest of Midian"This three-person family was the head of the nation: two men and a woman - a ruler, to his holy brother and his wife, who was a prophet. According to the Bible the children of Israel from slavery in Egypt led to the family, which consisted of three people: the Director, in his holy brother and his sister, who was a prophet .These Israeli leaders were children of Amram's children. Al-Masudin cited by the leaders of the tribe, who were saved by Mariban, Amir had children. Moses was a holy brother of Aaron, the brother of a sacred tribal chief was Amran. Moses' sister was Miriam, his wife was Sipora; Mariban prophet was Zeripha. Al-Masudin report of these three persons and their doings to remind a lot of astonishingly similar report on biblical Moses, Aaron and Miriam and the children of Israel. His report is one of the few, whose origin is not from the Bible or the traditions of the Jews. All current place names in the Sinai and the Negev, that link Israeli scientists are set by David Ben Gurion's request. The Egyptian language provides an etymology.4 The name Moses is related to common Egyptian names like Amenmose, Ramose and Thutmose,* which are formed of a god's name followed by mose.5 These compound names mean something like "Amen is born" or "Born of Amen" or

"The offspring of Ra" or "The child of Thoth." When the name Mose appears by itself, as it occasionally does in Egyptian, it simply means "the Child" or "the Offspring."6 But in Egyptian, Mose most frequently appears along with the name of a god as part of a compound name.

The Egyptian root in 'ms' meaning to be born. The linguistic root of the name Moses is shows itself in the Egyptian word Mos which means "child." But this word also had a much broader legal meaning— "the rightful son and heir."This account is excerpted from the Hellenistic Jewish historian Artapanus of Alexandria (2nd century BCE), as reproduced by Eusebius of Caesarea."Jealousy of Moses' excellent qualities induced Chenephres to send him with unskilled troops on a military expedition to Ethiopia, where he won great victories. After having built the city of Hermopolis, he taught the people the value of the ibis as a protection against the serpents, making the bird the sacred guardian spirit of the city; then he introduced circumcision. After his return to Memphis, Moses taught the people the value of oxen for agriculture, and the consecration of the same by Moses gave rise to the cult of Apis. Finally, after having escaped another plot by killing the assailant sent by the king, Moses fled to Arabia, where he married the daughter of Raguel, the ruler of the district. Chenephres in the meantime died from elephantiasis — a disease with which he was the first to be afflicted — because he had ordered that the Jews should wear garments that would distinguish them from the Egyptians and thereby expose them to maltreatment. The sufferings of Israel then caused God to appear to Moses in a flame bursting forth from the earth, and to tell him to march against Egypt for the rescue of his people. Accordingly he went to Egypt to deliberate with his brother Aaron about the plan of warfare, but was put into prison. At night, however, the doors of the prison opened of their own accord, while the guards died or fell asleep. Going to the royal palace and finding the doors open there and the guards sunk in sleep, he went straight to the king, and when scoffingly asked by the latter for the name of the God who sent him, he whispered the Ineffable Name into his ear, whereupon the king became speechless and as one dead. Then Moses wrote the name upon a tablet and sealed it up, and a priest who made sport of it died in convulsions. After this Moses performed all the wonders, striking land and people with plagues until the king let the Jews go. In remembrance of the rod with which Moses performed his miracles every Isis temple in Egypt has preserved a rod — Isis symbolizing the earth which Moses struck with his rod... He was eighty-nine years old when he delivered the Jews; tall and ruddy, with long white hair, and dignified. According to Biblical chronology, Moses fled Egypt 40 years after his birth Exodus 2:15The Egyptian root in 'ms' meaning to be born. The linguistic root of the name Moses is shows itself in the Egyptian word Mos which means "child." But this word also had a much broader legal meaning—"the rightful son and heir."Testament of Amram:'Who are you, that you are thus empowered over me?' They answered, 'We have been empowered and rule over all mankind.' They said to me, 'Which of us do you choose to rule you?' Sadly it is like a never ending battle with many chapters, on-going. Seed of Moses: Crown Prince Thutmose/Tutmosis' The king's son the sem-priest Djhutmose;eldest son of pharaoh Amenhotep III and Queen Tiye, as the successor to the Egyptian throne I am the servant of this noble god, his miller; Incense for the Ennead of the western necropolis. A religious reformation was occurring, that reached its pinnacle under the reign of Akhenaton, Thutmose's brother.Israelites were to be ruled by a Priest or "Levitical King ". Crown Prince Tuthmose, the eldest son of pharaoh Amenhotep III, who mysteriously disappears from all records. Could he have been the factual origin of the Biblical character Moses? The name of this prince - Thutmose - is very similar to Moses and The Key for its heritage and our understanding of the True Moses of the Bible, "The Moses that was married to Zipporrah. "Zipporah (zĭp`ərə), in the Bible, daughter of Jethro and wife of Moses. Yahya is usually understood to mean "he shall live", spiritually meaning that John will forever be remembered as a great prophet.Yahya (John the Baptist) was the son of Prophet Zakariyya The duties at the temple in Jerusalem alternated between each of the family lines that had descended from those appointed by king David (1st Chronicles 24:1–19).[2] Luke states that during the week when it was the duty of Zechariah's family line to serve at "the temple of the Lord", the lot for performing the incense offering had fallen to Zechariah (Luke 1:8–11).(Luke 1:8–11).:"Now we begin the story of Jesus . As a prelude we have the birth of Mary and the parallel story of John the Baptist, Yahya, the son of Zakariya. Yahya's mother, Elizabeth, was a cousin of Mary, the mother of Jesus, (Luke 1:36) and therefore John and Jesus were cousins by blood. And there was a spiritual cousinhood in their birth and career. Elizabeth was of the daughters of Aaron (Luke 1:5) of a priestly family which went back to Aaron, the brother of Moses and son of Imran. John the Baptist is described in the Gospel of Luke as a relative of Jesus[13] The Egyptian root in 'ms' meaning to be born. The linguistic root of the name Moses is shows itself in the Egyptian word Mos which means "child." But this word also had a much broader legal meaning—"the rightful son and heir. Nachash is the Hebrew word for SERPENT from which nashak the word for usury is derived. There was no specific Hebrew word for money as silver was considered money. The Law of Moses strictly prohibited usury"Until Shiloh Come" The passage in Jacob's prophecy I translate thus, ... for Moses, who was "king in Jeshurun," was of the tribe of Levi I thank Moses who was married to Zipporah (KETURAH (meaning incense, perfume), the second legal wife of Abraham, married after the death of Sarah ... Likewise Zipporah (Exodus 4:24-26) .Moses also had his brother and sister, the Moses of the Bible for everything I understand at this critical time. One day we will sing the Song of Moses no doubt!!!!!!! Grandfather of the Moses of the Bible: the king's son the sem-priest Djhutmose;eldest son of pharaoh Amenhotep III and Queen Tiye, as the successor to the Egyptian throne I am the servant of this noble god, his miller; Incense for the Ennead of the western necropolis./ImranThe 10.5 centimetres (4 in) schist recumbent mummiform bier has Thutmose prone with the Ba, Soul Bird upon his lower breast. The sides of the small statuette contain the following hieroglyphs, recording him as 'S-M Thoth-MS-S ', "True of Voice" '–SM (priest?) Tutmosis, "True of Voice"-("deserving", worthy, or "venerable").[7] "But this is the covenant which I will make with the house of Israel after those days," declares the Lord. "I will put My Law within them, and on their heart I will write it; and I will be their God, and they shall be My people. And they shall not teach again, each man his neighbor and each man his brother, saying 'know the Lord,' for they shall all know Me, from the least of them to the greatest of them," declares the Lord, "for I will forgive their iniquity, and their sin I will remember no more.Messiah Text (4Q285)This six-line fragment, commonly referred to as the "Pierced Messiah" text, is written in a Herodian script of the first half of the 1st Century and refers to a Messiah from the Branch of David, to a judgement The War of the Messiah Jesus:"Naz Seir". This hawk symbol represents the star Sirius in Canis Major. In Egyptian, "Naz" means "Sent", while "Seir" means "Prince" or "Chief." Therefore, the title "Naz Seir" can mean "Sent Prince." Since "Naz" and "Zar" both mean "Prince" in Hebrew. Hear Jesus and what he says about himself and the Biblical Moses he was an decendent himself of,The War of the Messiah is a series of Dead Sea scroll fragments describing the conclusion of a battle led by the Leader of the Congregation. The fragments that make up this document include 4Q285, also known as The Pierced Messiah Text, and 11Q14 with which it was found to coincide. It is possible that it also represents the conclusion of the War Scroll.[1] [edit]The Pierced Messiah Text (4Q285)This six-line fragment, commonly referred to as the "Pierced Messiah" text, is written in a Herodian script of the first half of the 1st Century and refers to a Messiah from the Branch of David, to a judgement The War of the Messiah (4Q285)(4Q285) The Roman Ruler Herod Antipas was the ruler of Galilee. He had an adulterous relations with Herodias, the wife of his brother Herod Philip. John the Baptist reproached him for this grave sin. Herod Antipas got annoyed and imprisoned him till his execution.The Sons of Light, consising of the sons of Levi, the sons of Judah, and the sons Joseph Understanding who you are in the End Times is important. Understanding how and why we are who we are is also important.

Moses the King of Jeshrun is the Shiloh mentioned by Jacob. Moses himself had the scepter when the people gathered to him from Egypt as a Levi.

"Moses commanded us a law, the inheritance of the congregation of Jacob. And he was king in Jeshurun, when the heads of the people and the tribes of Israel were gathered together."

JoAnn McFatter-Manifested Sons of God tells who we are Today and what we must do is be who we are. Who are you? Who am I? In the eyes of the Lord, does it matter? Why would it matter if I am not rich, or I am not pretty or hansom, is that what the Lord sees? We are in this world, but we are not Of this world. Please listen to JoAnn, it just may change your life on how you see yourself, and what your role may be in these End Times: Like No OTHER in that the Lord is VERY Subtle: thin, tenuous, or rarefied, as a fluid or an odor.requiring mental acuteness, penetration, or discernment: a subtle philosophy.characterized by mental acuteness or penetration: a subtle understanding. God's purpose and will (Matt. 26:39; John 5:30; 14:10, 24).Yeshua's prayer to the Father before his crucifixion, recorded in John 17, confirms this understanding of "one":JOHN 17:11 "Now I am no longer in the world, but these are in the world, and I come to You. Holy Father, keep through Your name those whom You have given Me, that they may be one as We are." And they worshiped the dragon which gave power unto the beast: and they worshiped the beast, saying, Who is like unto the beast? who is able to make war with him? Jesus: And he said unto them, I beheld Satan fallen as lightning from heaven. 19 Behold, I have given you authority to tread upon serpents and scorpions, and over all the power of the enemy: and nothing shall in any wise hurt you.Daniel 9:24-27 Jesus says, "On the Judgment Day the Queen of Sheba will stand up and accuse you, because she traveled all the way from her country to listen to King Solomon's wise teaching." Two accounts in the New Testament describe Jesus as born in Bethlehem. According to the Gospel of Luke,[15] Jesus' parents lived in Nazareth but traveled to Bethlehem for the census of AD 6, and Jesus was born there before the family returned to Nazareth.The Gospel of Matthew account implies that the family already lived in Bethlehem when Jesus was born, and later moved to Nazareth.[19][20] Matthew reports that Herod the Great, told that a 'King of the Jews' has been born in Bethlehem, ordered the killing of all the children aged two and under in the town and surrounding areas. Jesus' earthly father Joseph is warned of this in a dream, and the family escapes this fate by fleeing to Egypt and returning only after Herod has died. But being warned in another dream not to return to Judea, Joseph withdraws the family to Galilee, and goes to live in Nazareth.Early Christians interpreted a verse in the Book of Micah[21] as a prophecy of the birth of the Messiah in Bethlehem.[22] Mhany modern scholars question whether Jesus was really born in Bethlehem, and suggest that the different Gospel accounts were invented to present the birth of Jesus as fulfillment of prophecy and imply a connection to the lineage of King David.[23][24][25][26] The Gospel of Mark and the Gospel of John do not include a nativity narrative or any hint that Jraesus was born in Bethlehem, and refer to him only as being from Nazareth.[27]

As the Lord had provided for his chosen people it was the agricultural land's, and the all important patrilineal order rightfully assumed the responsibility for maintaining this critical ownership and thus validating the inheritance rights as well as tenure it was truly the source of actual wealth for the Israelite tribes. As the law should still be to this day it was the rights of administrative authority as well as

Territorial rights as well as collective rights assigned to the tribes allowed the members to own and use **tribal lands bequeathed to them in perpetuity.** There were actual Guaratees of tenure in the custom of the jubilee year, it was at this time in which any lands that were temporarily alienated through by means of theft, lease pawn or deception was required to be returned to the original owners (Leviticus 25).

Law one of an Israeilite: **among ancient Israelites, the inheritance is patrilineal.** It comes from the father, who bequeaths only to his male descendants (daughters don't inherit). The eldest son received twice as much as the other sons. The father gives his name to his children; for example: the sons of Israel are called Israelites, because the land belonged to the father, and every one of his twelve sons gave his name to his descendants.

The common Biblical phrase used to refer to the territories actually settled by the Israelites is "from Dan to Beersheba" (or its variant "from Beersheba to Dan"), which occurs many times in the Bible. It is found in the Biblical verses Judges 20:1, 1 Samuel 3:20, 2 Samuel 3:10, 2 Samuel 17:11, 2 Samuel 24:2, 2 Samuel 24:15, 1 Kings 4:25, 1 Chronicles 21:2, and 2 Chronicles 30:5.

[23] And the land shall not be sold in perpetuity; for the land is mine: for ye are strangers and sojourners with me.

[24] And in all the land of your possession ye shall grant a redemption for the land.

Leviticus 25:23-24

Isaiah 41:14

American Standard Version (ASV)

[14] Fear not, thou worm Jacob, and ye men of Israel; I will help thee, saith Jehovah, and thy Redeemer is the Holy One of Israel.

Therefore, behold, the days come, saith the LORD, that they shall no more say, The LORD liveth, which brought up the children of Israel out of the land of Egypt; But, The LORD liveth, which brought up and which led the seed of the house of Israel out of the north country, and from all countries whither I had driven them; and they shall dwell in their own land.

Jeremiah 23:7,8

And God said moreover unto Moses,

Thus shalt thou say unto the children of Israel,

the LORD God of your fathers,

the God of Abraham, the God of Isaac, and the God of Jacob,

hath sent me unto you:

this is my name for ever,
and this is my memorial unto all generations.
Exodus 3:15

"And it shall come to pass in that day, that the Lord shall set his hand again
the second time to recover the remnant of his people, which shall be left,
from Assyria, and from Egypt, and from Pathros, and from Cush,
and from Elam, and from Shinar, and from Hamath, and from
the islands of the sea. And he shall set up an ensign for the nations,
and shall assemble the outcasts of Israel, and gather together
the dispersed of Judah from the four corners of the earth."
Isaiah 11:11,12

"Therefore, behold, the days come, saith the LORD, that it shall no more be said,
The LORD liveth, that brought up the children of Israel out of the land of Egypt;
But, The LORD liveth, that brought up the children of Israel from the land of the north,
and from all the lands whither he had driven them:
and <u>I will bring them again into their land that I gave unto their fathers.</u>"
Jeremiah 16:14,15

Jacob and Esau were the sons of Isaac and Rebekah and the first twins mentioned in the Bible. Even before they were born, they were struggling together in the womb of their mother. Their prenatal striving foresohadowed later conflict (Genesis 25:21-26).

Both Old and New Testaments use the story of Jacob and Esau to illustrate God's calling and election. God chose the younger Jacob to carry on the Abrahamic Covenant

<u>Yet in Israel over 125,000 acres of land with more than 40 settlements have been purchased under the auspices of the Rothschild's *Palestine Jewish Colonization Association* (PICA).</u>

While not regarded as a dynasty, the **High Priests of Amun** at Thebes were nevertheless **of** such power and influence that they were effectively the rulers **of** Upper Egypt. The **High Priest of Amun** or First Prophet **of Amun** (hem netjer en tepy) was the highest ranking **priest** in the priesthood of the Ancient Kemetian god **Amun. Amun** the God. <u>**Amenmesse**</u> (**Moses**). **Amun** the Ram Title: The Hidden One King of Gods

Again from: From the book:

<u>THE HITTITES: THEIR INSCRIPTIONS AND THEIR HISTORY.</u>

<u>VOLUME I. BY JOHN CAMPBELL, M.A., LL.D.</u>

<u>Professor in the Presbyterian College^ Montreal.</u>

TORONTO : WILLIAMSON & CO 1890.

In Egypt, the Kenites adopted the Hebrew faith which the great Aahpeti received the knowledge of from his minister, Joseph. It is to them, therefore, and not to any Israelitish writer, that we owe the remarkable statement that Jabez called upon the God of Israel, and the prayer that accompanies it.This faith they still possessed when dwelling in Arabia Petraea, after their expulsion by the kings who knew not Joseph, for Jethro, the priest of Midian, was recognized by Moses as a worshipper of the true God- When Israel traversed the Sinaitic peninsula, a body of Kenites, under the leadership of Hobab, the son of Jethro or Raguel, and the brother-in-law of Moses, accompanied them as guides.^" They entered the land of promise and received an inheritance in the south of Judah, facing the Arabian land of their adoption.

"We are justified, therefore, in regarding the original copy of the summary of universal history contained in First Chronicles as the gift of Hobab, or his father Jethro, to Moses, who, being learned in all the wisdom of the Egyptians, would be able to appreciate it. From it, probably, the Hebrew lawgiver extracted that part of the 86th chapter of Genesis which contains the genealogies of the Horites, and the list of kings who ruled in Edom"

"From Banu Sulaim ibn Mansoor were descended Ra'l, Zakwan, 'Asiyyah ibn Khuyfaf ibn Imri' Al-Qais ibn Buhthah ibn Sulaim and Za'b ibn Malik ibn Khufaf ibn Imri' Al- Qais ibn Buhthah ibn Sulaim …" The name Bodhi here appears connected with Pothi'phar, while Khufaf sounds similar to Epaphus. Mansoor otherwise Manasse'ir is undoubtedly Manasseh son of Joseph.

El Nas and Ghatafan are mentioned as the Bible as the families of the Judaeans, Neziah and Hatipha in the Biblical book of Ezra 2:54 and Nehemiah 7:56. El Yas, brother of El Nas, was y Elias which is sometimes translated Elijah in the Bible. "Then Elijah said to them, Seize the prophets of Baal; do not let one of them escape." So they seized them; and Elijah brought them down to the brook Kishon, and slew them there." This is the brook from which the **"Ghusan Khasafa, brother of Ghatafan is apparently Hasupha or Chasupha of Ezra 2:43. They are classified as Levites or priests.**

The brother of Khasafa in Arabian tradition is Ghatafan who gave birth to the tribes of Assiyeh (whom Tabari 9th c. calls "the Israelite woman") and Rahil/Rukhayla (Rachel) and Ghatafan or Ghutayf (Hatepha). **Their South Arabian Azd ancestors were said to have fought against the people already in control of Misrah i.e. "the Amalekites" near Mecca under Moses (Muzaikiya) and Aaron.**

The Rechabites that were descended from Hobab the Kenite (See Khufaf) who had come from the family of Hammath who is elsewhere called Hammon. (1 Chron. 6:76). Hobab was a member of the sub-division of Midianites known as the Kenites. House of Israel, in the days of the Kings, were Kenites The Kenites Kenan (Cainan), the son of Enos (and thus the grandson of Seth and the great-grandson of Adam), this appears in the newer Strong's Concordance

The ancestor of the Soleym known as Khasafa has link to the name of Asaf (Joseph) and his father Kab or Qabus. Note that Yaqub -El is cited as a name on one of the Hyksos scarabs as is Apachnas or Apophis I and II. These names as well may be the precursors to Cephen and Epaphus.All this makes it very likely that this tribal history that was brought up to Syria by the Soleym bin Mansur (Manasseh) or

Suwaleim tribes whom are called Solymi by the Romans like Tacitus who are also equated with "Eastern Ethiopians" by Choerilus other writers and "spoke a Phoenician like" dialect. **Khufaf or Apophis the Hyksos (Epaphus whom tradition makes brother of Cepheus "King of Ethiopia")**

Banu Rakabiyyeh or Rikab (See Rechab the Kenite 1Chronicles 2:55) The Rechabites were descended from Hobab the Kenite (See Khufaf) who had come from the family of Hammath who is elsewhere called Hammon. (1 Chron. 6:76). Historically the Rulers had married the daughters of priests who served them. As we saw Joseph, Jacob's first-born son by Rachel had married Asenath who was the daughter of a priest of the Egyptian shrine at Heliopolis. Our Law giver Moses had done the very same with Zipporah. Zipporah was Moses' wife and a daughter of Jethro, Priest of Midian. **Moses met her at a well and as the Bible says** where she and the other women near the well were being harassed. **Zipporah was Moses half sister or cousin bride in Horite Priest fashion.**

The children of Amram's children: And the Mariban prophet was Zeripha (Zipporah) These Israeli leaders were the children of Amram's children who were saved by Mariban.Moses addresses God using the title Adon/Aten (Exodus 4:10,13; 5:22; 34:9; Numbers 14:17; Deuteronomy 3:23; 7:26; 10:17); Moses, himself, is addressed both by Aaron (Ex.32:22; Num.12:11) and by Joshua (Numbers 11:28) using the title Adon/Aten; and Joshua also addresses God using the title Adon/Aten (Joshua 5:14 b; 7:7).

Short biography and facts about **Moses, Ramses** and Seti! The name of this **prince - Thutmose** - is very similar to **Moses**; Who was Moses? What elements of this story relate to Egyptian facts and the myths from Ancient Egyptian religion?

Moses was portrayed as being brought up in the royal family but then he is cast out

There was a Prince Tuthmose who was the eldest son of pharaoh Amenhotep III, and who mysteriously disappears from all records. There are very many facts pointing to that he have been the factual origin of the Biblical Moses? The name of this prince - Thutmose - is very similar to Moses

Since Crown Prince Tuthmose and Kiya as well as 3 chidren all disapered, are there any possible traces of any of this very important history? Let's futher consider one piece of evidence of Kiyas children we do have and who she was: _Kiya Ta-sherit_

Mery-khiba or Mery-Amon (Kiya) - (Miriam)-_Kiya Ta-sherit was the_ daughter of Mery-khiba or Mery-Amon (Kiya)

According to the Book of Jubilees (9:5,6), the inheritance of the Earth to be bequeathed to the descendants of Aram included all of the land between the Tigris and Euphrates rivers "to the north of the Chaldees to the border of the mountains of Asshur and the land of 'Arara."[21

EGYPT TO MOSES-KIYA LINE TO DAVID – Ahmose-Sipairi, Thutmose I & Mutnefert, Thutmose II & Iset, Tutmose III & Meryetre, Amenhotep II & Tyo, Tuthmosis IV & Mutemwiy, Amenhotep III & Gilukhipa, Kiya (wife of Mose), Kiya-Tasharenti & Aram/Ram, Amminadab & Tora/Thehora, Naason/Nahshon & Simar, Salmon & Rahab (repentant prostitute), Boaz & Ruth (of Moab), Obed, Jesse/Abinadah Nahash & Habliar, King David.

The hero is Amr, the son of Amir, the son of Thalabah (Thutmose, the son of Amenhotep III, the son of Thutmoses IV), surnamed Mozaikiya.

Banu Rakabiyyeh or Rikab (See Rechab the Kenite 1Chronicles 2:55)

The Rechabites were descended from Hobab the Kenite (See Khufaf) who had come from the family of Hammath who is elsewhere called Hammon. (1 Chron. 6:76). **"Moses, a son of the tribe of Levi, educated in Egypt and initiated at Heliopolis, became a High Priest of the Brotherhood under the reign of Pharaoh Amenhotep.** He was elected by the Hebrews as their chief and he adapted to the ideas of his people the science and philosophy which he had obtained in the Egyptian mysteries; proofs of this are to be found in the symbols, in the Initiations, and in his precepts and commandments....The dogma of an 'only god' which he taught was the Egyptian Brotherhood interpretation and teaching of the Pharaoh who established the first monotheistic religion known to man." - Egyptian High Priest Manetho (3rd Century BC)

Historically the Rulers had married the daughters of priests who served them. As we saw Joseph, Jacob's first-born son by Rachel had married Asenath who was the daughter of a priest of the Egyptian shrine at Heliopolis. Our Law giver Moses had done the very same with Zipporah. Zipporah was Moses' wife and a daughter of Jethro, Priest of Midian. **Moses met** her **at a well and as the Bible says** where she and the other women near the well were being harassed. Zipporah was Moses half sister or cousin bride in Horite Priest fashion.

The children of Amram's children: And the Mariban prophet was Zeripha (Zipporah) These Israeli leaders were the children of Amram's children who were saved by Mariban. Moses addresses God using the title Adon/Aten (Exodus 4:10,13; 5:22; 34:9; Numbers 14:17; Deuteronomy 3:23; 7:26; 10:17); Moses, himself, is addressed both by Aaron (Ex.32:22; Num.12:11) and by Joshua (Numbers 11:28) using the title Adon/Aten; and Joshua also addresses God using the title Adon/Aten (Joshua 5:14 b; 7:7). Short biography and facts about **Moses, Ramses** and Seti! The name of this **prince - Thutmose -** is very similar to **Moses:** There was a Prince Tuthmose who was the eldest son of pharaoh Amenhotep III, and who mysteriously disappears from all records. There are very many facts pointing to that he have been the factual origin of the Biblical Moses? The name of this prince - Thutmose - is very similar to Moses **Since Crown Prince Tuthmose and Kiya as well as 3 chidren all disapered, are there any possible traces of any of this very important history? Let's futher consider one piece of evidence of Kiyas children we do have and who she was:** *Kiya Ta-sherit* Mery-khiba or Mery-Amon (Kiya) - (Miriam)-*Kiya Ta-sherit was the* daughter of Mery-khiba or Mery-Amon (Kiya)

"Moses, a son of the tribe of Levi, educated in Egypt and initiated at Heliopolis, became a High Priest of the Brotherhood under the reign of Pharaoh Amenhotep. He was elected by the Hebrews as their chief and he adapted to the ideas of his people the science and philosophy which he had obtained in the Egyptian mysteries; proofs of this are to be found in the symbols, in the Initiations, and in his precepts and commandments....The dogma of an 'only god' which he taught was the Egyptian Brotherhood interpretation and teaching of the Pharaoh who established the first monotheistic religion known to man."
- Egyptian High Priest Manetho (3rd Century BC)

Moses of the Bible was an Israelite, a Hebrew, born into the tribe of Levi.

14 And he said, Who made thee a prince and a judge over us? Thinkest thou to kill me, as thou killedst the Egyptian? And Moses feared, and said, Surely the thing is known.15 Now when Pharaoh heard this

thing, he sought to slay Moses. **But Moses fled from the face of Pharaoh, and dwelt in the land of Midian: and he sat down by a well.**
The Midianites may be though of as the "Pro-Hebrews" as they were the originators of Hebrew religion.

SUWALEIM /SOLEYMI/SULAYM – The ancient tribe they were the Ethiopian Solymi of Tacitus and other writers whom were the founders of Jerusalem as well as early "Pelasgian" inhabitants of the Taurus, Mediterranean and Aegean.AZD TRIBES -. KHAZRAJ, KHUZA'A, GHASSAN, BAHILA Groups traditionally descended from those who followed diviner Muzaikiyya from Marib in Yemen and wandered to other parts of Arabia. Muzaikiyya appears to parallel that of prophet Moses leading an exodus from Meriba in the Biblical book of Exodus

According to the Book of Genesis, the Midianites were descended from Midian, who was the son of the Hebrew patriarch Abraham by the latter's second wife, Keturah. Jethro, priest-leader of the Midianite sub-tribe known as the Kenites, and his daughter Zipporah (a wife of Moses), influenced early Hebrew thought: it was Yahweh, the lord of the Midianites, who was revealed to Moses as the God of the Hebrews.

Then came Tha'labah ibn-'Amr Muzaikiya with his son and followers to Yathrib whose people were Jews. Al-Aus and al-Khazraj. Al-Aus and al-Khazraj are the sons of Harithah ibn-Tha'labah 3 ibn-'Amr Muzaikiya ibn- 'Amir, and their mother was Kailah, daughter of al-Arkam. Some say she was a Ghassanide of al-Azd tribe, others say she was of 'Udhrah tribe. (She was a decendent of Arkam bin al-Arkam last king of Akk as this is how many battles have ended was by the marriage of the two sides as was the case here)

Again: The line of Muzaikiya is this:
Al-Aus and al-Khazraj. Al-Aus and al-Khazraj are the sons of Harithah ibn-Tha'labah ibn-'Amr Muzaikiya ibn- 'Amir, and their mother was Kailah, daughter of al-Arkam. Moses was Amr Ibn Amir, Then came Tha'labah ibn-'Amr Muzaikiya with his son The people of Amr bin Amir the soothsayer after being expelled by Akk bin Adnan disengaged and dispersed in idifferent directions. Jafna bin Amr bin Amir settled in Syria, Aus and Khazraj settled in Yathrib and Khuza'a went to Marra.

The actual historical origins of Hawazin bin Mansur, Mazin bin Mansur, and Sulaym bin Mansur is they actually are representative of the movement of the tribes of Manasseh (Manasse'ir)northward into the northern Hejaz and Syria in pre-Islamic times after the flood of their dam at Marib.

It really can not be overemphasized that the Azd are the people whose traditions parallel the Hebrew tradition of the Israelite Exodus and the leaders Moses and Aaron from Meriba. Again the tradition as recorded by Sa'id of Andalusia, and others goes that Azd is "a name borne by the most important section of the people who inhabited the country of Saba and its capital Ma'rib, at the time of the rupture of the dyke of 'Arim and of the ruin to which that portion of Yaman was in consequence reduced. All but a very small section of the Azdites had abandoned the country. The chief body went to the Tihamah of Yaman, inhabited by the tribes of 'Akk and Ash'ar. Here they

settled in the neighbourhood of a pool named Ghassan, situated between the rivers Zabid and Rima. After a lengthened stay, dissensions with the original occupants ' of the country compelled the Azdites to depart. A portion of the tribe established itself in Najran, in the neighbourhood of the Madhhijites who had long occupied and ruled the country." Yaman Its Early Medieval History , Umarah ibn Ali al Hakami and Ibn Khaldun. p. 216.

The genealogy of Suleym or Sulaym, Mazin and Hawazin are that they were the children of Mansur (Manasseh) son of Ikrima (Ikrima) bin Khasafa (Asaf or Hasepha) son of Qays son of Ailan. It is another way of showing historically that the clans of <u>Soleym and the Azd are descend from the original Israelite</u>/Canaanite people of the region south of Ta'if extending to the Sara'at in Asir

The (literally) central identification of the theory is that the geographical feature referred to as הירדן, the "Jordan", which is usually taken to refer to the Jordan River, although never actually described as a "river" in the Hebrew text, actually means the great West Arabian Escarpment, known as the Sarawat Mountains. The area of ancient Israel is then identified with the land on either side of the southern section of the escarpment that is, the southern Hejaz and 'Asir, from 2%Ta'if down to the border with Yemen.

Remember it was <u>in the final year of abundance when Asenath bore two children to Joseph: Manasseh and Ephraim.</u>

The Book of Deuteronomy (Deuteronomy 31:9 and Deuteronomy 31:24–26) records Moses saying "Take this book of the law, and put it by the side of the ark of the covenant of the LORD."

The Bible describes the Ark as made of acacia or shittah-tree wood. It was a cubit and a half broad and high, and two and a half cubits long (about 130 cm × 78 cm × 78 cm or 4.29 × 2.57 × 2.57 feet, for Egyptian royal cubit was most likely used). The Ark was covered all over with the purest gold.Further passages: **God communicated with Moses "from between the two cherubim" on the Ark's cover** (Ex. 25:22). **The Ark and its sanctuary were "the beauty of Israel"** (Lamentations 2:1).

YASIR'EL - name of ancient southwest Arabian tribesmen mainly of the Azd group who moved north from the Asir bringing their tribal tradition with them to Syria. And with this, the Patrlineal line of the children of Amram's children will also be behind Joseph as these lines are tied by blood and historically.

Sarawt Mountains seen from Habala Valley

Remember: YASIR'EL - name of ancient southwest Arabian tribesmen mainly of the Azd group who moved north from the Asir bringing their tribal tradition with them to Syria.

The northern part, running from about north of Ta'if through western Saudi Arabia until the southern tip of Saudi Arabia. Some argue that the mountains of Lebanon and Western Syria are a continuation of the chain. It is mostly a slightly higher elevated area that the rest of Saudi Arabia, with the exception of Asir, and obscure landforms can be found in this chain. Elevations average around 1200–2000 meters, although the highest points are around 2400 meters above sea level.

Marib the capital of ancient Saba was evidently the Meriba of the book of Exodus. The story of Jafna, Muzaikiya and Tha'labah is unmistakably too similar to that of Jephuneh and his father Caleb in the Bible to be coincidental. (Tha'labah is sometimes written Salabiyyah.) While the Midianites at the torrent of Kishon are the people known as Jokshan or Kushan or Midianites of Habakkuk, Chronicles and Genesis. They are the same as the Kushi in the tents of Kedar and the reason Ziphorah the Midianite is named "a Kushite" woman (later translated Ethiopian). It is also said that the brethren of Jafna, descendants of "Tha'labah bin 'Amr left his tribe Al-Azd for Hijaz and dwelt between Tha'labiyah and Dhi Qar. When he gained strength, he headed for Madinah where he stayed. Of his seed are Aws and Khazraj, sons of Haritha bin Tha'labah." And "Imran bin 'Amr

Sulaym and Mazin, three sons of Mansour, son of Ikrima, son of Khasafa, son of Al Nas or Qays Ailan. "From Mazin bin Mansour bin Ikrima were the Khazraj and Aus or Awza children of Tha'laba Muzaikiya or Salebiyya and Jafna Muzaikiya . " The tribes of Mansour or Manasse'ir had branched off from the Ma'adi who appear to have been the origin of the Ma'adi'ah a family of priests (Levites) named in (Nehemiah 12).

It will be shown that Mansour or Manasse'ir is the same as Manasseh, child of Joseph and that in genealogy of Arabia most of Mansour's descendants figure among the **children of Levi** in the Bible who had been later captured by Bukht al Nasir (Nebuchadnezzar) the Chaldean in charge of Babylon centuries before the Christian era.

"ORIGINS: Biblical References to Soleym ibn Mansur, who was Manasseh son of Joseph whose brother was Levi.Levi's wife, his children's mother, is named as Milkah, a daughter of Aram.

Some great catastrophe in the area of Arim/Yarim (Aram) in ancient Saba forced the tribes of Azd to go scattering over the peninsula, some entering Africa. Hence the phrases "divided as the Sabaeans" and "wandering Aramaeans". Among these tribes were the Canaani and the Israelites under their leaders Muzaikiya of Marib (the Meriba of Exodus), the prophetess Zarifa (Ziphorah),Jafna (Jephunneh) and Caleb. ."Num. 10:29-32 Northern Hedjaz and the land of Midian. Zipporah who was the half sister or cousin bride of Moses is mentioned in Exodus 2:15-16 and in Exodus 18:1-6. Zipporah was the daughter of "the priest of Midian"

The Egyptian language provides an etymology.4 The name Moses is related to common Egyptian names like Amenmose, Ramose and Thutmose,* which are formed of a god's name followed by mose.5 These compound names mean something like "Amen is born" or "Born of Amen" or "The offspring of Ra" or "The child of Thoth." **When the name Mose appears by itself, as it occasionally does in Egyptian, it simply means "the Child" or "the Offspring."**6 But in Egyptian, Mose most frequently appears along with the name of a god as part of a compound name.

The Egyptian root in 'ms' meaning to be born. The linguistic root of the name Moses is shows itself in the Egyptian word Mos which means "child." But this word also had a much broader legal meaning—"the rightful son and heir."

Remember the Tale of Two Brothers

The Aten, bore the name Imram. In the Bible, Moses is referred to as the son of Amram, the Hebrew equivalent.

The name Mozaikiya does not appear to have been Arabic, but Egyptian origin.

The tribes are as listed here in Revelation 7:5   *God's People will Be Preserved*

1After this I saw four angels standing at the four corners of the earth, holding the four winds of the earth, that no wind should blow on the earth, or on the sea, or upon any tree. 2And I saw another angel ascend from the sunrising, having the seal of the living God: and he cried with a great voice to the four angels to whom it was given to hurt the earth and the sea, 3saying, Hurt not the earth, neither the sea, nor the trees, till we shall have sealed the servants of our God on their foreheads.

144,000 Sealed

4And I heard the number of them that were sealed, a hundred and forty and four thousand, sealed out of every tribe of the children of Israel:

5Of the tribe of Judah were' sealed twelve thousand: Of the tribe of Reuben twelve thousand; Of the tribe of Gad twelve thousand; 6Of the tribe of Asher twelve thousand; Of the tribe of Naphtali twelve thousand; Of the tribe of Manasseh twelve thousand; 7Of the tribe of Simeon twelve thousand; Of the tribe of Levi twelve thousand; Of the tribe of Issachar twelve thousand; 8Of the tribe of Zebulun twelve thousand; Of the tribe of Joseph twelve thousand; Of the tribe of Benjamin were' sealed twelve thousand.

Praise from the Great Multitude

9After these things I saw, and behold, a great multitude, which no man could number, out of every nation and of all tribes and peoples and tongues, standing before the throne and before the Lamb, arrayed in white robes, and palms in their hands; 10and they cry with a great voice, saying, Salvation unto our God who sitteth on the throne, and unto the Lamb. 11And all the angels were standing round about the throne, and about the elders and the four living creatures; and they fell before the throne on their faces, and worshipped God, 12saying, Amen: Blessing, and glory, and wisdom, and thanksgiving, and honor, and power, and might, be unto our God for ever and ever. Amen.

13And one of the elders answered, saying unto me, These that are arrayed in white robes, who are they, and whence came they? 14And I say unto him, My lord, thou knowest. And he said to me, These are they that come of the great tribulation, and they washed their robes, and made them white in the blood of the Lamb. 15Therefore are they before the throne of God; and they serve him day and night in his temple: and he that sitteth on the throne shall spread his tabernacle over them. 16They shall hunger no more, neither thirst any more; neither shall the sun strike upon them, nor any heat: 17for the Lamb that is in the midst of the throne shall be their shepherd, and shall guide them unto fountains of waters of life: and God shall wipe away every tear from their eyes.

Amen and Amen It is likely that Melchizedek was the brother-in-law of Joktan, Abraham's father-in-law. In reality, Melchizedek did have an earthly father, probably Sheba the Elder.: It was historically The ruler-priestly lines of the two first-born sons intermarried, thus preserving the bloodline of those to whom Seth Ben Adam Ben Jehovah God made the promise that a woman of their people would bring forth the Seed who would crush the serpent's head and restore Paradise. The firstborn son of the cousin/niece wife ascended to the throne of his maternal grandfather, after whom he was named.

So Isaac ruled over Abraham's territory by Joktan ruled over the territory of Joktan the Elder, Ketu-rah's father. The two lines continued to intermarry according to a pattern that is traceable, using the Biblical genealogies, to Jesus Christ.   The heirs of God's promise that the Son of God would come through their lines.(Jesus)This strongly suggests that the ruling lines were aware and believed the promise made in Eden (Gen. 3:15) concerning the Woman's Seed who would crush the serpent's head, deliver from death and receive the Father's Kingdom. This line is traced through Jesse and David, but because of the very exclusive intermarriage pattern of the Kushite clans, it is also traced through Sheba and Joktan.   Indeed The Messiah himself Hashem Jesus Christ completely fulfilled what was the   eternal promise to the line of Moses as the King of Jeshurun. Jesus being a descendant of David verifies David's descent from Moses. In history, four of the most famous divine bloodlines are: Abraham, Moses, David, Jesus On the night of my night journey I passed by Moses b. 'Imran "For lo! That day is at hand, burning like an oven. All the arrogant and all the doers of evil shall be straw, and the day that is coming – said HaShem of Hosts – shall burn them to ashes and leave them neither stock nor boughs. But for you who revere My Name the son of righteousness shall rise to bring healing. You shall go forth and stamp like stall fed calves, and you shall trample the wicked to a pulp, for they shall be dust beneath your feet on the day that I am preparing. Be mindful of the Torah of Moshe whom I charged at Horeb with laws and rules for all of Israel. How can we even say his name or that of Hashem even without loving the Truth with all our hearts?" Alas! for that day is great, so that none is like it: it is even the time of Jacob's trouble; but he shall be saved out of it"

Genesis 3:15American Standard Version (ASV)

15 and I will put enmity between thee and the woman, and between thy seed and her seed: he shall bruise thy head, and thou shalt bruise his heel.

Revelation 12American Standard Version (ASV)

12 And a great sign was seen in heaven: a woman arrayed with the sun, and the moon under her feet, and upon her head a crown of twelve stars;

2 and she was with child; and she crieth out, travailing in birth, and in pain to be delivered.

3 And there was seen another sign in heaven: and behold, a great red dragon, having seven heads and ten horns, and upon his heads seven diadems.

4 And his tail draweth the third part of the stars of heaven, and did cast them to the earth: and the dragon standeth before the woman that is about to be delivered, that when she is delivered he may devour her child.

5 And she was delivered of a son, a man child, who is to rule all the nations with a rod of iron: and her child was caught up unto God, and unto his throne.

6 And the woman fled into the wilderness, where she hath a place prepared of God, that there they may nourish her a thousand two hundred and threescore days.

7 And there was war in heaven: Michael and his angels going forth to war with the dragon; and the dragon warred and his angels;

8 And they prevailed not, neither was their place found any more in heaven.

9 And the great dragon was cast down, the old serpent, he that is called the Devil and Satan, the deceiver of the whole world; he was cast down to the earth, and his angels were cast down with him.

10 And I heard a great voice in heaven, saying, Now is come the salvation, and the power, and the kingdom of our God, and the authority of his Christ: for the accuser of our brethren is cast down, who accuseth them before our God day and night.

11 And they overcame him because of the blood of the Lamb, and because of the word of their testimony; and they loved not their life even unto death.

12 Therefore rejoice, O heavens, and ye that dwell in them. Woe for the earth and for the sea: because the devil is gone down unto you, having great wrath, knowing that he hath but a short time.

13 And when the dragon saw that he was cast down to the earth, he persecuted the woman that brought forth the man child.

14 And there were given to the woman the two wings of the great eagle, that she might fly into the wilderness unto her place, where she is nourished for a time, and times, and half a time, from the face of the serpent.

15 And the serpent cast out of his mouth after the woman water as a river, that he might cause her to be carried away by the stream.

16 And the earth helped the woman, and the earth opened her mouth and swallowed up the river which the dragon cast out of his mouth.

17 And the dragon waxed wroth with the woman, and went away to make war with the rest of her seed, that keep the commandments of God, and hold the testimony of Jesus:

This Historical understanding is cristical for Mankind, so I have been pai staking in my Historical analysis and proof of the Fathers Kingdom because this understanding is critical for our current times Blesses are those for theirs is the Kingdom of God.

Seth Ben Adam Ben Jehovah's heritage and bloodline still exist within the Seed of the Woman "Adam" direct decendents of Seth Ben Adam Ben Jehovah. Why else would Go (Jehovahs make the promise he made because the Fathers Kindom is Seth ben Adam Ben Jehovahs Kingdom.

It is critical that the Seed of the woman "Adam " finally knows who they are, I know because my son is traced %100 the Revleaion 12 Rod of Iron, but I know there are many more males that carry the Seed of the Woman "Adam " as they are all decendents of the Tribes of Israel and all tribes of Israel are decendents of Seth Ben Adam Ben Jehovah. They have to be rescued because they are the decendents of the Seed of the woman "adam" that Seth Ben Adam Ben JEhvovah God made the promise that the Seed of the Woman Adam will Cruush the Serpent seed of Cain and inherite Seth Ben Adam Ben Jehovahs Kingdom, and the Nasrid dynasty has been attached now to Seth Ben Adam Ben Jehovahs Endd Days Kindom because it Originated with Seth Ben Adam Ben Jejhovah and was rtraced %100 patrilineally and my son is a direct malle line decendent of the Nasrid dynasty so he is the Seed of the Woma Ada that has to crush the Serrpent seed of Cain and inherite his Fathres Kindom and that is Seth Ben Adam bEn Jehovahs Kindom because the Nasrid dynasty originated with Seth Ben Adam Ben Jehovah and and now been proven it was traced %100 though time to this day.

Though it feels impossible task a labor of Love is has to be achieved because when God (Jehovahs makes a promise he cannot lie and did not lie. Seth Ben Adam Ben Jehovahs End days Kindom now needs to raise one Million dollars to rescue the Seed of the Woman "Adam, the tribes of Israel decendents because the Bible says threr will be 144,000, 12,000 of Each and every tribe and as many as the Sands of the Sea.   I cannot allow Genesis 3:15 is the same as Revleaion 12 to be killed because Seth Ben Adam Ben Jehovah's Kingdom is the only way to survie Revelation 13, and that is Seth Ben Adam Ben Jehovahs Kingdom 100% verifiable that the seed of the woman "Adam " is Seth Ben Adam Ben Jehovahs Kingdom because the seed of the woman "Adam" decends from Seth Ben Adam Ben Jehovah and Jejhovahs is his own Kingdom he originalted is his own Kingdom and is his own Seed of the woman "Adam and His own Emnity. The Nasrid dynasty %100 traces to current times is Seth Ben Adam Ben Jehovahs End days Kingdom and the Revleaion 12 Rod of Iron My son that will rule all nations with a Rod of Iron is a direct male patrilineal decendent of the Nasrid Dynasty that originated with Seth Ben Adam Ben Jehovahs then led to Hashem Moses then lead to King David and carried the Required Y Chromosome and the required "Seed of the Woman "adam "heritage it requires to inherit the Father's Kingdom.

I am having to take special measures to not allow humans to Kill Seth Ben Adam Ben Jehovah's Kingdom the Fathers Kingdom because it clearly is the Seed of the woman "adam" only that is to inherit the Fathers Kingdom originated by Seth Ben Adam Ben Jehovah and this book is the %100 proof that it has always existed with the Seed of the Woman Adam to this very day. I left out the closest male line decedents names to protect the Current Heirs of Seth Ben Adam Ben Jehovah's Kingdom   my son and he is a direct decedent traced %100 from the Nasrid Dynasty so again relation to Seth Ben Adam Ben

Jehovah, Hashem Moses, and King David via Jehoachim. It is King David's Kingdom forever hence the Rod of Iron (Root of David)